# Praise for

"An informative and helpful study for thos[...] ing of a dozen of our Lord's precious word pictures. Dr. MacArth[...] of justification by faith alone based on the parable of the tax collector and the Pharisee is outstanding."

— Dr. Joel R. Beeke, president of Puritan Reformed Theological Seminary, Grand Rapids, Michigan

"Everything you thought you knew about the parables is reoriented in this new work by John MacArthur to explain their meaning and show their relevance in the lives of believers. Teaching these vividly profound stories for those inside the kingdom of Christ, MacArthur argues that the parables do not reveal the truth to outsiders, but actually conceal it. *Parables* is intriguing and stimulating as it pierces through a thick cloud of exegetical misunderstanding about the illustrative teaching of Jesus. John MacArthur stands as a watchman on the ramparts, pointing us back to the protective refuge of Christ inside the walls of truth."

— Steven J. Lawson, president of OnePassion Ministries and the Professor of Preaching, The Master's Seminary

"After over 40 years of faithful pastoral ministry, John MacArthur has proven himself to be a sure guide through Scripture and a faithful expositor of God's Word. This new book, *Parables: The Mysteries of God's Kingdom Revealed Through the Stories Jesus Told*, is a rich biblical, theological, and devotional treatment of our Lord's parables."

— R. Albert Mohler, Jr., president of the Southern Baptist Theological Seminary

"No one has given a more heroic and consistent defense of the authority and inspiration of Scripture in this generation than John MacArthur. I consider him one of the finest biblical expositors of our day. Few have given more careful attention to interpreting and applying the words of Jesus in the Gospels. I wholeheartedly recommend *Parables* as a landmark achievement by a beloved and seasoned pastor."

— Dr. R. C. Sproul, founder and chairman of Ligonier Ministries

# PARABLES

# PARABLES

*The Mysteries of God's Kingdom Revealed*

*Through the Stories Jesus Told*

JOHN MACARTHUR

NELSON
BOOKS

An Imprint of Thomas Nelson

© 2015 by John MacArthur

All rights reserved. No portion of this book may be reproduced in any form without the written permission of the copyright owner, except for brief excerpts quoted in critical reviews.

Published in association with the literary agency of Wolgemuth & Associates, Inc.

Edited by Phillip R. Johnson

All Scripture quotations in this book, except those noted otherwise, are from the New King James Version. © 1982 by Thomas Nelson, Inc. Used by permission. All rights reserved.

Quotations marked NASB are from the New American Standard Bible, ©1960, 1962, 1963, 1968, 1971, 1972, 1973, 1975, 1977, 1988, and 1995 by The Lockman Foundation, and are used by permission.

Quotations marked KJV are from the King James Version of the Bible, public domain.

Quotations marked ESV are from THE ENGLISH STANDARD VERSION. © 2001 by Crossway Bibles, a division of Good News Publishers.

ISBN: 978-1-4002-0350-5 (eBook)
ISBN: 978-0-7180-4208-0 (IE)
ISBN: 978-0-7180-8231-4 (TP)

**Library of Congress Cataloging-in-Publication Data**

MacArthur, John, 1939–
    The parables of Jesus : Jesus' theology of salvation in stories / John MacArthur.
        pages cm
    Includes bibliographical references and index.
    ISBN 978-1-4002-0348-2
    1. Jesus Christ--Parables. I. Title.
    BT375.3.M33 2015
    226.8'06--dc23                                                                          2014040263

*Printed in the United States of America*

24 25 26 27 28  LBC  26 25 24 23 22

*To Marshall Brackin, a loyal friend who personifies the apostle Paul's admonition in 1 Corinthians 16:13–14: "Be on the alert, stand firm in the faith, act like men, be strong. Let all that you do be done in love."*

# Contents

CONTENTS

# Why did Jesus teach in parables, and how can we interpret them rightly?

Jesus' parables were ingeniously simple word pictures with profound spiritual lessons. His teaching was full of these everyday stories. Some of them were no more than fleeting remarks about commonplace incidents, objects, or persons. In fact, the most compact of all Jesus' short stories does not even fill a complete verse of Scripture. It is found in Matthew 13:33: "The kingdom of heaven is like leaven, which a woman took and hid in three measures of meal till it was all leavened." In the original Greek text, that parable is just nineteen words. It is the most ordinary of anecdotes about the most common of activities told in the fewest possible words. But it contains a profound lesson about the mysteries of the kingdom of heaven. Like all Jesus' parables, it captivated His hearers and has sustained the interest of Bible students for two thousand years.

Jesus was the master storyteller. There is not a truism so familiar or a doctrine so complex that He could not give it new depth and insight through the telling of a simple story. These narratives epitomize the plain, powerful profundity of His message and His teaching style.

## Sloppy Thinking About the Parables

Despite the popularity of the parables, both the method and the meaning behind Jesus' use of these stories are frequently misunderstood and misrepresented, even by Bible scholars and experts in literary genre.

Many assume, for example, that Jesus told parables for one reason only: to make His teaching as easy, accessible, and comfortable as possible. After all, the parables were full of familiar features—easily recognizable scenes, agricultural and pastoral metaphors, household items, and common people. This would naturally make His words simpler for His provincial audience to relate to and grasp. It was without question a brilliant teaching method, unveiling eternal mysteries for simple minds. Jesus' parables certainly do show that even the simplest stories and illustrations can be effective tools for teaching the most sublime truths.

Some suggest that Jesus' use of parables proves storytelling is a *better* method for teaching spiritual truth than didactic discourses or sermonic exhortation. Stories, they say, "pack more punch than sermons. Want to make a point or raise an issue? Tell a story. Jesus did it."[1]

Some go further still, contending that the default form of discourse in the church should always be narrative, not hortatory or didactic. They point to Mark 4:33–34, which describes Jesus' public teaching during the latter part of His Galilean ministry this way: "With many such parables He spoke the word to them as they were able to hear it. But without a parable He did not speak to them." Therefore, the argument goes, storytelling should be every pastor's preferred method—if not the *only* style of preaching we ever use. In the words of one writer:

> A sermon is not a doctrinal lecture. It is an *event-in-time*, a narrative art form more akin to a play or novel in shape than to a book. Hence we are not engineering scientists; we are narrative artists by professional function.
>
> Does it not seem strange to you that in our speech and homiletical training we seldom considered the connection between our work and

that of the playwright, novelist, or television writer? . . . I propose that
we begin by regarding the sermon as a homiletical plot, a narrative art
form, a sacred story.[2]

Indeed, that is precisely the kind of preaching that now dominates
many evangelical and megachurch pulpits. In some cases, the pulpit is
totally gone, replaced by a stage and a screen. The key people on the
church staff are those whose main task is directing the drama team or
the film crew. Declaring truth in propositional form is out. What's now
in vogue is telling stories—or acting them out—in a way that encourages people to fit themselves into the narrative. Stories are supposedly
more hospitable, more meaningful, and more genteel than brute facts or
unambiguous truth claims.

That perspective on preaching has steadily gained acceptance
for three or four decades, alongside other pragmatic church-growth
strategies (a trend that I have critiqued elsewhere[3]). Here's how a religious publisher advertises an influential book dealing with the late
twentieth-century revolution in preaching and ministry philosophy: "Preaching is in crisis. Why? Because the traditional, conceptual
approach no longer works. . . . It fails to capture the interest of listeners."[4]
The book itself says, "The old topical/conceptual approach to preaching
is critically, if not terminally ill."[5]

Countless recent books on preaching have echoed that assessment,
or something similar. The remedy? We are told again and again that
preachers need to see themselves as storytellers, *not* teachers of doctrine.
Here's a typical sample:

Contrary to what some would have us believe, story, not doctrine, is
the Bible's main ingredient. We do not have a doctrine of creation;
we have stories of creation. We do not have a concept of the resurrection, we have marvelous narratives of Easter. There is relatively little in
either the Old Testament or the New Testament that does not rest on
narrative or story of some form.[6]

Statements such as those are dangerously misleading. It is sheer folly to set story against doctrine as if one were hostile to the other, or (worse yet) to pit narrative against proposition as if they were somehow mutually exclusive.* The idea that "a doctrine of creation" or "a concept of the resurrection" cannot be conveyed through narrative is simply and obviously untrue. It is likewise patently false to claim that "we do not have a concept of the resurrection" taught in Scripture apart from the narrative accounts. See, for example, 1 Corinthians 15—a long chapter, all of which is devoted to a systematic, pedagogical, and polemical defense of the doctrine of bodily resurrection, replete with exhortations, arguments, syllogisms, and an abundance of propositional statements.

Furthermore, there is a clear and significant difference between a *parable* (a story made up by Jesus to illustrate a precept, proposition, or principle) and *history* (a chronicle of events that actually happened). The parable helps explain a truth; history gives a factual account of what happened. Although history is told in story form, it is not illustrative fiction but reality. One of the main ways the essential propositions of Christian truth have been preserved and passed down to us is by including them in the infallible record of biblical history. Again, that is the very principle on which Paul built his argument about the truth of bodily resurrection in 1 Corinthians 15.

His defense of that doctrine begins with a recounting of historical facts that were amply confirmed by multiple eyewitnesses. In fact, the doctrines deemed "of first importance" (v. 3 NASB) were all key points in the story of that final Passover weekend: "... that Christ died for our sins according to the Scriptures, and that He was buried, and that He rose again the third day according to the Scriptures" (vv. 3–4).

The notion that stories are always better and more helpful than straightforward truth claims is a shopworn postmodern canard. To differentiate stories from propositions with such a hard line and set one against the other (as if it were possible to tell stories *without* propositional

---

* The Appendix answers the common misconception that doctrine and story are fundamentally opposed to one another.

statements) is sheer nonsense—rhetorical sleight of hand. That kind of intellectual gibberish is a typical tool of language deconstruction. The real goal of such an exercise is to confound meaning, eliminate certainty, and overthrow dogma.**

But the flagrant mistreatment of Jesus' parables by modern commentators sometimes gets even worse than that. An even more radical view, rapidly gaining popularity in these postmodern times, is the notion that stories by their very nature have no fixed or objective meaning; they are entirely subject to the hearer's interpretation. By this way of thinking, Jesus' use of parables was a deliberate repudiation of propositions and dogma in favor of mystery and conversation. One commentator says it like this: "It is the nature of narrative to lend itself to an auditor's imagination and become whatever the auditor wants it to be—in spite of the narrator's intention. Narratives are essentially polyvalent, and therefore subject to a wide range of readings."[7]

That same author cites other commentators' varying interpretations of Jesus' parables and cynically declares, "Parables work any way interpreters and auditors want them to work—in spite of whatever Jesus may have intended with them . . . We simply do not know how Jesus used parables and clearly have no hope of ever discovering his intention."[8]

He's not finished:

Interpreters of parables are not telling readers what Jesus actually meant with the parable; they simply do not, and cannot, know that. Interpreters describe what *they think* Jesus meant—something vastly different. An explanation is evoked in a particular reader's mind from an engagement with a parable, and responses depend as much on what that interpreter brings to the parable as on what the parable itself says—perhaps more so. Had the interpreter been present in

---

** For a succinct explanation and analysis of postmodernity see John MacArthur, *The Truth War* (Nashville: Thomas Nelson, 2007). In short, postmodern philosophies are dominated by the notion that truth is subjective, hazy, uncertain—perhaps even unknowable. Or, to use a brief statement from *The Truth War*, "Postmodernism in general is marked by *a tendency to dismiss the possibility of any sure and settled knowledge of the truth*" (10).

the audience when Jesus first spoke the parable, the situation would have been no different. My hypothetical modern interpreter, whom I have just taken back in time to the feet of Jesus, would still have to make sense of the parable as interpreters do today. Then as now, others in the audience would have had rather different responses. In this sense the situation with interpretations of parables today is identical to what would have been the case in the first century. Thus, no "right" interpretations of the parables of Jesus ever existed. By "right" I mean interpretations that capture Jesus' intent. Given the nature of narrative, no one explanation of a parable can rule out all others.[9]

Why anyone who holds such a view would bother writing a book on the parables is a mystery to me, I confess. If a person rejects the propositional truth being illustrated by a parable, *of course* it remains an open riddle. The problem is not that the parable has no true meaning but that those who come to the story with a heart fixed in unbelief have already rejected the truth the parable was given to illustrate.

The view that author is advocating is an exaggerated version of *reader-response criticism*, another favorite tool of postmodern language deconstruction. The underlying idea is that the recipient, not the author, is the one who creates the meaning of any text or narrative. It's a two-edged sword. If applied consistently, that approach to hermeneutics would expose the incomprehensibility of the commentator's own prose. At the end of the day, it is just another expression of the postmodern agenda to confound rather than clarify meaning—motivated by a stubborn rejection of biblical authority and inerrancy.

## Why Parables?

All the above views are wrong—and dangerously so—because they take only part of the truth into account. Consider, for example, the common belief that the sole reason Jesus used parables was to make hard truths as clear, familiar, and easy to grasp as possible. When Jesus Himself explained why He spoke in parables, He gave practically the opposite reason:

> The disciples came and said to Him, "Why do You speak to them in parables?"
>
> He answered and said to them, "Because it has been given to you to know the mysteries of the kingdom of heaven, but to them it has not been given. For whoever has, to him more will be given, and he will have abundance; but whoever does not have, even what he has will be taken away from him. Therefore I speak to them in parables, because seeing they do not see, and hearing they do not hear, nor do they understand. And in them the prophecy of Isaiah [6:9–10] is fulfilled, which says:
>
> > 'Hearing you will hear and shall not understand,
> > And seeing you will see and not perceive;
> > For the hearts of this people have grown dull.
> > Their ears are hard of hearing,
> > And their eyes they have closed,
> > Lest they should see with their eyes and hear with their ears,
> > Lest they should understand with their hearts and turn,
> > So that I should heal them.'" (Matt. 13:10–15)

While the parables do illustrate and clarify truth for those with ears to hear, they have precisely the opposite effect on those who oppose and reject Christ. The symbolism hides the truth from anyone without the discipline or desire to seek out Christ's meaning. That's why Jesus adopted that style of teaching. It was a divine judgment against those who met His teaching with scorn, unbelief, or apathy. In chapter 1, we'll look more closely into this idea, and we'll examine the circumstances that prompted Jesus to begin speaking in parables.

This is not to suggest that the parables were *merely* a reflection of the severity with which God condemns unbelief; they were also an expression of His mercy. Notice how Jesus (citing Isaiah's prophecy) described the unbelievers among those who followed Him. They had stopped up their own ears and held their own eyes tightly closed "lest they should understand with their hearts and turn, so that I should heal them" (v. 15). Their unbelief was stubborn, deliberate, and by their own choice irrevocable. The more they heard Christ, the more truth they were accountable for. The more they hardened their hearts against the truth, the more severe their judgment would be, for "to whom much is given, from him much will be required" (Luke 12:48). Thus by concealing spiritual lessons in everyday stories and symbols, Jesus was keeping them from piling guilt upon guilt on their own heads.

There were surely other merciful benefits of this teaching style. The parables (like any good illustration) would naturally arouse interest and increase attention in the minds of people who were not necessarily hard-set against the truth but simply lacked a measure of aptitude or had no taste for hearing doctrine expounded in plain, dogmatic language. No doubt the parables had the effect of awakening the minds of many such people who were struck by the simplicity of Jesus' parables and therefore became eager to discover the underlying meanings.

For others (including, surely, some whose first exposure to the truth may have provoked skepticism, indifference, or even rejection), the graphic imagery of the parables helped keep truth rooted in the memory until it sprang forth in faith and understanding.

Richard Trench, a nineteenth-century Anglican bishop, wrote one of the most widely read works on Jesus' parables. He highlights the mnemonic value of these stories:

> Had our Lord spoken naked spiritual truth, how many of his words, partly from his hearers' lack of interest in them, partly from their lack of insight, would have passed away from their hearts and memories, and left no trace behind them. But being imparted to them in this form, under some lively image, in some short and perhaps seemingly paradoxical sentence, or in some brief but interesting narrative, they

aroused attention, excited inquiry, and even if the truth did not at the moment, by the help of the illustration used, find an entrance into the mind, yet the words must thus often have fixed themselves in their memories and remained by them.[10]

So there were several good and gracious reasons for Jesus to package the truth in parables in the face of widespread unbelief, apathy, and opposition to His ministry (cf. Matt. 13:58; 17:17).

When explained, the parables were illuminating illustrations of crucial truths. And Jesus freely explained His parables to the disciples.

For those who remained unyielding in their refusal to hear, however, the unexplained parables remained riddles without clear meaning, so the parables further obscured Jesus' teaching from their already dull hearts. Thus Jesus' immediate judgment against their unbelief was built right into the form of discourse He used when He taught publicly.

In short, Jesus' parables had a clear twofold purpose: *They hid the truth* from self-righteous or self-satisfied people who fancied themselves too sophisticated to learn from Him, *while the same parables revealed truth* to eager souls with childlike faith—those who were hungering and thirsting for righteousness. Jesus thanked His Father for both results: "I thank You, Father, Lord of heaven and earth, that You have hidden these things from the wise and prudent and have revealed them to babes. Even so, Father, for so it seemed good in Your sight" (Matt. 11:25–26).

One more common misunderstanding needs to be cleared up: Our Lord did not *always* speak in parables. Most of the Sermon on the Mount is precisely the kind of straightforward sermonic exhortation some of today's more stylish homileticians repudiate. Though Jesus closes the sermon with a short parable (the wise and foolish builders, Matthew 7:24–27), the substance of the message, starting with the Beatitudes, is delivered in a series of direct propositional statements, commandments, polemical arguments, exhortations, and words of warning. There are many vivid word pictures in the mix—a courtroom and prison scene (5:25); the amputation of offending eyes or hands (5:29–30); the eye as the lamp of the body (6:22);

lilies arrayed in finery that surpasses Solomon in all his glory (6:28–29); the plank in the eye (7:3–5); and so on. But these aren't parables. In fact, Matthew's account of the sermon is 107 verses long and only 4 verses near the very end could technically be described as parable.

Luke does include one saying not found in Matthew's record of the Sermon, and Luke expressly calls it a parable: "Can the blind lead the blind? Will they not both fall into the ditch?" (Luke 6:39).*** That, of course, is not a classic narrative-style parable. It's a maxim framed as a question. Luke calls it a parable no doubt because of the way it invokes such a vivid picture that could easily be recast as narrative. But even after raising the parable count in Jesus' Sermon on the Mount to two, we are still left with the fact that Jesus' best-known public discourse is simply not an example of narrative discourse. It is a classic *sermon,* dominated by doctrine, reproof, correction, and instruction in righteousness (cf. 2 Tim. 3:16). It is not a story or a string of anecdotes. The few scattered word pictures simply illustrate the sermonic material.

Elsewhere, we see Jesus preaching and exhorting the multitudes with no suggestion whatsoever that He used a narrative style. Some of the longest, most detailed records of Jesus' public sermons are found among the discourses recorded in John's gospel, and none of them includes any parables. There are no parables mentioned in the record of Jesus' teaching in the synagogues at Nazareth (Luke 4:13–27) or Capernaum (vv. 31–37). So it simply is not accurate to imply that He employed narrative preaching more than any other style, much less to say that He *always* spoke in parables.

What, then, does that statement in Mark 4:33–34 mean: "without a parable He did not speak to them"? That's a description of Jesus' *public* teaching style *only during the final year or so of His public ministry.* It

---

*** This was undoubtedly a common saying of Jesus, because Matthew 15:14 does record a similar statement, but this time it is a comment made in private to the Twelve, and it comes at a much later point in the Galilean ministry (Matt. 15:14). Peter immediately responds, "Explain this parable to us" (v. 15), but the saying Jesus explains is an earlier statement made to the multitudes: "Not what goes into the mouth defiles a man; but what comes out of the mouth, this defiles a man" (v. 11). This broad usage of the word *parable* exemplifies how the Bible's own use of the word makes Jesus' parables very difficult to distinguish, define, and count precisely.

refers to that intentional change in teaching style that took place about the same time Jesus' Galilean ministry entered its final phase. As noted earlier, we'll open chapter 1 by examining the events that provoked Jesus to adopt that style. It was a sudden and striking shift, and a response to hard-hearted, deliberate unbelief and rejection.

So it's quite true that the parables *do* help illustrate and explain truth to simple people who listen with faithful hearts. But they also conceal truth from unwilling and unbelieving auditors—by neatly wrapping the mysteries of Christ's kingdom in familiar symbols and simple stories. This is not an incidental point. By His own testimony, the main reason Jesus suddenly adopted the parabolic style had more to do with hiding the truth from hard-hearted unbelievers than explaining the truth to simple-minded disciples. It was Jesus' own declared purpose thus to "utter things kept secret"—and His parables still serve that same dual purpose today. If it seems the stories Jesus told are capable of endless interpretations and therefore devoid of any discernible objective meaning, that's because truly understanding them requires faith, diligence, careful exegesis, and a genuine desire to hear what Christ is saying.

It is important also to know that all unbelievers lack that capacity. Jesus' parables "speak the wisdom of God in a mystery, the hidden wisdom which God ordained before the ages for our glory, which none of the rulers of this age knew; for had they known, they would not have crucified the Lord of glory" (1 Cor. 2:7–8). No unbeliever will ever grasp the mysteries of the kingdom by filtering these stories through the sieve of human wisdom. Scripture is clear on that. The carnal, unbelieving "'eye has not seen, nor ear heard, nor have entered into the heart of man the things which God has prepared for those who love Him.' *But God has revealed them to us through His Spirit.* For the Spirit searches all things, yes, the deep things of God" (vv. 9–10, emphasis added).

In other words, faith, prompted and enabled by the work of the Holy Spirit in our hearts, is the necessary prerequisite for understanding the parables. These stories *do* have objective meaning. They have a divinely intended, and therefore correct, interpretation. Jesus Himself explained some of the parables in detail, and the hermeneutic He employed gives us a model to follow as we learn from the rest of His stories. But we must come to the parables as believers, willing to hear—not as skeptics with hearts hardened against the truth.

## Some Definitions and Details

In the chapters that follow, we'll examine a dozen of Jesus' most notable parables. It would require multiple volumes to cover *all* the parables in sufficient depth. There are roughly forty of them woven into the gospel record. (A precise number depends on the method of counting.) My basic comments on any of Jesus' parables can be found in the corresponding volumes of *The MacArthur New Testament Commentary* series. Also, more than twenty-five years ago, I included a digest of seven gospel-themed parables in a major book examining Jesus' evangelistic message.[11] A few of those same parables are included here in all-new, more in-depth chapters. Although the parable of the prodigal son is one of the most rich, memorable, and important of all Jesus' stories, it is not included in this book, since I've already written a full volume on that passage.[12] The aim of this book is to unfold the depth of meaning in a representative sampling of Jesus' parables, and to analyze the ingenious way He illustrated vital truths with everyday stories.

Before looking at specific parables, it would be good to consider the genre. What is a parable, and how does it differ from other illustrative forms—metaphors, similes, fables, allegories, and the like? A parable is not merely a simple analogy. It's an elongated simile or metaphor with a distinctly spiritual lesson contained in the analogy. Short figures of speech like "as strong as a horse" or "as quick as a rabbit" are plain similes—simple and straightforward enough not to require an explanation. A parable extends the comparison into a longer story or more complex metaphor, and the meaning (always a point of spiritual truth) is not necessarily obvious. Most of Jesus' parables demanded some kind of explanation.

But giving a technical definition that fits all Jesus' parables is notoriously difficult, partly because of the range of sayings expressly labeled parables in the gospel accounts. In Matthew 15:15, for example, Peter asks Jesus to explain "this parable" recorded in verse 11: "Not what goes into the mouth defiles a man; but what comes out of the mouth, this defiles a man." That's actually a pair of simple propositions stated as a kind of proverb. It has none of the distinctive elements of story or narrative—no plot, no characters, no series of events. Yet Scripture calls it a parable (not only in Matthew 15, but also in Mark 7:17).

Furthermore, in Luke 4:23, Jesus cites a proverb: "Physician, heal yourself!" In the Greek text, the word He uses to refer to that saying is *parabolē*, the same word normally translated "parable."

Obviously, then, the biblical idea of a parable is broader than most of the technical definitions proposed by various commentators, and this is why getting an exact count of biblical parables is tricky.

The word *parable* is used four times in the New King James Version of the Old Testament: Psalm 78:2 and Ezekiel 17:2; 20:49; and 24:3. The Hebrew word in those texts is *mashal*, which can refer to a prophetic saying, a proverb, a riddle, a discourse, a poem, a short story, a similitude—almost any kind of pithy maxim or anecdote. The word is used some forty times in the Hebrew Scriptures, usually translated "proverb" (though it's rendered "oracle" throughout the book of Numbers, and "discourse" in the book of Job). Only in the three Old Testament texts cited above does the word in context seem to refer to anything resembling the type of parables Jesus was known for telling.

The Greek word translated "parable" throughout the Synoptic Gospels (Matthew, Mark, and Luke) is *parabole*, and it's used fifty times in forty-eight verses of the New Testament. Twice the word is used in the book of Hebrews to signify figurative speech: "[The first Tabernacle] was symbolic [*parabole*] for the present time" (9:9); and "[Abraham believed] God was able to raise [Isaac] up, even from the dead, from which he also received him in a figurative sense [*parabole*]" (11:19).

All forty-eight other occurrences of the term in the New Testament are found in the Synoptics, where the word is always translated "parable" or "parables"—always in reference to Jesus' stories.

The word comes from two Greek roots: *para* ("beside") and *ballō* ("throw"). Literally, it means "to place alongside." It suggests a comparison between two things that are alike in some way. (This idea is retained even in the English derivative, *parabola*, which describes a curve where one side precisely mirrors the other.) The derivation of the word *parable* therefore refers to the analogy being drawn between some commonplace reality and a profound spiritual truth. That juxtaposition of common things alongside transcendental truth is what's most distinctive about a parable—not the plot, length, form, literary devices, or narrative style. To put it as simply as possible, a parable is an illustrative figure of speech made for comparison's sake—and specifically for the purpose of teaching a spiritual lesson. A parable might be long or short. It might employ metaphor, simile, proverb, or some other type of word picture. (It might even contain elements of allegory.) But it always makes a comparison that applies to some truth in the spiritual realm.

The lesson revealed in the comparison is always the central (and often the *only*) point of the parable. A parable is not an allegory like *Pilgrim's Progress*, in which every character and virtually every plot point conveys some cryptic but vital meaning. Parables are not to be mined for layer upon layer of secret significance. Their lessons are simple, focused, without much embellishment. (We'll return to this point shortly.)

Another important distinctive of Jesus' parables is that they never feature elements of myth or fantasy. They are nothing whatsoever like Aesop's fables, where personified forest creatures teach moral lessons. The parables of Jesus are all believable, true-to-life illustrations. They could in fact all be true.

So for our purposes in this book, the simple definition with which I began this introduction is as good as any: *a parable is an ingeniously simple word picture illuminating a profound spiritual lesson.*

Although Jesus was not the first to use the form, He was surely the first to teach in parables so extensively. Leading rabbis prior to Christ's era had made frugal use of parables. Hillel the Elder, for example, one of the most famous and still-influential rabbis of all time, lived a generation before the birth of Christ, and he is said to have spoken occasionally in parables. The Midrash is a collection of rabbinical homilies, commentaries, anecdotes, and illustrations explaining various biblical texts. The text of the Midrash dates from the second century AD, but includes a few older parables thought to predate the ministry of Christ. What's clear from the record, however, is that parabolic teaching increased dramatically in the rabbinical tradition during and after the time of Christ.[13] No one was better than He at telling parables, and other rabbis soon adopted the form.

Jesus' parables are found only in the Synoptic Gospels. Not a single parable is recorded anywhere in the gospel of John. Parables are scarce in Mark; he includes only six,**** and just one of those (4:26–29) is given *only* in Mark. In other words, all but one of Jesus' recorded parables are found in Matthew and Luke.*****

It is also worth noting that Matthew and Luke have somewhat different ways of recounting Jesus' parables. Matthew tells the stories with as much brevity as possible and just the facts. Luke's accounts tend to give the characters in the stories more life and personality. Simon J. Kistemaker sums up the stylistic differences between Matthew and Luke:

---

**** The parables Mark records are the sower (4:3–20); the scattered seed (4:26–29); the mustard seed (4:30–32); the wicked vinedressers (12:1–9); the fig tree (13:28–32); and the doorkeeper (13:34–37). Some commentators include simple figurative expressions in their lists of parables. Brief figures of speech don't necessarily fit the classic story form that distinguishes a true parable, so I have not included them in the above list. But it's worth noting that there are numerous ways to count the parables in Mark. Some lists, for example, include Jesus' statement about fasting with the bridegroom present (Mark 2:19–20); the imagery of wine in new wineskins (2:21–22); the lamp under a basket (4:21)—and so on. A case could likewise be made for including the binding of the strong man (3:27) and the salt that has lost its savor (9:50). That's why lists of Mark's parables vary, generally from six to as many as eleven. The wide divergence illustrates the practical impossibility of making a definitive list of all Jesus' parables—and that is why I haven't attempted to include such a list in this book. A thorough discussion of the fine distinctions between simple analogies and full-fledged parables would make an excellent academic thesis, but it is far beyond the scope of this volume.

***** Some say *two* parables are unique to Mark, citing both the scattered seed (4:26–29) and the doorkeeper (13:34–37). But the latter text is simply an abbreviated account of the same parable told in Matthew 24:42–51.

From the storehouse of Jesus' parables, Matthew has selected those that he presents in black and white sketches. For instance, the pearl merchant is an ordinary person who fails to come to life. By contrast, the parables Luke has selected sparkle in their crispness, are vivid in the portrayal of life, and are colorful in design. In these parables the people talk, as in the case of the rich man who, reaping a bumper crop, built bigger and better barns (Luke 12). Even in the parable of the lost sheep recorded by both Matthew and Luke, this difference is obvious. Upon finding the lost sheep, the shepherd, filled with joy, returns home and calls together his friends and neighbors and says, "Rejoice with me; I have found my lost sheep" (Luke 15:6). Matthew merely records that the man is happy (Matt 18:13). It almost seems as if Matthew is taking his pictures on film that is black-and-white while Luke uses color.[14]

This is not by any means to suggest that Matthew's approach is somehow inferior or less inspired than Luke's. One fact to be borne in mind about Jesus' parables is that they are simple on purpose, and the lessons they teach are likewise uncomplicated. We touched on this fact earlier when we were considering the distinctions between parable and allegory. But the point is too important to pass by so quickly, and it's a good note on which to end this introduction:

*The symbolism in Jesus' parables is never thickly layered, and rarely even multidimensional.* In most cases, the parables make one simple point. Trying to find meaning in every story element is an exercise in bad hermeneutics. Even the most detailed parables (like the good Samaritan and the prodigal son) usually teach fairly straightforward, uncomplicated lessons. Minor elements in the story are not to be laden with spiritual meaning.

For example, the oil and wine the good Samaritan used to dress the traveler's wounds (Luke 10:34) have no necessary symbolic or spiritual significance beyond showing that the Samaritan gave the man tender, time-consuming care. Neither is there any need to inject some secret spiritual meaning into "the pods that the swine ate" in the prodigal son's story (Luke 15:16). That detail is given because it shows vividly in just a few words how far the boy had fallen into the utter poverty of a defiled and degrading lifestyle.

Again, the important thing in every parable is the central lesson, and in those cases where the symbolism is more complex (such as the parable of the soils and the parable of the tares), Jesus almost always explains the symbolism for us.

As we study Jesus' parables together in the pages to come, let's commit ourselves to being true disciples, carefully seeking wisdom and understanding with obedient hearts. The lessons Christ has built into His word pictures are truly profound and well worth our close attention. As Jesus said privately to those first disciples, "Blessed are the eyes which see the things you see; for I tell you that many prophets and kings have desired to see what you see, and have not seen it, and to hear what you hear, and have not heard it" (Luke 10:23–24). Built into these stories, then, is a promise of blessedness to the one who understands the truth they teach.

*The Saviour . . . knew what he meant when he spoke. Some people, when they speak, do not know what they mean; and, when a man does not make you understand what he means, it generally is because he does not himself know the meaning of what he says. Indistinct speaking is usually the result of indistinct thinking. If men think clouds, they will preach clouds; but the Saviour never spoke in that style which, at one time, was so common in our pulpits;—a style imported partly from Germany, and which was excessively cloudy and smoky, though it was thought by some people to be wonderfully profound and to be the very trademark of intellect.*

*But there was not a sentence of that kind in all Christ's teaching. He was the clearest, most straightforward, and most outspoken of all speakers. He knew what he meant to say, and he meant his hearers also to know.*

*It is true that the Jews of his day did not comprehend some of his teaching, but that was because judicial blindness had fallen upon them. The fault was not in the light, but in their bleared eyes.*

*Turn to his teaching, and see if anyone else ever spoke so simply as he did. A child can comprehend his parables. There are, in them, hidden truths which are a mystery even to Christ's deeply-taught disciples; but Christ never mystified his hearers. He talked to them like a child. . . . He never laid aside the simplicity of childhood, though he had all the dignity of fully-developed manhood.*

*He wore his heart upon his sleeve, and spoke out what was in his mind in such plain, clear language that the poorest of the poor, and the lowest of the low were eager to listen to him.*

CHARLES HADDON SPURGEON[15]

# 1

# One Ominous Day in Galilee

*It has been given to you to know the mysteries of the
kingdom of heaven, but to them it has not been given.*

—MATTHEW 13:11

One very busy day near the end of Jesus' second year of public ministry, He
had an encounter with some hostile Pharisees, and the whole character of
His teaching suddenly changed. He no longer preached straightforward
sermons peppered with key prophetic texts from the Old Testament. From
that point on, whenever He taught publicly, He spoke in parables. Such an
abrupt shift in Jesus' teaching style was a portent of judgment against the
religious elite of Israel and all who followed their lead.

## The Pharisees and the Sabbath

Matthew introduces the turning point in Jesus' public ministry by
recounting a series of very public conflicts provoked by Jewish religious
leaders who were desperate to discredit Jesus.

The main fight they chose to pick had to do with the proper observance of the Sabbath—the symbol of their legalistic system. The Pharisees fancied themselves specialists and law-enforcement officers when it came to strict observance of the Sabbath. They had overlaid the inspired Old Testament Sabbath statutes with a long list of petty, manmade restrictions. They made this their signature issue, and they were militant in their attempts to impose an extremely rigorous brand of Sabbatarianism on the whole nation.

The Pharisees' original rationale, evidently, was that in order to avoid careless or accidental infractions on the Sabbath, it was best to prohibit everything doubtful and restrict Sabbath activities to the barest inventory of absolute necessities. Whatever their original aim, they had turned the Sabbath into an oppressive inconvenience. Worse, their rigid system became a point of immense pride to them—and a weapon of abuse with which they tormented others. The day of "rest" became one of the most onerous ordeals in a long list of "heavy burdens, hard to bear" that the Pharisees were determined to lay on other people's shoulders (Matt. 23:4).

Sabbath observance in the Old Testament was never supposed to be burdensome; it was meant to be the exact opposite: "a delight" (Isa. 58:13) and a respite for weary people. The canonical commandments regarding the Sabbath were thorough but sharply defined. The seventh day was set aside as a gracious, weekly reminder that humanity has a standing summons to enter the Lord's rest (Heb. 4:4–11). Scripture introduces this theme right at the outset. It is the crown and culmination of the creation story: "The heavens and the earth, and all the host of them, were finished. And on the seventh day God *ended His work* which He had done, and He *rested* on the seventh day from all His work which He had done. Then God *blessed* the seventh day and *sanctified* it, because in it He rested from all His work which God had created and made" (Gen. 2:1–3, emphasis added).

The progression of verbs in that text is significant. When God finished His creative work, He rested—not because He needed relief or recovery, but because His work was finished.* He then declared the Sabbath holy—as a favor to humanity. Work is a drudgery. That is a result of the curse humanity's sin brought upon all creation (Gen. 3:17–19). Furthermore, a man left to himself will discover "there is no end to all his labors" (Eccl. 4:8). The Sabbath is a celebration of *the Lord's* finished work, and all humanity is urged to enter into the Lord's rest. This truth was first pictured in the Lord's own rest on the last day of creation week. But the full glory of the Sabbath was finally unveiled in the finished work of Christ (John 19:30).**

So the Sabbath is vitally important in the biblical story of redemption. It was supposed to be a weekly reminder of the grace of God, which always stands in stark contrast to human work.

A number of precepts governing Sabbath observance were included in Moses' law. But the primary command to remember and sanctify the Sabbath is the fourth of the Ten Commandments. It is the last commandment in the first table of the Decalogue. (The first table features the commandments that define our duty with respect to God. The second table—encompassing the fifth through tenth commandments—spells out our duty with respect to our neighbors.)

Covering four full verses in Exodus 20, the fourth commandment is the longest one in the Decalogue. (The second commandment is three verses long. All eight others are stated in a single verse each.) But despite its extraordinary length, the Sabbath ordinance is not inherently complex. It says, simply:

---

* "Behold, He who keeps Israel shall neither slumber nor sleep" (Ps. 121:4). "Have you not known? Have you not heard? The everlasting God, the LORD, the Creator of the ends of the earth, neither faints nor is weary" (Isa. 40:28).

** That explains why Colossians 2:16 includes formal Sabbath observance in a list of Old Testament ceremonies that are not binding on Christians. Such things were "a shadow of things to come, but the substance is of Christ" (v. 17). Everything the Sabbath signified has been completely fulfilled in the finished work of Christ. That is why the apostle Paul suggests it is legitimate to esteem every day alike (Rom. 14:5). For the Christian, every day is a celebration of the Sabbath principle. We have entered into the spiritual rest provided for us by the finished work of Christ (Heb. 4:10–11). In other words, when Jesus declared, "The Son of Man is also Lord of the Sabbath" (Luke 6:5), and "I will give you rest" (Matt. 11:28), He not only repudiated the Pharisees' self-appointed rule over the Sabbath and affirmed His own deity; He also signified that the ultimate fulfillment of everything the Sabbath offered humanity is found in the repose of the soul who trusts in Christ's finished work.

Six days you shall labor and do all your work, but the seventh day is the Sabbath of the LORD your God. In it you shall do no work: you, nor your son, nor your daughter, nor your male servant, nor your female servant, nor your cattle, nor your stranger who is within your gates. For in six days the LORD made the heavens and the earth, the sea, and all that is in them, and rested the seventh day. Therefore the LORD blessed the Sabbath day and hallowed it. (Ex. 20:9–11)

Notice: the unusual wordiness of the fourth commandment is owing to the fact that it expressly prohibits landowners and heads of households from sidestepping the restriction by making others do their work for them. All such loopholes are closed. Then the text gives the biblical and doctrinal basis for the commandment, stressing how the Sabbath pictures entering into *God's* rest.

Aside from that, the fourth commandment is simple. What was forbidden on the Sabbath was *work*—specifically, the toil of everyday life. All labor was to be suspended; even beasts of burden were exempt from work on this day devoted to rest. The Sabbath was a gift and a blessing from God to His people, ordained by Him to keep earthly life from seeming like one long, unbroken, arduous grind.

Israel sinned repeatedly throughout her history by ignoring the Sabbaths and permitting business as usual straight through the end of the week. This negligence was motivated either by a desire for financial gain, sheer indifference about spiritual things, apostasy, idolatry, or some sinister combination of the above. Nehemiah 13:15–22 describes Nehemiah's struggle to get the people of his era to observe the Sabbath. Jeremiah 17:21–27 is a record of Jeremiah's pleading with the citizens of Jerusalem to rest on the Sabbath. They refused, and Jeremiah received a prophetic message from the Lord threatening the destruction of the city if the people would not repent of defiling the Sabbath.

By Jesus' time, however, the pendulum had swung to the opposite extreme, thanks to the preaching and politicking of the Pharisees. The people of Israel were obliged to observe the Sabbath by the strictest possible code of scruples, supposedly for the honor of God—yet not with joy and gratitude as the Lord intended, but under the Pharisees' stern compulsion and oversight. The Sabbath became a vexing, taxing, legalistic *work*—a cumbersome ritual rather than a true day of rest. People lived in fear that if they accidentally violated or neglected some trivial Sabbath rule, the Pharisees would call them on the carpet and threaten them with excommunication or, in the worst cases, stoning. That is precisely what happened to Jesus and His disciples.

## Jesus' Conflict with the Religious Elite

Matthew 12 begins with a major confrontation provoked by a Pharisaical Sabbath-enforcement squad. The disciples were hungry and had plucked some heads of grain to eat while walking through a field of wheat or barley on the Sabbath. The Pharisees were up in arms and contended with Jesus over the propriety of what His disciples had done (Matt. 12:1–2). According to the Pharisees' rules, even casually plucking a handful of grain was a form of gleaning, and therefore it was work. This was precisely the kind of seemingly inconsequential act that the Pharisees routinely targeted, turning even the bare necessities of life into a thousand unwritten Sabbatarian taboos. Their system was a veritable minefield for the average person.

Jesus replied by showing the folly of a rule that forbids an act of human necessity on a day set aside for the benefit of humanity: "The Sabbath was made for man, and not man for the Sabbath" (Mark 2:27). He rebuked the Pharisees for condemning the guiltless, and then added that famous declaration of His own divine authority: "The Son of Man is Lord even of the Sabbath" (Matt. 12:8).

The Pharisees were infuriated. But they were not through challenging Jesus about the Sabbath.

Luke 6:6 says, "Now it happened on another Sabbath, also, that He entered the synagogue and taught. And a man was there whose right hand was withered." The Pharisees were there, too, and they were prepared to escalate the conflict over the Sabbath. Pointing to the man with the disabled hand, they more or less dared Jesus to break their Sabbath rules once more in the presence of a synagogue full of witnesses. "And they asked Him, saying, 'Is it lawful to heal on the Sabbath?'—that they might accuse Him" (Matt. 12:10). They had seen Jesus do miracles many times before and knew that He had power to heal any and every kind of affliction. They had also seen ample proof (again and again) that He was indeed the promised Messiah.

But He was not the kind of Messiah they had always hoped for. He clearly opposed their vast body of man-made religious traditions. He boldly challenged their authority and claimed supreme authority for Himself. They knew that if He took His rightful place on the throne as Israel's Messiah, their status and influence over the common people would be removed. In a secret conclave, discussing what to do with Jesus, they candidly admitted what the real issue was. They were concerned about losing their own power and political status: "If we let Him alone like this, everyone will believe in Him, and the Romans will come and take away both our place and nation" (John 11:48). They were already losing favor with rank-and-file citizens in Galilee.

No wonder. "The common people heard [Jesus] gladly" (Mark 12:37). But the religious leaders' blind hatred was such that they frankly did not care whether His messianic credentials were legitimate or not; they were determined to dissuade people from following Him no matter what it took.

So when Jesus responded to their challenge by instantly healing the man with the disfigured hand, the Pharisees stormed out of the synagogue to have one of those private parleys, consulting with one another about what they might do with Him. Their ultimate goal was already clear: "The Pharisees went out and plotted against Him, how they might destroy Him" (Matt. 12:14).

The hatred of the entire Jerusalem-based religious regime had now literally reached a murderous level, and Jesus knew their intentions. Therefore, because His hour had not yet come, He immediately became more discreet in His movements and more guarded in His public ministry. Matthew says, "When Jesus knew [their intent to destroy Him], He withdrew from there. And great multitudes followed Him, and He healed them all. Yet He warned them not to make Him known" (Matt. 12:15–16).

Matthew follows his account of the Sabbath conflicts with a quotation from Isaiah 42:1–4:

> Behold! My Servant whom I have chosen, My Beloved in whom My soul is well pleased! I will put My Spirit upon Him, and He will declare justice to the Gentiles. He will not quarrel nor cry out, nor will anyone hear His voice in the streets. A bruised reed He will not break, and smoking flax He will not quench, till He sends forth justice to victory; and in His name Gentiles will trust. (Matt. 12:18–21)

Matthew's point (and Isaiah's) is that contrary to all expectations, Israel's Messiah would not arrive on the scene as a military conqueror or powerful political figure, but with a gentle, quiet approach. The "bruised reed" refers to a handmade musical instrument—a pipe or flute made from the thick stalk of a cane plant that grew on water's edge. When the flute became too worn or soggy to make music, it would be snapped in half and discarded. The "smoking flax" refers to a lamp wick that could no longer sustain a flame and thus was useless for giving light. A smoldering wick would typically be snuffed out so that the burnt edge could be trimmed in order to make the lamp efficient again.

The bruised reed and smoking flax in Isaiah's prophecy are symbolic of broken and dysfunctional people. Instead of rejecting and discarding the outcasts, Israel's Messiah would embrace them, teach them, heal them, mend them, and minister to them. Even the Gentiles would learn to trust in Him.

That prophecy from Isaiah is the bridge between Matthew's recounting of these twin Sabbath controversies and the explosive conflict that dominates the second half of Matthew 12. The writers of all four gospels sometimes arrange anecdotes from Jesus' earthly ministry in topical, rather than chronological, order. Whenever time clues are given, they are important, but sometimes the chronological relationship between one incident and the next is not crucial and therefore is not recorded in the text. That's the case between the first and second halves of Matthew 12. The plucking of the grain, followed by the healing of the man with the withered hand are told as if they occurred in quick succession. The two incidents are told in close sequence not only in Matthew 12, but also in Mark 2:23–3:5 and in Luke 6:1–11. But Luke 6:6 makes it clear that the two incidents happened on separate Sabbaths. Mark and Luke immediately follow their account of those incidents with the record of Jesus calling the Twelve, so the two Sabbath conflicts seem to have occurred early in Jesus' Galilean ministry.

Matthew is more concerned with the topic than with the timing, and his point in his chapter 12 is to show how the Sabbath controversies provoked extreme hostility against Jesus from the Jewish religious leaders. The utter contempt they had for Him finally culminated in a determination to destroy Him, which intention they sealed with an unforgivable blasphemy.

Matthew 12:22–37 recounts the shocking blasphemy and Jesus' response to it. This incident became the final straw that provoked Jesus to change His teaching style. Piecing together the chronology from all the gospel accounts, we know that this happened several months after the two Sabbath disputes. The word *then* at the start of verse 22 therefore moves us from the Isaiah prophecy to a new day near the end of Jesus' Galilean ministry. This was a pivotal day in more ways than one. In fact, this is one of the most thoroughly documented days of Jesus' Galilean ministry.

## A Remarkable Healing and Deliverance

The day started ominously when Jesus was presented with a desperately needy man—one of the most complex, heartbreaking, seemingly

ONE OMINOUS DAY IN GALILEE

impossible cases of human misery imaginable. This was a vastly more
difficult case than the man with a withered hand. This poor man's very
*soul* was withering. He was not only in dire need of physical healing; he
was also in permanent bondage to some evil spirit. He was precisely the
kind of bruised reed and smoking flax pictured in Isaiah's prophecy.

As Matthew describes it, "one was brought to Him who was
demon-possessed, blind and mute" (Matt. 12:22). Here was the living
epitome of "those who are sick" and in "need of a physician" (Mark
2:17). The man was unable to see, unable to communicate, and most
cruelly trapped in enslavement to a powerful demon. The very best phy-
sicians and doctors of divinity working together could not have helped
him by any means known to them. What could be more hopeless? Or
more urgent?

Scripture recounts in the simplest, least sensational language what
Jesus did: "He healed him, so that the blind and mute man both spoke and
saw" (Matt. 12:22). There was no delay and no period of rehabilitation.
This was a complete and instantaneous deliverance. It was undeniably
an act of God—one of the most stunningly glorious examples of Jesus'
power both to heal and to cast out demons.

Nevertheless, Matthew gives scant attention to the details of the
miracle itself. That's because what is most remarkable in this particular
incident is the aftermath. Jesus had of course already done countless
miracles of healing and deliverance all over Galilee. As Mark says,
"He healed many, so that as many as had afflictions pressed about
Him to touch Him. And the unclean spirits, whenever they saw Him,
fell down before Him and cried out, saying, 'You are the Son of God'"
(Mark 3:10–11). Countless people had already watched Jesus heal and
deliver people. There was no question about the source of His power.
Even the demons who were cast out gave testimony that Jesus was the
Son of God.

Mark further tells us that the people who crowded around Jesus
included many who had come from all over Galilee and its border

regions—specifically, from Syria to the north; from Decapolis and Perea to the east; and from Jerusalem and Judea to the south. In Matthew's words,

> Jesus [had traveled] about all Galilee, teaching in their synagogues, preaching the gospel of the kingdom, and healing all kinds of sickness and all kinds of disease among the people. Then His fame went throughout all Syria; and *they brought to Him all sick people who were afflicted with various diseases and torments, and those who were demon-possessed, epileptics, and paralytics; and He healed them.* Great multitudes followed Him—from Galilee, and from Decapolis, Jerusalem, Judea, and beyond the Jordan. (Matt. 4:23–25, emphasis added)

This spectacle of miracles became the main reason so many people wanted to be in Jesus' presence (John 6:2). The miracles were not done in a corner or only on rare occasions. They were not the vague and invisible ailments today's fake faith healers seem to specialize in. Nor was there any shortage of eyewitness testimony to the power of Jesus. Dramatic healings and other miracles became commonplace events for those who followed Jesus closely.

Again, however, the most noteworthy feature of *this* healing was the response of the religious rulers. Mark indicates that among them were "scribes who came down from Jerusalem" (Mark 3:22). These were not common Pharisees, but the chief religious scholars in all Israel—priestly aristocrats. They had made the four-day journey from Jerusalem to Galilee, it seems, specifically to try to find some fault with Jesus. Remember: according to Matthew 12:14, they were already secretly plotting to destroy Him. This was the initial phase of the conspiracy that finally culminated in His death on the cross.

The instant healing of this wretched demoniac in front of a crowd of eyewitnesses was clearly an impediment to the Pharisees' strategy. People were already responding with wonder and amazement, saying aloud, "Could this be the Son of David?" (Matt. 12:23). The crowd seemed on the verge of trying to make Him their king by force (cf. John 6:15).

The leading Pharisees quickly responded, "This fellow does not cast out demons except by Beelzebub, the ruler of the demons" (Matt. 12:24).

That was the precise moment when everything changed. What immediately follows in Matthew 12 is a short discourse that culminates in this warning about unpardonable sin: "Anyone who speaks a word against the Son of Man, it will be forgiven him; but whoever speaks against the Holy Spirit, it will not be forgiven him, either in this age or in the age to come" (v. 32).

## The Unpardonable Sin

Jesus' words, as always, must be read attentively. He was not saying that any and every blasphemy invoking the Holy Spirit's name is unpardonable. He was not announcing that there is some broad, ambiguously defined category of unpardonable transgressions we need to live in fear of—lest we carelessly or accidentally speak words that place us forever beyond the reach of divine grace. In fact, Jesus specifically said, "every sin and blasphemy will be forgiven men [*except*] the blasphemy against the Spirit" (Matt. 12:31). Thus His solemn warning about this one extraordinary act of unforgivable blasphemy was purposely prefaced by a comprehensive statement declaring every other imaginable kind of "sin and blasphemy" forgivable.

Jesus was not saying, of course, that anyone's sin is forgiven automatically without regard to whether the person repents and believes or not. Every sin is damnable as long as the sinner remains impenitent and unbelieving. "He who does not believe is condemned already, because he has not believed in the name of the only begotten Son of God" (John 3:18).

But even the vilest sin is *forgivable*—and complete forgiveness is guaranteed to every sinner who renounces his love of sin and turns to Christ as Savior. "If we confess our sins, He is faithful and just to forgive us our sins and to cleanse us from *all* unrighteousness" (1 John 1:9, emphasis added). In other words, when we agree with God concerning our own guilt, the atoning blood of Christ cleanses us from every kind of sin or blasphemy—no matter how abominable. Jesus Himself made this promise: "Most assuredly, I say to you, he who hears My word and believes in Him who sent Me has everlasting life, and shall not come into judgment, but has passed from death into life" (John 5:24).

But one very specific sin is instantly and permanently damnable. Every detail of Jesus' statement about the unpardonable sin makes it clear that He was talking about a singular, flagrantly malicious, deliberately evil act of blasphemy: "*the* blasphemy against the Spirit" (Matt. 12:31, emphasis added). The definite article is crucial. There's a clear and significant contrast between "every [other] sin and blasphemy" versus this one particular sin that "will not be forgiven . . . either in this age or in the age to come" (v. 32).

The context of Matthew 12 clearly indicates what Jesus was referring to. It was the blasphemy this haughty band of religious hypocrites had just uttered.

The Pharisees themselves did not—*could* not—really believe their own ruse. After all, they were standing in the very presence of Christ when He put His power and glory on display. Nowhere do they deny His miracles. And here they were up-close eyewitnesses to another indisputable wonder. They clearly knew the full truth about Him, but they not only rejected Him anyway; they actively tried to turn others away from Him as well. Still worse, they tried to discredit Him with a blatant blasphemy—claiming that His miracles were being accomplished with Satan's power.

The hard-hearted intentionality of the Pharisees' sin is the main factor that made it unpardonable. Why would they credit Satan with what Jesus had done through the power of the Holy Spirit? They had just watched Him vanquish demons. They fully grasped who Jesus was and with what authority He spoke and acted (Luke 6:10–11; John 11:47–48; 12:9; Acts 4:16)—and yet they hated Him with a devilish hatred anyway. It's clear that they were lying when they said *He* was the devilish one.

Jesus was speaking directly to them when He said, "Brood of vipers!
. . . by your words you will be condemned" (Matt. 12:34, 37). That was
His final, breathtaking reply to these lying, blaspheming religious pho-
nies. Their sin was so heinous and so hateful that Jesus damned them
forever on the spot. In essence, He gave the entire multitude a preview of
His accusers' final judgment. The One to whom all judgment has been
committed (John 5:22) formally pronounced them guilty. His verdict
against them was rendered publicly, emphatically, and with absolute
finality. They were now sealed forever in the darkness and hardness of
heart they had chosen for themselves.

Why was their statement such a grievous offense against the Holy
Spirit? For one thing, the demoniac's healing was as much a work of
the Holy Spirit as it was a work of Christ. All Jesus' miracles were done
according to the will of the Father through the power of the Holy Spirit
(Luke 4:14; John 5:19, 30; 8:28; Acts 10:38). Therefore to attribute our
Lord's miracles to Satan was to credit Satan with the Holy Spirit's work.
Because they knew better, the Pharisees' abominable insult was a direct,
deliberate, diabolical blasphemy against the Spirit of God.

Furthermore, the Holy Spirit is the one who confirms the testimony
of Christ and makes His truth known (John 15:26; 16:14–15). "It is the
Spirit who bears witness, because the Spirit is truth" (1 John 5:6). For
those with ears to hear, the Holy Spirit's testimony about Christ was
thunderously and definitively the polar opposite of what these Pharisees
claimed. Again: *the Pharisees knew it.* The signs and wonders they had
seen were real and incontrovertible. They uttered their blasphemy with
full awareness that they were opposing God, lying about His anointed
Servant, and blaspheming His Holy Spirit.

So that was it for them. There was now no hope for them, "either in
this age or in the age to come" (Matt. 12:32). They had deliberately closed
their eyes and stopped their ears to the truth for too long. Rejecting the
most powerful possible testimony to the truth, they chose a lie instead.
After this, Jesus would peremptorily conceal the truth from them by the
use of parables in His public teaching.

## The Pivotal Day Continues

The day was not nearly over yet. Mark 4:35, speaking of this same twenty-four-hour period, says, "On that day, when evening had come, he said to them, 'Let us go across to the other side.'"\*\*\* That was the evening when Jesus stilled a storm on the Sea of Galilee. Later yet, when "they came to the other side of the sea" (5:1), He delivered two demoniacs who were living among the tombs there—sending the demons into a herd of pigs who promptly committed suicide by running into the sea and drowning themselves (Matt. 8:28–34).\*\*\*\*

But the heart of that day was given to teaching the multitudes—and it was on that very day that Jesus began to speak to the crowds in parables.

Matthew 13:3 marks the point in that gospel where Jesus began teaching in parables. The first parable Matthew records is the parable of the soils—followed by Jesus' private explanation of the parable. (We'll examine it closely in the chapter that follows.) Matthew 13 goes on to record a few more key parables about the kingdom of heaven. Then (in a very close parallel to Mark 4:33–34) Matthew 13:34–35 says, "All these things Jesus spoke to the multitude in parables; and without a parable He did not speak to them, that it might be fulfilled which was spoken by the prophet, saying: 'I will open My mouth in parables; I will utter things kept secret from the foundation of the world.'"

By deliberately rejecting the truth, the sworn enemies of Christ had lost the privilege of hearing any more plain truth from His lips. That is precisely what Jesus meant when He said, "Whoever has, to him more

---

\*\*\* "It is called 'the Busy Day,' not because it was the only one, but simply that so much is told of this day that it serves as a specimen of many others filled to the full with stress and strain." Archibald Thomas Robertson, *Word Pictures in the New Testament*, 6 Vols (Nashville: Broadman, 1930), 1:100.

\*\*\*\* Matthew's account is not given to us in strict chronological order, but the statement in Mark 4:35 makes clear that the stilling of the storm occurred "On the same day, when evening had come." Then the sequence in both Mark 4–5 and Matthew 8 indicates that the deliverance of the two demoniacs likewise happened immediately after the storm had been stilled and the disciples' boat reached its destination.

will be given; and whoever does not have, even what he seems to have will be taken from him" (Luke 8:18).

The shift in Jesus' teaching style was immediate and dramatic. Everything He taught in public from that day forward would be concealed from everyone except those with willing ears to hear.

# 2

# A Lesson About
# Receiving the Word

*He who has ears to hear, let him hear!*

—LUKE 8:8

The decisive clash with the leading Pharisees had taken place in someone's home close to the shore of Galilee. Shortly after the dispute ended, Matthew 13:1–2 says, "*On the same day* Jesus went out of the house and sat by the sea. And great multitudes were gathered together to Him, so that He got into a boat and sat; and the whole multitude stood on the shore" (emphasis added). Luke, describing the same event, likewise stresses the size and diversity of the crowds that gathered: "They had come to Him from every city" (Luke 8:4).

Jesus twice fed swarms of followers numbering in the thousands. The official tallies would typically include only adult men, so the crowds could actually have been twice as large as the number given. No matter how heads were counted, we know that Jesus drew massive throngs of people, all pressing to get as close to Jesus as possible. The safest way for

Him to teach without being crushed in the press of teeming people was to get into a small fishing boat and push out from the shore. (Rabbis typically taught from a seated position anyway, so there was nothing unusual about the fact that He sat.) The crowds would line the shore to listen. The hills overlooking parts of the Galilean shore would form a natural amphitheater, and if there were even a slight onshore breeze, Jesus' voice would carry so that thousands might hear Him clearly.

But from this point on, only those willing to listen faithfully would get the message.

## A Surprisingly Simple Story

On this occasion, Jesus began with a story that would have been immediately familiar to everyone within earshot. In fact, from that place on the shore of the Sea of Galilee, they might have been able to view a scene that matched precisely what Jesus was saying:

> A sower went out to sow his seed. And as he sowed, some fell by the wayside; and it was trampled down, and the birds of the air devoured it. Some fell on rock; and as soon as it sprang up, it withered away because it lacked moisture. And some fell among thorns, and the thorns sprang up with it and choked it. But others fell on good ground, sprang up, and yielded a crop a hundredfold. (Luke 8:5–8)

No one would be mystified by the story itself. Only those of us who are accustomed to a world of pavement would find the imagery unfamiliar. For Jesus' actual listeners, living in an agricultural society, this was everyday life.

Fields in first-century Israel were long, narrow strips marked off and surrounded by footpaths, not fences or hedges. The sower used a broadcasting method, taking one handful of seed at a time out of a seed-bag at his side and flinging the seed over a wide swath. The arc of dispersal might have looked indiscriminate, and to a large degree it certainly was, but the method had the advantage of covering large areas of ground with evenly scattered seed. A skilled sower would not waste seed by letting it fall in concentrated patches or mound up in little piles. He would throw the seed as widely and as evenly as possible. The goal was to cover the whole plowed field, with no margins on the perimeter left unseeded.

Of course, it's impossible to throw seed by hand like that at the edges of a field yet guarantee that it stays within the boundaries. Some of the broadcast seed would inevitably fall outside the perimeter of the plowed field. Even the seed cast on the interior of the field might find patches of ground where the soil for agriculture wasn't ideal. Only the seed that found its way into good soil would ever yield produce worth harvesting. Everyone who had ever cultivated a crop fully understood this principle. It was not a complex point.

Jesus names four different types of soil.

First is the *roadside soil:* "Some fell by the wayside." That refers to those well-beaten footpaths that separated the fields. The soil there remained unplowed, of course, and in that arid climate, the pathways (when dry) were as hard as concrete. As the sower threw seed at the outer edges of the plowed field, some of the seed would inevitably end up on the hard-baked earth of the wayside.

Seed that landed on the wayside had no hope of penetrating the hard layer of the footpath. It would lie there and either be trampled underfoot or eaten by birds. The seed would never even have a chance to sprout.

Birds are surprisingly intelligent and relentlessly aggressive when it comes to snatching away scattered seed. I once tried to seed a bare patch left by foot traffic on my lawn, and I was repeatedly frustrated in that effort by the birds. One thing I learned is that putting extra seed on the bare area doesn't help. On the hard, impenetrable earth of a walkway, some seed will be trampled and fatally crushed, and the birds will devour every last trace of what's left.

The second kind of soil Jesus names is *rock* (v. 6). That isn't referring to a rocky slab on the surface of the ground. Nor does it mean "rocky soil" (as some translations have it), suggesting a patch of ground fairly full of large rocks. No self-respecting farmer would leave stones in his farmland. When the field was plowed, whatever rocks came to the surface would be removed and carried away.

What Jesus is describing is a rock bed under the field's surface, covered by a shallow layer of good soil on top. The underlying rock would be invisible to the farmer when the field was plowed, because the plowshare penetrated only about eight to ten inches deep. A layer of limestone rock bed a foot beneath the surface would be hard to detect, but such a shallow layer of soil would not be deep enough or stay moist enough to sustain crops—especially in a dry climate.

In such soil the seed goes in and germinates. But almost as soon as it begins to look lush, it will wither away from a lack of sufficient water. The roots cannot get past the rock layer. For a while, the crop might look healthy and full of potential, but when the sun comes out and the water is gone, it dies out as quickly as it sprang up.

This kind of land would be the bane of a farmer who had done everything he could to plow his field without knowing that a layer of rock lay underneath. That part of the crop would at first seem to grow more rapidly than the rest because there is no room for roots to go. The plant's abundant topside growth would also appear especially leafy. An experienced farmer would know right away that's not a good sign; it means the crops are not developing an adequate root system.

The third category Jesus names is *weed-infested soil*, full of useless, wild vegetation—thorns, nettles, thistles. The Greek word for "thorns" is *akantha*. It's the same Greek word used in the biblical crucifixion narratives to describe the crown of thorns that was placed on Jesus' head to mock Him. The word has been transliterated to form the English word *acanthus*. That's the name of a Mediterranean shrub with spiny leaves. In Greek architecture, the ornaments on Corinthian capitals were images of acanthus leaves. But thorns and thistles are useless for any agricultural purpose. In fact, they are harmful to crops, because they take over the field and choke out everything else. (That's another key feature of the curse in Genesis 3:17–19. Weeds grow better and faster than anything else.)

Seed sowed in a field of weeds will not mature to a healthy harvest. Plow up a field of weeds and many more new weeds will grow, even from the mutilated remnants of the old roots. Freshly plowed, weed-infested soil has a deceptively promising appearance. On the surface it may look rich, loamy, well cultivated, and ready for seed. But underneath there's a tragic reality. Dense roots and tiny seeds left over from the noxious weeds are still under the soil and alive, ready to spring forth with copious but worthless foliage. Those weeds will suck up the soil's moisture, drain out the nutrients, block the sunlight from the crops, and thus choke the life out of everything growing in the field that might be beneficial.

Finally, there is *fertile soil*. The seed that lands in the plowed field flourishes. It can get down into the soil (out from underfoot, and out of the birds' sight). Its roots will penetrate deeply. This is clean soil, free from weeds, with room for the crop to thrive. It is in every sense *prepared* soil. The seed that lands here produces an abundant crop. Matthew 13:8 and Mark 4:8 are parallel passages recording this same parable, and in those passages, Jesus says the seed brings forth thirtyfold, sixtyfold, or even a hundredfold. Luke 8:8 says only that this soil "yielded a crop a hundredfold."

Genesis 26 describes an incident where Isaac and Rebekah were forced by famine to dwell in the land of the Philistines for a time. Verse 12 says, "Isaac sowed in that land, and reaped in the same year a hundredfold; and the LORD blessed him." So a hundredfold signified extraordinary blessing from God. The next verse says of Isaac, "he became very prosperous."

"A hundredfold" is not a reference to the number of seeds each seed would ultimately yield. (A single pumpkin seed, for example, can produce ten to fifteen pumpkins. The total number of seeds they contain will be far more than a hundred. A hundredfold *in seeds* would be a fairly poor harvest.) The expression speaks of the return on the farmer's original financial investment. For every denarius spent on seed, he earns a hundred denarii in the sale of his crops. Tenfold would thus be quite a healthy return. Thirty or sixty would be something spectacular. "A hundredfold" was a staggering profit.

## Some Subtle Points to Notice

As Jesus tells the story, several things become clear: First, nothing is said about the sower and his skill. There's only one sower in the story. The key difference between the seed that bears a hundredfold harvest and the seed that is devoured by the birds has nothing to do with the method the sower uses when he casts the seed.

Second, nothing is said about the quality of the seed. It all comes from the same source. The seed that survives and bears fruit is the very same kind of seed that gets choked out by weeds. There's no problem with the quality of the seed.

*The lesson Jesus is teaching is all about the soil.* This is a simple story whose meaning on the surface is not the least bit mysterious. But following the plot of the story isn't the same as understanding what it refers to. The true significance of what Jesus is teaching is not immediately obvious. The parable needs to be explained.

Jesus therefore urges His hearers to investigate the true meaning of the parable. That is made clear by a statement in the second half of Luke 8:8: "When He had said these things He cried, 'He who has ears to hear, let him hear!'" The verb tense in the Greek is imperfect, which usually signifies repeated or continuous action. The New American Standard Bible translates the verse this way: "As He said these things, He would call out, 'He who has ears to hear, let him hear'"—implying that as He told the parable, He stressed more than once the need to pay attention, listen with a believing heart, and look beyond the surface for the true meaning. Jesus later would reinforce that point, shortly after explaining this parable, saying, "Take heed how you hear" (Luke 8:18).

## Take Heed How You Hear

The disciples took Him at His word. The Twelve and a few other close followers were apparently the only ones in the multitude who did. Mark 4:10 says, "When He was alone, those around Him with the twelve asked

Him about the parable." That is a clear indication of who did have ears to hear. They were the ones who truly believed in Him. They were the ones who followed Jesus' teaching, rather than merely chasing His miracles.

Luke 8:9–10 picks up the story at that point:

> Then His disciples asked Him, saying, "What does this parable mean?"
>
> And He said, "To you it has been given to know the mysteries of the kingdom of God, but to the rest it is given in parables, that
>
> 'Seeing they may not see,
>
> And hearing they may not understand.' "

When Jesus speaks of "mysteries," He is not talking about some gnostic-style clandestine teaching that only certain advanced or enlightened votaries are privy to. He is not describing esoteric secrets. When the New Testament speaks of "mysteries," the meaning is simple, and quite narrow: a biblical *mystery* is some spiritual truth that was obscure or totally hidden under the old covenant but now has been fully revealed in the new. The fact that Gentiles would be fellow heirs and partakers in the gospel was one such mystery, "which in other ages was not made known to the sons of men, as it has now been revealed by the Spirit to His holy apostles and prophets" (Eph. 3:5). The gospel itself was a mystery (Eph. 6:19). The incarnation of Christ was likewise a mystery, "the mystery of Christ" (Col. 4:3). Those are all truths that were not fully revealed in the Old Testament but have now been made clear in the New. Paul seems to quote from an early-church hymn or a familiar confession of faith when he describes the entire earthly ministry of Christ (everything from His incarnation to His ascension) as "the mystery of godliness:

> *God was manifested in the flesh,*
> *Justified in the Spirit,*
> *Seen by angels,*
> *Preached among the Gentiles,*
> *Believed on in the world,*
> *Received up in glory." (1 Tim. 3:16)*

So a "mystery" (in the sense Jesus is using the term) is something either partially or completely hidden at one time that has now been fully revealed. Our Lord was about to start taking the lid off everything the Old Testament had kept shrouded in typology, symbolism, and prophetic hints.

But the unveiling was purposely subtle, so that the only people who got it were authentic believers who were eager to learn the truth—those who had ears to hear. They understood the truths Jesus was teaching, not by some special clairvoyance or preternatural ability, but because they had enough interest to ask Jesus for the interpretation. To the rest, the mysteries remained cloaked in parabolic symbolism.

To the disciples He said privately, "To you it has been given to know the mysteries of the kingdom of God" (Luke 8:10). To those with ears to hear, He was saying, in effect, "You are elect; you are chosen; you are blessed." It was a staggering privilege for a group composed largely of fishermen from a remote Galilean village.

Although Jesus was presenting the parables in a way that would obscure the truth from unbelieving ears, no one was excluded against his or her will. Anyone who truly wanted to understand could have asked. Remember, Jesus urged every person in earshot to seek understanding: "Therefore take heed how you hear. For whoever has, to him more will be given; and whoever does not have, even what he seems to have will be taken from him" (Luke 8:18). The listeners' response would separate those who believed from those who didn't. Those who believed would seek the truth, and find it. For those who did not believe, the parables would only further conceal the truth. Their spiritual blindness was compounded by their own unbelief and then further deepened by divine judgment.

But to the inquisitive disciples, Jesus said, "Blessed are your eyes for they see, and your ears for they hear; for assuredly, I say to you that many prophets and righteous men desired to see what you see, and did not see it, and to hear what you hear, and did not hear it" (Matt. 13:16–17). Years later, Peter was still in awe of such a privilege. He wrote,

Of this salvation the prophets have inquired and searched carefully, who prophesied of the grace that would come to you, searching what, or what manner of time, the Spirit of Christ who was in them was indicating when He testified beforehand the sufferings of Christ and the glories that would follow. To them it was revealed that, not to themselves, but to us they were ministering the things which now have been reported to you through those who have preached the gospel to you by the Holy Spirit sent from heaven—things which angels desire to look into. (1 Peter 1:10–12)

Truths that were mysterious—not only to the Old Testament prophets but even to the angels—were about to be explained to Peter and his companions.

## The Explanation

This parable gives us an important template for how we should read and interpret Jesus' storytelling. Jesus' explanation is as simple and straightforward as the parable itself:

Now the parable is this: The seed is the word of God. Those by the wayside are the ones who hear; then the devil comes and takes away the word out of their hearts, lest they should believe and be saved. But the ones on the rock are those who, when they hear, receive the word with joy; and these have no root, who believe for a while and in time of temptation fall away. Now the ones that fell among thorns are those who, when they have heard, go out and are choked with cares, riches, and pleasures of life, and bring no fruit to maturity. But the ones that fell on the good ground are those who, having heard the word with a noble and good heart, keep it and bear fruit with patience. (Luke 8:11–15)

The seed represents God's Word. Specifically in view here is the gospel message (the good news of the kingdom). The Word of God (the gospel message in particular) is likewise pictured as seed in James 1:18–21 and 1 Peter 1:23–25. There's a hint of this same imagery in a couple of familiar Old Testament texts. Isaiah 55:11 pictures God's Word going out by some means analogous to the sower's method of broadcasting: "My word . . . shall not return to Me void." The principle of Psalm 126:5–6 certainly applies to the work of the evangelist who spreads the gospel:

> Those who sow in tears
> Shall reap in joy.
> He who continually goes forth weeping,
> Bearing seed for sowing,
> Shall doubtless come again with rejoicing,
> Bringing his sheaves with him.

This, then, is the key that unlocks the meaning of the parable: "The seed is the word of God."

The sower is not specifically identified. Some think he is supposed to represent Christ Himself, because when Jesus explained the parable of the tares, He said, "He who sows the good seed is the Son of Man" (Matt. 13:37). But these are different parables, and the imagery is not the same. One important rule to bear in mind when interpreting parables is not to mix the details. For example, in the parable of the soils, we're expressly told that the seed represents the Word of God, and (as we shall observe shortly) the plowed field represents a human heart properly prepared to receive the Word. But just a few verses later, in the parable of the tares (Matt. 13:24–30), the good seed represents "the sons of the kingdom" (the true inhabitants of the kingdom of God), and "the field is the world" (v. 38). So we must be careful not to mingle the symbolism of the parables.

The sower in the parable of the soils isn't expressly identified, because his identity is simply not important. He represents anyone who distributes the seed. That's anyone who proclaims the Word of God, whether by preaching, personal evangelism, in an individual testimony, or whatever. The sower is whoever disperses God's Word or the gospel message.

The point of the parable has to do with the soil. You cannot get the gist of this parable without understanding that the soil is a picture of the human heart. Specifically, the parable highlights four different kinds of hearts in varying degrees of receptivity. Luke 8:12 gives incontrovertible proof that the soil in the parable represents the human heart: "Those by the wayside are the ones who hear; then the devil comes and takes away the word *out of their hearts,* lest they should believe and be saved" (emphasis added).

That word *hearts* makes a proper interpretation of the parable fairly easy. The heart is, of course, where the seed of God's Word ought to take root. In the words of Luke 8:15: "the *good ground* are those who, having heard the word with a noble and *good heart,* keep it and bear fruit with patience" (emphasis added).

So the parable is about hearts in assorted stages of preparedness. All four kinds of soil consist of the same minerals. They are organically and intrinsically identical. What makes them distinct from one another is whether they are in a suitable condition for producing fruit or not.

Again we see that the point Jesus is teaching has nothing to do with the skill of the sower or the quality of the seed. The seed is perfect, and eternally unchanging. Any attempt to improve the harvest by using different seed is a misguided dereliction of the sower's duty. The point of the activity is not merely to produce dense but fruitless foliage. If that were the goal, he could sow dandelions or tumbleweeds. It's quite true that these would germinate and grow more easily in the shallow, hard, or already weedy places.

But woe to the tiller of ground who seeks a harvest that way.

The unadulterated Word of God is the only true and legitimate seed. The sower is anyone who disseminates the message of God's Word (epitomized in the proclamation of the gospel). Jesus doesn't even mention the weather, but the weather would be the same for all four types of soil, and the implication of a hundredfold harvest is that the weather in this case was just fine. The one factor that differentiates between an abundant harvest and the hard, dry, desolate barrenness of the wayside ground is simply and only the condition of the soil.

Here, then, is the lesson of this first parable: A person's response to the Word of God is dependent on the condition of that person's heart. Furthermore, *fruit* is the only evidence that one has heard the Word rightly.

It is not without significance that when Jesus began to unveil the mysteries of the kingdom, this is the first truth He taught. It is a foundational truth, and one that the church today desperately needs to be reminded of. Evangelicals constantly adopt all kinds of bizarre and unbiblical methodologies because they think they can elicit a better response from hard, shallow, or worldly hearts. Some *alter the seed*, or manufacture synthetic seed. They try to update the message, tone down the offense of the cross, leave the hard or unpopular parts out. Many simply replace the gospel with a totally different message.

Some abandon the sower's task. They decide that throwing seed around is primitive and unsophisticated—and imagine that they can devise a better use for the field. Why not use it to host a music festival, or turn it into a drive-in theater?

But the parable is not about enhancing the quality of the seed, improving the skill of the sower, or finding a more elegant use for the farm. It's all about the condition of the soil. Whether the Word of God bears fruit in the life of a hearer or not depends ultimately on the condition of that person's heart. The various heart conditions Jesus illustrates cover the whole range of human possibilities.

## The Wayside Hearer

The pressed-down, dry, and hardened soil by the wayside pictures a heart that is impervious to biblical truth. This is perhaps the most disturbing and hopeless of all the conditions Jesus depicts. Unbelief and a love of sin have made the heart a dense, rocklike environment where truth cannot possibly penetrate, much less take root. The hearer is therefore oblivious, hopeless, spiritually dead—and totally susceptible to the stratagems of Satan.

Jesus explains: "Those by the wayside are the ones who hear; then the devil comes and takes away the word out of their hearts, lest they should believe and be saved" (Luke 8:12). That verse, by the way, explains the true goal symbolized in the work of the sower. His aim is that people might "believe and be saved." There is only one way to sow the proper seed for such a goal: by proclaiming the gospel of Jesus Christ (which is, after all, the ultimate point and the real focus of the entire Bible). The sower is an evangelist. He is hoping for a harvest of souls.

Inevitably, he encounters hearers whose hearts are like concrete. The Old Testament calls them "stiff-necked" (Ex. 32:9; 2 Kings 17:14). The clear implication is that such people have deliberately hardened their own hearts. "They have stiffened their necks that they might not hear My words" (Jer. 19:15). Of Zedekiah, the evil young king who "did evil in the sight of the LORD his God" (2 Chron. 36:12), Scripture says, "He stiffened his neck and hardened his heart against turning to the LORD God of Israel" (v. 13). He deliberately steeled his own will against repentance. Men like that were the ones who stoned Stephen, and he called them on it: "You stiff-necked and uncircumcised in heart and ears! You always resist the Holy Spirit; as your fathers did, so do you" (Acts 7:51).

Such a person is depicted by the well-worn, barren footpath around the field. This heart is a thoroughfare, crossed by the mixed multitude of iniquities that continually traverse it. It is not fenced, so it lies exposed to all the evil stomping of everything wicked that comes along. It is never plowed by conviction. It is never cultivated with any kind of self-searching, self-examination, contrition, honest assessment of guilt, or true repentance. The heart is as hardened against the sweet beckoning of grace as it is against the dreadful terrors of judgment. Indifference, insensibility, and a love for sin have made this person's heart dense, dry, and impenetrable.

This is the fool of Proverbs—the person who despises wisdom and instruction (Prov. 1:7) and "has no delight in understanding, but in expressing his own heart" (18:2). What's interesting here is that Jesus is not describing atheists. He is speaking to people in a highly religious culture, and the hardest of all hearts in His audience this day are the religious aristocracy—the top scribes and Pharisees, the same ones who had so recently blasphemed the Holy Spirit, cutting themselves off from grace altogether. Their sin epitomizes the absolute ultimate in hard-heartedness. The rank atheist is in a better state spiritually than they are. Elsewhere, Jesus said to them, "You are of your father the devil, and the desires of your father you want to do" (John 8:44).

Here, He again says hardened hearts are utterly at the mercy of the evil one. "The devil comes and takes away the word out of their hearts, lest they should believe and be saved" (Luke 8:12).

How does the devil snatch the Word of God away from a heart? He has many devices, and we should not be ignorant of them (2 Cor. 2:11). If you think Satan and his works are always obviously diabolical, you are going to be defrauded by him. He uses deceit. "He is a liar and the father of it" (John 8:44). He transforms himself and his servants as angels of light and ministers of righteousness (2 Cor. 11:14–15). He confuses people through false teachers who come in Christ's name but subtly attack or undermine the truth of the gospel. He also exploits sinful human passions: fear of what others might think, pride, stubbornness, prejudice, or various lusts. He appeals to the fallen heart's love for the pleasures of sin. He knows that people love "darkness rather than light, because their deeds [are] evil" (John 3:19), and he takes advantage of that. It is easy for him to make himself appealing to those who love darkness. Then having gained the sinner's trust and attention, he diverts the mind from the truth of the Word, effectively snatching it away from the person's consciousness.

## The Shallow Hearer

The soil spread thinly over a layer of rock illustrates a shallow-hearted person who responds immediately but only superficially. "The ones on the rock are those who, when they hear, receive the word with joy; and these have no root, who believe for a while and in time of temptation fall away" (Luke 8:13). Without deep roots, vegetation cannot live long in a dry climate. It grows green and leafy quickly, but dies just as quickly, before reaching fruit-bearing maturity. Such growth is useless for any profitable purpose.

Psalm 129:6 similarly compares the wicked to "the grass on the housetops, which withers before it grows up." In the thin layer of dust that accumulates on a flat roof, grass or weeds may sprout and even look lush for a short season, but it is in a location that cannot sustain long-term life. It is doomed as soon as it sprouts—and even the dead straw left in the end is useless for any good purpose. The psalm goes on to say that "the reaper does not fill his hand [with it], nor he who binds sheaves, his arms" (v. 7).

In the area where I live, barren hills and mountains surround us. During the rainy season they suddenly spring to life with luxuriant-looking greenery. But in a very short while they revert to a parched brown. The green that looked so promising turns into lifeless scrub, good for nothing but for feeding California's wildfires as tinder.

That's a perfect parable for the way some people respond to the gospel. They are the polar opposite of the hard-hearted hearers. They *seem* receptive. They show a keen interest. Jesus says they "receive the word with joy" (Luke 8:13). They are exhilarated by it. But all that enthusiasm obscures the fact that there is no root. They "believe for a while." That's an important fact to acknowledge: intellectually, at least, they are receptive, affirmative—even quite enthusiastic. There is a kind of temporary credence that is not authentic faith, precisely because it is superficial—shallow, rootless, totally at the mercy of the hostile elements that are sure to test its viability.

It's not a question of *if* but *when* such "faith" will fail. It usually (but not always) happens sooner rather than later. Each person who responds positively to the Word of God will face a "time of temptation." The Greek word translated "temptation" in Luke 8:13 can also refer to a trial or a test—and that is clearly the sense here. The new disciple's faith will eventually be put to the test under the threat of persecution, by one of life's calamities, or by the sheer difficulty of maintaining the pretense of deep, abiding belief. If it's superficial, rootless, heartless faith, no matter how enthusiastic the response may have seemed in the beginning, that person will "fall away"—meaning she will abandon the faith completely.

Jesus said in John 8:31, "If you abide in My word, you are My disciples indeed." Hebrews 3:14 says, "We have become partakers of Christ if we hold the beginning of our confidence steadfast to the end." The apostle Paul said you can know you are truly reconciled to God "if indeed you continue in the faith, grounded and steadfast, and are not moved away from the hope of the gospel which you heard" (Col. 1:23).

Those whose faith is merely temporary hear the gospel and respond, quickly and superficially. Perhaps they have some selfish motive (thinking Jesus will fix their worldly problems or make life easy for them). They don't truly count the cost. For a while they bask in some emotion—a feeling of relief, exhilaration, euphoria, or whatever. There are tears of joy, embraces, high fives, and a lot of activity—at first. That tends to convince other believers that this is a true conversion, well rooted in genuine conviction. We might even be inclined to think that's a better response than the quiet restraint of some genuine believer who is so deeply convicted about his sin and unworthiness that all he feels is a profound sense of meekness and quiet gratitude.

An outburst of joy is not the distinguishing feature of an authentic conversion. Joy is a fine and appropriate response, of course. All heaven is filled with rejoicing when a soul is converted. "There will be more joy in heaven over one sinner who repents than over ninety-nine just persons who need no repentance" (Luke 15:7). But as Jesus makes clear in our parable, great joy sometimes accompanies false conversion. Neither hyperactive joy nor grateful quietude proves anything one way or another about whether someone's profession of faith is an expression of superficial, temporary belief or deep and lasting conviction. The person's fruit (or lack of it) will reveal that. "A tree is known by its fruit" (Matt. 12:33).

It doesn't ultimately matter how much enthusiasm the shallow hearer shows in that initial response to the Word of God: if it's a shallow conviction with no real root, that person will eventually fall away. And when that happens, it proves definitively that in spite of all that apparent joy and zeal, the person never truly believed in the first place. "They went out from us, but they were not of us; for if they had been of us, they would have continued with us; but they went out that they might be made manifest, that none of them were of us" (1 John 2:19).

## The Worldly Hearer

The third type of soil, the weedy soil, represents a heart too enthralled or too preoccupied with worldly matters. Jesus explains, "Now the ones that fell among thorns are those who, when they have heard, go out and are choked with cares, riches, and pleasures of life, and bring no fruit to maturity" (Luke 8:14).

Those who fit this category (like the shallow-soil hearers) may seem to respond positively at first. The analogy suggests that there will most likely be some initial sign of receptivity. Seed sown among weeds *would* germinate. These people, "when they have heard, go out"—meaning, apparently, that they give every sign of pursuing the way of faith. Mark seems to suggest that at first they seem to have every potential to be fruitful, but then at some point afterward, "the cares of this world, the deceitfulness of riches, and the desires for other things entering in choke the word, and it *becomes* unfruitful" (Mark 4:19, emphasis added).

This is not a hard-hearted unbeliever or a shallow, emotional person. This time the soil itself is well plowed and deep enough. But there are all kinds of impurities in it. Weeds native to that soil have already germinated under the surface. They will always grow stronger and faster than the good seed. The Word of God is a foreigner in such a heart. Weeds and thorns own that ground.

This person is too in love with this world—too obsessed with the "cares, riches, and pleasures of life"—*this* life (Luke 8:14). That's the key. The values of the temporal world (sinful pleasures, earthly ambitions, money, prestige, and a host of trivial diversions) deluge the heart and muffle the truth of God's Word.

This is "a double-minded man, unstable in all his ways" (James 1:8). As Jesus taught, "No servant can serve two masters; for either he will hate the one and love the other, or else he will be loyal to the one and despise the other. You cannot serve God and mammon" (Luke 16:13).

Indeed, in Matthew's account, the stress is on the worldly hearer's love of money: "The deceitfulness of riches choke the word" (Matt. 13:22). Writing to Timothy, the apostle Paul said, "Those who desire to be rich fall into temptation and a snare, and into many foolish and harmful lusts which drown men in destruction and perdition. For the love of money is a root of all kinds of evil, for which some have strayed from the faith in their greediness, and pierced themselves through with many sorrows" (1 Tim. 6:9–10). Nothing is more hostile to the truth of the gospel than love for the riches and pleasures of this world. To those whose main wish is to spend their resources on worldly pleasures, James 4:4 says, "Adulterers and adulteresses! Do you not know that friendship with the world is enmity with God? Whoever therefore wants to be a friend of the world makes himself an enemy of God."

The apostle John condemned worldliness with equal severity. He wrote, "Do not love the world or the things in the world. If anyone loves the world, the love of the Father is not in him" (1 John 2:15). Did he mean it is a sin to love mountains and flowers or good food and people? Of course not. He is talking about the values and the vices of this world, everything embodied in the world's pathological and self-destructive enmity toward God: "All that is in the world—the lust of the flesh, the lust of the eyes, and the pride of life—is not of the Father but is of the world" (v. 16).

That is precisely what the weeds and thorns in the parable represent: selfishness, sinful desire, and the unholy belief system that dominates this world. Values such as those—not the natural features of the created world itself—are what suffocate the truth of God's Word in fallen hearts and make this world unworthy of our love.

Don't miss the point. Material wealth is not inherently evil, nor is pleasure. When properly prioritized, wealth and pleasure should be received with thanksgiving as gracious gifts from the hand of God, who is generous with such blessings (Deut. 8:18; Eccl. 5:18–19; Hos. 2:8). But it is evil to love the gifts more than the Giver, or to value tangible and temporal benefits more highly than spiritual blessings. Paul told Timothy, "Command those who are rich in this present age not to be haughty, nor to trust in uncertain riches but in the living God, who gives us richly all things to enjoy" (1 Tim. 6:17).

One classic New Testament example of the worldly hearer is the rich young ruler. He came to Jesus eagerly seeking eternal life, but he was a materialist and a lover of the world—and Jesus knew it. Scripture says the young ruler "went away sorrowful, for he had great possessions" (Matt. 19:22). He loved worldly values more than he loved God. Another example, of course, is Judas, who made every pretense of following Jesus from the time Jesus called the Twelve until Judas finally betrayed Christ for thirty pieces of silver. Scripture tells us that Judas's besetting sin was the love of money. "He was a thief, and had the money box; and he used to take what was put in it" (John 12:6). He was the most sinister kind of weedy-soil hearer.

Here's what the wayside hearer, the shallow hearer, and the worldly hearer all have in common: They "bring no fruit to maturity" (Luke 8:14). The whole purpose of agriculture is to produce a harvest. Soil that fails to produce a crop is of no value. The hardened wayside will remain perpetually hard, the shallow soil will most likely not be seeded again, and the weedy soil will be burnt. If it cannot be completely cleared, purged of weeds, and cultivated again, it will be abandoned as wasteland.

All three varieties of fruitless soil are emblematic of unbelievers—including those who originally showed some promise but failed to bear fruit.

## The Fruitful Hearer

The final soil is well cultivated and produces the desired crop. Jesus says this symbolizes "those who, having heard the word with a noble and good heart, keep it and bear fruit with patience" (Luke 8:15). This is the truly prepared heart. In Matthew 13:23, Jesus says the good soil pictures a person "who hears the word and understands it." In Mark 4:20, He says it is a symbol of "those who hear the word, *accept* it, and bear fruit" (emphasis added).

He is describing someone with a heart so well prepared that when the person hears the gospel, he receives it with true understanding and genuine faith. The expression Luke uses ("[they] keep it and bear fruit with patience") suggests a tenacious hold on the truth, and perseverance in the faith.

Perseverance with fruit is the necessary sign of genuine, saving trust in Christ. This is one of the key lessons of the whole parable: *the mark of authentic faith is endurance.* Jesus said, "If you abide in My word, you are My disciples indeed" (John 8:31). Temporary faith is not true faith at all.

The "fruit" spoken of in the parable includes, of course, the fruit of the Spirit—"love, joy, peace, longsuffering, kindness, goodness, faithfulness, gentleness, self-control" (Gal. 5:22–23). It encompasses all "the fruits of righteousness which are by Jesus Christ, to the glory and praise of God" (Phil. 1:11). A truly believing heart will naturally produce worship—"the fruit of . . . lips, giving thanks to His name" (Heb. 13:15). And the apostle Paul spoke of people whom he had led to Christ as fruit of his ministry (Rom. 1:13). All of these are examples of the kinds of fruit Jesus had in mind when He said the good soil represents people who "bear fruit with patience."

The expectation is that they will also bear fruit *abundantly.* Matthew and Mark both say "some thirtyfold, some sixty, and some a hundred" (Mark 4:20; cf. Matt. 13:23). As we noted earlier in this chapter, anything over tenfold would be an immense return on the farmer's investment. While Jesus is clearly teaching what we know from experience—that Christians are not all equally fruitful—He is simultaneously suggesting that an abundance of fruit is the expected result of faith. The spiritual fruit in our lives should be copious and obvious—not so scarce that it's hard to find. After all, we are "created in Christ Jesus for good works, which God prepared beforehand that we should walk in them" (Eph. 2:10). Jesus said, "Every branch in Me that does not bear fruit [the Father, who is the vinedresser] takes away; and every branch that bears fruit He prunes, that it may bear more fruit" (John 15:2). Fruitfulness—a divinely wrought, abundant harvest—is the expected outcome of saving faith.

That can occur only in a heart that is clean and well cultivated.

It is each person's *duty* to have a prepared heart, ready to "receive with meekness the implanted word" (James 1:21)—and then to nurture that seed to full fruitfulness. The Old Testament tells us that Rehoboam, Solomon's foolish son and heir to the throne, "did evil, *because he did not prepare his heart* to seek the LORD" (2 Chron. 12:14, emphasis added). Also, to the backslidden people of Judah and Jerusalem in Old Testament Israel, God gave this command through His prophet: "Break up your fallow ground, and do not sow among thorns" (Jer. 4:3). The context makes it perfectly clear that He was commanding them to prepare their hearts to receive the word (cf. v. 4). That is the duty of every person.

But here is the problem: We cannot accomplish that for ourselves. We are already hopelessly unclean. We are fallen, guilty sinners with shallow, weedy, rebellious hearts. Left to ourselves we would just grow harder. Every exposure to the light would bake the hardness in even more, until we became as impervious to God's Word as a concrete walkway is to grass seed. "The carnal [unregenerate, fleshly] mind is enmity against God; for it is not subject to the law of God, nor indeed can be. So then, those who are in the flesh cannot please God" (Rom. 8:7–8).

Only God Himself can plow and prepare a heart to receive the Word. He does it through the regenerating and sanctifying work of His Holy Spirit, who convicts the world "of sin, and of righteousness, and of judgment" (John 16:8). For those who believe, he awakens them spiritually (Rom. 8:11). He enlightens their minds to the truth (1 Cor. 2:10). He washes them clean (Ezek. 36:25). He removes the stony heart and gives them a new heart (v. 26). He indwells His people and motivates them unto righteousness (v. 27). He engraves the truth of God on their hearts (Jer. 31:33; 2 Cor. 3:3). He pours the love of God into their hearts (Rom. 5:5). We who believe in Christ are totally dependent on the indwelling Spirit's work in our hearts to keep us tender, receptive, and ultimately fruitful.

And we must remain faithfully dependent on Him.

Like David, who prayed, "Create in me a clean heart, O God, and renew a steadfast spirit within me" (Ps. 51:10), we must approach God with trust and submission, allowing Him to do the necessary work in our hearts that we cannot do ourselves.

Finally, this parable is a reminder that when we proclaim the gospel or teach the Word of God to our neighbors and loved ones, the results will always vary according to the condition of the hearts of our hearers. Success or failure does not hinge on our skill as sowers. Some of the seed we disperse will fall on hard, shallow, or weedy ground. But there's nothing wrong with the seed. If you are faithful at the task, some of the seed you throw *will* find well-cultivated soil, and the result will be abundant fruit.

# 3

# A Lesson About the
# Cost of Discipleship

*If anyone desires to come after Me, let him deny himself,*
*and take up his cross daily, and follow Me.*

—LUKE 9:23

Perhaps the most unnecessary extreme activity is high mountain climb-ing. Every year (compounding as each year passes) the slopes of Mount Everest are littered with the dead bodies of failed climbers. The effort is costly, all-consuming, and dangerous. Prior to 1996, one in four who made the attempt died in the process. The numbers are a little better today, but still on average fourteen people die for every one hundred who reach the summit. One in ten who do make it to the top die on the way down. More than 225 people have perished in the past three decades try-ing to make the climb. April 2014 saw the deadliest day in the mountain's history when an avalanche swept sixteen people to their deaths. What other sport claims the lives of so many participants?

It is an expensive expedition, too, costing anywhere from thirty thousand dollars to four times that just to make one attempt. Training for the climb takes eight to twelve months full time—minimally. Several years of climbing experience is considered absolutely necessary by most experts.

Considering the high cost of the hobby and the dire outcome that is possible, it is astonishing how many people will risk everything they have and even their own lives to accomplish a feat that offers them no tangible reward beyond self-satisfaction and pride. It is certainly not a commitment to be entered into lightly.

Our Lord said something similar to those who showed a superficial interest in following Him. Discipleship is not a lifestyle to be embarked on heedlessly. He told two parables in Matthew 13 that illustrate the necessity of counting the cost of entering His kingdom.

## What Is the Kingdom?

The kingdom of heaven is a frequent theme in Jesus' parables. It is the realm over which Christ Himself is the undisputed King of kings and Lord of lords. It is the domain in which His lordship is even now fully operative. In other words, all who truly belong to the kingdom of heaven have formally yielded to Christ's lordship. To enter the kingdom, therefore, is to enter into eternal life. In short, the kingdom is synonymous with the sphere of salvation—that eternal realm where the redeemed have their true citizenship (Phil. 3:20).

At present, the kingdom is a spiritual dominion, not an earthly geopolitical realm. Jesus described the current state of the kingdom as intangible and invisible: "The kingdom of God does not come with observation; nor will they say, 'See here!' or 'See there!' For indeed, the kingdom of God is within [or among] you" (Luke 17:20–21). He also said, "My kingdom is not of this world" (John 18:36).

This is not the full and final expression of Christ's kingdom, of course. The earthly culmination of the kingdom awaits His bodily return. Then all "the kingdoms of this world [will] become the kingdoms of our Lord and of His Christ, and He shall reign forever and ever!" (Rev. 11:15). The first phase of that eternal rule is the thousand-year reign of the Lord Jesus on earth promised in Revelation 20:1–7. That is followed by the creation of the new heaven and the new earth over which His eternal reign continues (Rev. 21:1–8).

That is what Jesus taught us to pray for: "Your kingdom come. Your will be done on earth as it is in heaven" (Matt. 6:10). When the kingdom is finally manifest in the new creation, it will be visible, universal (spanning heaven and earth), and never ending. In the meantime, the kingdom is absolutely real; it is present; and it is constantly, quietly growing, as sinners are redeemed and graciously granted kingdom citizenship for all eternity. Jesus illustrated all those truths in His parables.

The kingdom is called by several names in Scripture: "the kingdom of Christ and God" (Eph. 5:5); "the kingdom of God" (Mark 4:11); and "His [Christ's] kingdom" (Matt. 13:41; 16:28). The common notion that "the kingdom of heaven" and "the kingdom of God" are separate realms is a fallacy. Matthew always used the expression "kingdom of heaven," and he is the only writer in the New Testament who used that phrase. All the other gospels routinely say "kingdom of God." The terms are synonymous, as you can see by a comparison of cross-references (cf. Matt. 5:3 and Luke 6:20; Matt. 19:24 and Mark 10:23; or Matt. 11:11 and Luke 7:28). Matthew was writing for the benefit of Jewish readers. He always said "kingdom of heaven" rather than "kingdom of God" because Jewish readers tended to be overscrupulous about the use of God's name, and he did not want to put an unnecessary stumbling block in his readers' way.

## Is Entrance to the Kingdom Free, or Is There a Cost?

Nothing in the universe could ever match the priceless value of the kingdom. It's worth more than any mere mortal could ever imagine—which means it is infinitely beyond the price range any of us could ever even think to afford. If you gave everything you ever had and everything you ever will have, it still would be nowhere near enough to merit entry into the kingdom. This is crystal clear in Scripture: you simply cannot buy your way in.

In fact, it actually works the other way. People who are rich in this world's goods are severely disadvantaged from the perspective of the heavenly kingdom. Jesus said, "It is easier for a camel to go through the eye of a needle than for a rich man to enter the kingdom of God" (Matt. 19:24). Scripture says, "The love of money is a root of all kinds of evil" (1 Tim. 6:10). To be enthralled with material wealth makes a person unfit for the kingdom—even if the person *isn't* wealthy. In Jesus' words, "How hard it is for those who trust in riches to enter the kingdom of God!" (Mark 10:24). Nor does the kingdom belong to self-righteous people or those who think their religion, morality, education, humanitarianism, philanthropy, environmentalism, political viewpoint—or anything else—might earn merit with God (cf. Luke 18:10–14).

The demand of God's law is very straightforward. Jesus summed it up in a single statement: "You [must] be perfect, just as your Father in heaven is perfect" (Matt. 5:48). James says it this way: "Whoever shall keep the whole law, and yet stumble in one point, he is guilty of all" (James 2:10). So the law condemns us all, because we all fall far short of that measure. It is the very height of arrogant presumption to imagine that fallen sinners could sufficiently satisfy God's perfect standard of righteousness or somehow win His favor by trying to cover our guilt with our own imperfect works. "We are all like an unclean thing, and all our righteousnesses are like filthy rags" (Isa. 64:6).

We could sooner buy all the palaces and mansions on earth than we could earn entry into the kingdom of heaven by our own merits. In fact, the characteristic attitude of all true kingdom citizens is that they are "poor in spirit" (Matt. 5:3). They recognize and confess their own utter spiritual poverty. They know that they are unworthy sinners (1 Tim. 1:15).

That, by the way, is not one of the kingdom mysteries kept hidden until it was finally revealed in the New Testament. It is a basic truth that should have been perfectly clear already:

*Those who trust in their wealth*
*And boast in the multitude of their riches,*
*None of them can by any means redeem his brother,*
*Nor give to God a ransom for him—*
*For the redemption of their souls is costly.* (Ps. 49:6–8)

That's why Jesus—the perfect, spotless, sinless Lamb of God—had to make the only possible atonement for sinners. "[God] made Him who knew no sin to be sin for us, that we might become the righteousness of God in Him" (2 Cor. 5:21). In effect, Christ paid the kingdom's entry fee in full for those who believe on His name—because He is the only one who could ever pay such an unimaginably high price.

And it was indeed an exorbitant price—worth infinitely more than all earth's gold and material riches combined. "You were not redeemed with corruptible things, like silver or gold . . . but with the precious blood of Christ, as of a lamb without blemish and without spot" (1 Peter 1:18–19).

He paid the price *in full*. That's what His final words on the cross signified: "It is finished!" (John 19:30). "By one offering He has perfected forever those who are being sanctified" (Heb. 10:14).

Therefore all who enter the kingdom do so freely, "without money and without price" (Isa. 55:1), by grace through faith—not by any merit or virtue of their own (Eph. 2:8–9).

Yet as we are about to see in this pair of pithy illustrations, genuine faith never fails to appreciate the true cost of salvation—what our deliverance from sin's curse and bondage cost Christ; what it means to be bought by Christ and bow to His lordship; and (above all) how valuable redemption is in terms of its eternal worth to the sinner.

Further, and paradoxically, though the Lord Jesus paid the price in full, it is *not* inconsistent to urge people to count the cost of entering the kingdom. That is, in fact, the very point Jesus is making in these two brief parables recorded in Matthew 13:44–46. He urges all who would enter the kingdom to consider what it will cost them.

What *is* the cost to a sinner who enters God's kingdom?

# Hidden Treasure

The first parable is so simple it is contained in a single verse: "The kingdom of heaven is like treasure hidden in a field, which a man found and hid; and for joy over it he goes and sells all that he has and buys that field" (Matt. 13:44).

A story that simple implies that Jesus was dealing with familiar imagery. The hearers would understand the legal and cultural context with no explanation. But for us some background is necessary. Let's start with a recent and strikingly similar story that went viral on the Internet in February 2014. A Northern California couple were walking their dog on their own property when they spotted something beginning to emerge from under the dirt of the pathway. It was a corroded tin can that had been buried years before. Digging it up, they found more cans, all containing gold coins—more than fourteen hundred coins total, valued at more than ten million dollars. The coins had been minted in San Francisco at various times between 1847 and 1894—dates that span the California gold rush era. One particularly rare coin in the collection was valued at more than a million dollars. It was believed to be the most valuable hidden treasure ever uncovered in the United States.[1] Most of the network news reports covering the story stressed the fact that the odds of winning the lottery are several thousand times better than the chance of finding such a rare treasure.

Hiding treasure in a field was perhaps more common in our Lord's time than it is today. People today put their money in the savings and loan, or invest in stocks, bonds, securities, or real estate. Other valuables are typically locked away in safe-deposit boxes. In Jesus' time, money changers and moneylenders operated in connection with the temple rather than in banks. And they did not offer safe places to store one's wealth. Wealth was typically tied up in land and possessions. Only the extremely rich would have a surplus of coins, jewels, or other valuable treasure, and it was up to the individual who owned such a cache to find a way to hide it.

In lands where wars and political upheavals were fairly common events, burying one's riches was a convenient means of protecting the family wealth. Conquering armies always believed they were entitled to the spoils of war. Some took this as a right to steal, loot, and plunder from local inhabitants. If a battle was on the horizon, a prudent person might take whatever jewelry or money was kept in the house, bury it in an earthen jar, and remember the place so it could be retrieved when the danger was over. Josephus wrote about the aftermath of Jerusalem's destruction by Rome under Titus Vespasian in AD 70:

> No small quantity of the riches that had been in that city [were] still found among its ruins; a great deal of which the Romans dug up: but the greatest part was discovered by those who were captives, and so they carried it away. I mean the gold, and the silver, and the rest of that most precious furniture which the Jews had, and which the owners had treasured up under ground, against the uncertain fortunes of war.[2]

People sometimes buried valuables out of craven fear, distrust, or slothfulness. Jesus makes reference to this in Matthew 25:18, where one of His parables describes a lazy steward who "dug in the ground, and hid his lord's money"—rather than investing it or putting it to work for some profitable purpose. He should have at least returned the money with interest, Jesus said. Burying it when he had the opportunity to earn something with it was foolish and unfaithful. (We'll examine that parable in chapter 7.)

So here is a man who discovers a buried treasure in a field that belongs to someone else. He might have been employed by the owner of the field to cultivate the land. As he is plowing, he unearths a buried treasure. Immediately, he puts it back where he found it. Then he goes and sells everything he possesses in the world, liquidates all that he has, and buys that field in order that he may gain the treasure hidden in it.

We are not told precisely what the treasure was—only that it was immensely valuable.

Readers sometimes wonder if what the man did was ethical. He discovers a treasure that does not belong to him, then buries it again without telling the person who owned the field. Did he not have a duty to report his finding to the landowner?

He did not. Jewish rabbinic law was very specific about such things. When an object of value whose owner was unknown was found outdoors (even just outside the threshold of the house), the landowner had no necessary claim to it. Here's a sample from a modern collection of ancient sources:

> [If] he found [an object] between the boards [at the threshold of the doorway to the house], [if the object was located] from the door-jamb and outward, it belongs to [the finder]. If it was located from the door-jamb and inward, it belongs to the householder. [If] one found an object in a hole or new wall, if the object was located from the mid-point and outward, it belongs to [the finder]. [If the object was located] from the mid-point and inward [toward the inside of the house], it belongs to the householder . . . [If the wall or hole] was open wholly outward, even if the object was located from the mid-point toward the inside of the house, it belongs to the finder. [If the wall or hole] was open wholly inward, even if the object was located from the mid-point toward the outside of the house, it belongs to the householder.[3]

The treasure found in the field clearly did not belong to the landowner. (If it had been his, he would have dug it up before selling his field to someone else. The fact that he didn't know it was there meant he had no prior right to it.) Therefore, by Jewish law, it belonged to the finder.

If the man who found the treasure had been less than scrupulous, he might have simply grabbed it and split. Or he could have simply taken part of the treasure and used it to buy the field containing the rest of the stash. He didn't do that. Nor did he unnecessarily provoke a debate about who the rightful owner was. He simply took the treasure he had found and put it right back in the ground. Then he sold everything he had on the face of the earth and bought the entire field just so that he would have undisputed ownership of that treasure.

That is the point of the parable: A man found something so valuable that he sold everything he owned in order to get it. He was so overjoyed, so overwhelmed by the value of his discovery that he was eager to surrender everything he had in order to gain that treasure.

## The Pearl of Great Price

The second parable makes the same point: "Again, the kingdom of heaven is like a merchant seeking beautiful pearls, who, when he had found one pearl of great price, went and sold all that he had and bought it" (Matt. 13:45–46).

This man was likely a wholesaler. (The word for "merchant" is *emporos* in the Greek text. It is the same word from which the English *emporium* is derived.) He would travel from city to city, searching through markets, fishing ports, trade fairs, looking for high-grade pearls to buy for resale. People do the same thing nowadays with antiques. They search through old barns and attics and attend estate sales, hoping to find among all the secondhand furniture an overlooked treasure that they can pick up at a bargain.

In Jesus' time, pearls were the equivalent of diamonds today. Well-formed pearls were as valuable as any precious gem. Pearls also made wealth very portable. If you had fine pearls, you owned a fortune. Free divers (working without scuba masks, wetsuits, proper weights, or breathing apparatus) would gather them from dangerous depths in the Red Sea, the Persian Gulf, and the Indian Ocean. Many died in such dives. Pearl divers would tie rocks to their bodies, take one long, deep breath, jump off the side of a boat, and scour the bottom mud for oysters.

A single pearl of perfection, size, and beauty could be of immense value. When Jesus said, "Do not . . . cast your pearls before swine" (Matt. 7:6), He was painting an absurd word picture to illustrate the folly of attempting to reason with people who clearly have nothing but contempt for the truth. Who would ever expect the lowest of unclean brute beasts to appreciate something as valuable as pearls?

This merchant sought fine pearls to sell because they were a reliable investment; they increased in value as time went by. As is true today, wise investors would diversify: put some money in the ground, some in pearls, some in real estate. The one thing smart investors did not typically do was put everything into one commodity.

In light of that, it is significant that in both of these parables the main characters did precisely what most savvy investment advisors would strongly warn us against. The first man sold everything and bought one field. The second man sold everything and bought one pearl.

## Six Vital Truths About the Kingdom

These two simple parables are not about principles of investment. They make a point that is spiritual: everything this world deems worthwhile or important counts as sheer loss compared to the surpassing value of knowing Christ and being part of His kingdom (Phil. 3:7–8). That one point summarizes several underlying lessons about the kingdom that are woven into these parables.

First is a truth we have touched on already: *The kingdom is priceless in value.* In Christ and His kingdom we have an eternal treasure that is rich beyond comparison. This treasure is incorruptible, undefiled, unfading, eternal, and reserved in heaven for believers (1 Peter 1:4).

Both parables feature a fortune of incomparable value that represents the kingdom of God. Keep in mind how we have defined the kingdom: it is that realm where Christ graciously rules over and eternally blesses willing, loving subjects who gladly embrace Him as Lord by faith. It is the realm of salvation. Christ is the undisputed sovereign here, and His glory is the kingdom's centerpiece.

That alone would be sufficient to establish the kingdom's infinite value, but that's not all. The kingdom consists of everything that is eternal, everything that has true and intrinsic value, everything that is permanently incorruptible and undefiled. Everything else will pass away, while the blessedness of the kingdom can never fade or diminish. Indeed, "of the increase of His government and peace there will be no end" (Isa. 9:7). To paraphrase a favorite hymn, the peace of the kingdom is perfect, but it flows fuller every day; perfect, but it grows deeper all the way.[4]

The kingdom is a heavenly treasure lying in the field of this poverty-stricken, bankrupt, accursed world. It is a prize sufficient to make every one of earth's poor, miserable, blind, sinful inhabitants immeasurably rich for all eternity. The treasure includes salvation, forgiveness, love, joy, peace, virtue, goodness, glory, eternal life in heaven, the presence of God under His smile, and Christ Himself. Literally everything of eternal value is encompassed in the treasure of the kingdom.

That is why this is the most valuable commodity that can ever be found, and only an absolute fool would be unwilling to relinquish everything he owns to gain it.

A second lesson here: *The kingdom is not superficially visible.* The treasure was hidden; the pearl had to be sought. They weren't obvious to the casual observer. That's exactly like the parables themselves. The true meaning is not immediately manifest. It's there for those who seek it, but it is not prominent and unmistakable so that someone whose interest is merely tepid will take notice.

Likewise, Jesus said the kingdom of God does not come with fanfare; most pay no attention to it whatsoever (Luke 17:20). Spiritual realities cannot be naturally perceived and are therefore not appreciated in any way by unregenerate humanity. "No one knows the things of God except the Spirit of God" (1 Cor. 2:11). "The natural man does not receive the things of the Spirit of God, for they are foolishness to him; nor can he know them, because they are spiritually discerned" (v. 14). "Unless one is born again, he cannot see the kingdom of God" (John 3:3). So the kingdom and its true worth remain hidden from carnal minds. That's why the treasure of salvation is not highly esteemed or ever even discovered by most. After all, "the carnal mind is enmity against God" (Rom. 8:7).

That also explains why worldly people don't understand or appreciate why Christians are passionate about the glory of God. They don't understand why we prize the kingdom of heaven so highly when it means nothing to them. Unregenerate people simply have no sense of what divine glory entails. They can't fathom why someone would willingly submit to the lordship of Jesus Christ. They don't understand why anyone would repudiate sin and its pleasures in order to pursue righteousness, sacrificing earthly delights for heavenly joys. That goes against every instinct and every desire of the fallen human heart.

People are quite simply blind to the riches of the kingdom. Scripture says, "the god of this age has blinded [the minds of those] who do not believe, lest the light of the gospel of the glory of Christ, who is the image of God, should shine on them" (2 Cor. 4:4). Christ, who is the light of the world, "was in the world, and the world was made through Him, and the world did not know Him. He came to His own, and His own did not receive Him" (John 1:10–11).

To a large degree, that explains the moral deterioration of our culture today. Sinners are not naturally inclined to seek God. In fact, Scripture says, "There is none who seeks after God" (Rom. 3:11). But only those who do seek will find. And those who do seek, do so because God graciously draws them to Christ (John 6:44)—not dragging them against their will, but drawing them "with gentle cords, with bands of love" (Hos. 11:4). He invites (and urges) all to "Seek the LORD while He may be found, call upon Him while He is near" (Isa. 55:6). And Christ Himself promises, "Ask, and it will be given to you; seek, and you will find; knock, and it will be opened to you. For everyone who asks receives, and he who seeks finds, and to him who knocks it will be opened" (Matt. 7:7–8).

Here's a third lesson from these two parables: *The kingdom is personally appropriated.* The key figure in both parables is an individual. Each finds something of great value specifically for himself and appropriates it. The imagery is vital, because Jesus was teaching people who were prone to think because they were part of national Israel, they were automatically members of the Messiah's kingdom. Likewise lots of people think that because they were baptized, attend church, or even formally join the membership of a church, that is what gives them entrance to Christ's kingdom. It is even theologically trendy today to think of people coming into the kingdom collectively, rather than as individuals, because their tribe, nation, or clan formally associates with some form of Christianity.

Not so. "They are not all Israel who are of Israel" (Rom. 9:6). "He is not a Jew who is one outwardly, nor is circumcision that which is outward in the flesh; but he is a Jew who is one inwardly; and circumcision is that of the heart, in the Spirit" (Rom. 2:28–29). You are not yet a citizen of the kingdom of heaven until you have personally been brought into union with Christ by the Spirit of God, and thereby appropriated the treasure for yourself. The fruit and necessary proof of that union is true love for Christ, surrender to His authority, and a wholehearted trust in Him as both Lord and Savior. "If anyone does not love the Lord Jesus Christ, let him be accursed" (1 Cor. 16:22).

Lesson four: *The kingdom is the true source of real joy*. Matthew 13:44 says it was "for joy" that the man went and sold everything in order to buy the field with the buried treasure. The mention of joy in such a context is highly significant. For one thing, the Lord is acknowledging the basic desire of all human beings to be happy. Joy is a good thing. Jesus Himself said in John 15:11, "These things I have spoken to you, that My joy may remain in you, and that your joy may be full." Later, teaching them how to pray, He said, "Until now you have asked nothing in My name. Ask, and you will receive, that your joy may be full" (16:24). The apostle John echoed those words years later: "These things we write to you that your joy may be full" (1 John 1:4). Romans 14:17 puts joy on the same level as righteousness and peace: "The kingdom of God is . . . righteousness and peace and joy in the Holy Spirit." And in his benediction to the Romans, Paul wrote, "Now may the God of hope fill you with all joy and peace in believing" (15:13). Joy is, of course, the natural result of appropriating such a treasure for oneself. So if you own the treasure, "Rejoice in the Lord always. Again I will say, rejoice!" (Phil. 4:4).

A fifth lesson: *Not everyone comes to the kingdom by the same approach*. We hardly need to point out the obvious similarities in the two parables. In both cases you have an individual. Each of them finds something of great value. Each understands its worth. And each is willing to give up everything to obtain the treasure.

But there is also a difference in the two stories.

In the first parable, the man just stumbles across the treasure. In the second parable, the merchant seeks the pearl, knowing exactly what he's looking for.

There is no reason to think the man in the field was looking for treasure. He was merely going through whatever routine he normally followed, working, walking, plowing a field, building something, or otherwise doing something that perhaps involved digging or cultivating a crop. And while in the field, going about his business, he stumbled across a fortune.

Lots of people enter the kingdom just like that. The apostle Paul, for example, was not seeking to enter the kingdom. He assumed he was in it, and he was on his way to Damascus to persecute Christians. The next thing he knew, God blasted him from heaven, he landed in the dirt, and he was redeemed. He was, in fact, quite satisfied with his own self-righteousness until he stumbled into a fortune that made his own religious accomplishments look like a sack of manure (Phil. 3:8).

Likewise, the Samaritan woman came to the well because she needed water. Not seeking an encounter with Christ, she providentially met Him and went home redeemed. She, the man born blind (John 9), the apostle Matthew (Matt. 9:9), and countless others have unexpectedly stumbled into the kingdom.

The merchant, on the other hand, was on a search specifically for valuable pearls. He knew what he was seeking. He wanted something of genuine, lasting value. He is like the Ethiopian eunuch of Acts 8, Cornelius in Acts 10, or the Bereans in Acts 17. He represents someone who is knowingly seeking the kingdom. He is being drawn to Christ in a conscious quest for eternal life.

Some seem to come into the kingdom almost by accident; others, being drawn, spend time consciously seeking. In both cases, it is God who sovereignly ordains their discovery of Christ. He deals with all people as individuals, ordering the steps of each one in accord with His plan, graciously granting to sinful hearts the will and the wisdom to see and appreciate the infinite value of the kingdom, and thereby motivating them to esteem Christ greater than all the riches of the world. That is saving faith.

Sixth: *Saving faith has a high cost.* Notice that in both of these parables, the prize is purchased. Jesus was not teaching, of course, that eternal life can be purchased with money or merited by human works. We've already pointed out that such a thought is contrary to everything Scripture teaches about grace, faith, and salvation. Of course, the Lord Jesus Christ paid salvation's price in full. He made full atonement for the sins of His people. Eternal life is free to the repentant sinner; it is a gift received by faith alone, not a reward to be earned or purchased by works of any kind.

But to say that eternal life can be freely received by faith is not to suggest that such faith is simple knowledge or notional assent to certain facts. Saving faith is not a physical act like walking an aisle or raising a hand. Genuine faith is not a mere idea or a selective acquiescence to Jesus' teaching. It means letting go of everything else and giving up all trust that anything or anyone else can gain us merit with God. It is total surrender to the person and work of the Savior. As the classic hymn says, "Nothing in my hand I bring; simply to Thy cross I cling."[5]

Authentic faith is a "saving grace whereby we receive [Jesus Christ] and rest upon him alone for salvation as he is offered to us in the gospel." Those words are borrowed from the *Westminster Shorter Catechism* (question 86). The larger catechism (question 72) says,

> Justifying faith is a saving grace, wrought in the heart of a sinner by the Spirit and Word of God, whereby he, being convinced of his sin and misery, and of the disability in himself and all other creatures to recover him out of his lost condition, not only assents to the truth of the promise of the gospel, but receives and rests upon Christ and

his righteousness, therein held forth, for pardon of sin, and for the accepting and accounting of his person righteous in the sight of God for salvation.

In simpler terms, saving faith is an exchange of all we are for all Christ is. Christ took the place of the believing sinner when He bore the penalty of sin on the cross. Sinners take their place "in Christ" *by faith* when the Holy Spirit brings them into perfect, permanent union with Christ through a spiritual baptism (1 Cor. 12:13). That transaction is what is pictured in these parables.

Authentic saving faith yields unconditionally to Christ as both Lord and Savior. That's not to suggest that the moment we believe we can expect to immediately lose every sinful tendency or gain instant victory over every bad habit. It does mean that from the heart we repudiate sin and gain a love for righteousness. That change of heart is the fruit of regeneration and the proof of our spiritual union with Christ. Those who never repent and who lack any true love for righteousness have never truly believed. The proof of true salvation is a life of loving submission to the Lord and His Word.

Jesus frequently turned people away when their faith proved superficial, lacking in real commitment. In Luke 9:57–62, for example, we read this exchange:

Now it happened as they journeyed on the road, that someone said to Him, "Lord, I will follow You wherever You go."

And Jesus said to him, "Foxes have holes and birds of the air have nests, but the Son of Man has nowhere to lay His head."

Then He said to another, "Follow Me."

But he said, "Lord, let me first go and bury my father."

Jesus said to him, "Let the dead bury their own dead, but you go and preach the kingdom of God."

And another also said, "Lord, I will follow You, but let me first go and bid them farewell who are at my house."

But Jesus said to him, "No one, having put his hand to the plow, and looking back, is fit for the kingdom of God."

In Matthew 10:37–39, Jesus gives a detailed description of what kind of transaction genuine faith entails: "He who loves father or mother more than Me is not worthy of Me. And he who loves son or daughter more than Me is not worthy of Me. And he who does not take his cross and follow after Me is not worthy of Me. He who finds his life will lose it, and he who loses his life for My sake will find it." In other words, if you are unwilling to give up whatever needs to be given up in order to be faithful to Christ, then you are not worthy of Christ.

We read the same thing in fewer words in Matthew 16:24: "Jesus said to His disciples, 'If anyone desires to come after Me, let him deny himself.'" That is the transaction. It is an exchange wherein I step aside and acknowledge Christ as the only rightful ruler of my life. That is what distinguishes authentic faith from all superficial and counterfeit varieties of religious profession.

That, then, becomes the guiding principle of the kingdom citizen's life. Obviously, people don't comprehend all the ramifications of that self-surrender at the moment they are saved. But true believers "grow in the grace and knowledge of our Lord and Savior Jesus Christ" (2 Peter 3:18), and that is the evidence that they are truly saved.

The need to count the cost is not stressed often enough in today's evangelism. In Luke 14:28, Jesus says, "which of you, intending to build a tower, does not sit down first and count the cost, whether he has enough to finish it." Three verses later, He adds, "Or what king, going to make war against another king, does not sit down first and consider whether he is able with ten thousand to meet him who comes against him with twenty thousand?"

He is making the same point in these two parables: Count the cost of following Him. And if you do that thoughtfully, you will surely realize that the pearl is so valuable and the treasure so rich that it is worth letting go of every temporal treasure.

# 4

# A Lesson About Justice and Grace

*What shall we say then? Is there unrighteousness*
*with God? Certainly not!*

—ROMANS 9:14

Have you ever considered the stark contrast between Judas Iscariot and the thief on the cross? One was a close disciple of Jesus Christ and gave three years of his life to the best, most intensive religious instruction available anywhere. *But he lost his soul forever.* The other was a hardened, lifelong criminal who was still mocking everything holy while being put to death for his crimes. *But he went straight to paradise forever.*

The difference in the two men could hardly be more pronounced—nor could the endings to their respective life stories be more surprising. Judas was a disciple in Christ's closest circle of twelve. He preached, evangelized, ministered, and was even given power to "cure diseases" (Luke 9:1). He seemed like a model disciple. When Jesus predicted that one of the Twelve would betray Him, no one pointed the finger of suspicion at Judas. He was so thoroughly trusted by the other disciples that they had made him their treasurer (John 13:29). They evidently saw nothing in his character or attitude that seemed questionable, much less diabolical. But he betrayed Christ, ended his own miserable life by suicide, and entered into eternal damnation laden with horrific guilt. Christ's words about him in Mark 14:21 are chilling: "Woe to that man by whom the Son of Man is betrayed! It would have been good for that man if he had never been born."

The thief on the cross, on the other hand, was a career criminal—a serious enough malefactor that he had been sentenced to die by the slowest, most painful form of capital punishment known. He's called a "robber" in Matthew 27:38, using a Greek word that speaks of a brigand or a highwayman. He was being crucified with a partner. They were both originally slated to be executed along with Barabbas, an insurrectionist and killer (Luke 23:19). All of that indicates that he was part of a gang of cutthroat ruffians who stole by violence and lived by no law but their own passions. He was clearly vicious, mean-spirited, and aggressive, because in the early hours of the crucifixion both he and his cohort in crime were taunting and reviling Jesus along with the mocking crowd (Matt. 27:44). But as that thief watched Jesus die silently—"oppressed . . . afflicted, yet He opened not His mouth; . . . led as a lamb to the slaughter" (Isa. 53:7)—the hardened criminal had a remarkable last-minute change of heart. Literally in the dying moments of his wretched earthly life, he confessed his sin (Luke 23:41), uttered a simple prayer: "Jesus, remember me when you come into your kingdom" (v. 42 ESV)—and was ushered that very day into paradise (v. 43), clothed in perfect righteousness, all his guilt borne and paid for in full by Christ.

Those who think heaven is a reward for doing good might protest that this was throwing justice out the window. The thief had done nothing whatsoever to merit heaven. If it's possible to forgive such a man so completely in the dying moments of a wretched lifetime filled with gross sin, wouldn't it also be proper for Judas's one act of treachery to be canceled (or mitigated) on the basis of whatever good works he had done while following Christ for three years? People do occasionally raise questions like that. The Internet is dotted with comments and articles suggesting Judas was dealt with unfairly or judged too harshly.

Judas himself seemed to be the type of person who kept score on such matters. He protested, for example, when Mary anointed the feet of Jesus with a costly fragrance. He knew the precise value of the ointment (equal to a year's wages), and he complained, "Why was this ointment not sold for three hundred denarii and given to the poor?" (John 12:5 ESV). He no doubt would have also thought the grace Jesus showed to the thief was too extravagant.

People who have devoted their lives to religion do sometimes seem to resent it when God reaches out and graciously redeems someone whom they deem unworthy of divine favor.

What we have to bear in mind is that all people are totally unworthy. No one *deserves* God's favor. We are all guilty sinners who deserve nothing more than damnation. No one who has sinned has any rightful claim on the kindness of God.

God, on the other hand, has every right to show mercy and compassion to whomever He chooses (Ex. 33:19). Furthermore, when He shows mercy it is always in lavish abundance. As He told Moses, He is "the LORD, the LORD God, merciful and gracious, longsuffering, and abounding in goodness and truth, keeping mercy for thousands, forgiving iniquity and transgression and sin" (34:6–7).

People who protest that God is unfair or unjust when He shows grace to the least deserving people simply do not understand the principle of grace. Undiluted justice would mean immediate death for every sinner, because "the wages of sin is death" (Rom. 6:23). The truth is, we don't really want what is "fair." We all desperately need grace and mercy.

On the other hand, grace is not unjust, because Christ made full atonement for the sins of those who trust Him—and thereby turned justice in their favor. "If we confess our sins, He is faithful *and just* to forgive us our sins and to cleanse us from all unrighteousness" (1 John 1:9, emphasis added). Because Christ took the penalty of sin on Himself, God can justify believing sinners (even notorious sinners like the thief on the cross) without compromising His own righteousness. "He [is both] just and the justifier of the one who has faith in Jesus" (Rom. 3:26).

What if God shows mercy to a wretched thief in his death throes while condemning someone with a religious track record like Judas? "Is there unrighteousness with God? Certainly not!" (Rom. 9:14). "He has mercy on whom He wills" (v. 18).

God's mercy must never be thought of as a reward for good works. Heaven is not a prize for people who deserve it. God "justifies the ungodly" (Rom. 4:5). Grace is by definition *undeserved*. But it is not unjust or "unfair." Don't try to subject God's grace to childish notions about fair play and equity. No one has any rightful claim on God's mercy. He is perfectly free to dispense His grace however He sees fit. As He told Moses, "I will have mercy on whomever I will have mercy, and I will have compassion on whomever I will have compassion" (Rom. 9:15).

In Matthew 20:1–15, Jesus tells a parable that illustrates those principles:

> The kingdom of heaven is like a landowner who went out early in the morning to hire laborers for his vineyard. Now when he had agreed with the laborers for a denarius a day, he sent them into his vineyard. And he went out about the third hour and saw others standing idle in the marketplace, and said to them, "You also go into the vineyard, and whatever is right I will give you." So they went. Again he went out about the sixth and the ninth hour, and did likewise. And about the eleventh hour he went out and found others standing idle, and said to them, "Why have you been standing here idle all day?" They said to him, "Because no one hired us." He said to them, "You also go into the vineyard, and whatever is right you will receive." So when evening had come, the owner of the vineyard said to his steward, "Call the laborers and give them their wages, beginning with the last to the first." And when those came who were hired about the eleventh hour, they each received a denarius. But when the first came, they supposed that they would receive more; and they likewise received each a denarius. And when they had received it, they complained against the landowner, saying, "These last men have worked only one hour, and you made

them equal to us who have borne the burden and the heat of the day." But he answered one of them and said, "Friend, I am doing you no wrong. Did you not agree with me for a denarius? Take what is yours and go your way. I wish to give to this last man the same as to you. Is it not lawful for me to do what I wish with my own things? Or is your eye evil because I am good?"

Like all parables, this one aims to teach a profound spiritual truth. Jesus is not making a point about fair labor laws, minimum wage, equity in our business dealings, or any other earthly principle. He is describing how grace works in the sphere where God rules.

This parable belongs to the later ministry of Christ, when He was ministering in Perea, east of the Jordan River, opposite Jericho. This was the same region where John the Baptist's ministry had flourished. Jesus had retreated there after some leading Pharisees tried to seize Him (John 10:39–40). The weeks He spent in Perea were some of the most fruitful of His earthly ministry. The area was a barren wilderness, but throngs came to hear Jesus from all over Galilee and Judea. "Many came to Him and said, 'John performed no sign, but all the things that John spoke about this Man were true.' And many believed in Him there" (vv. 41–42).

## The Parable

The parable of the vineyard introduces us to a "landowner." The word in the Greek text is *oikodespotes* (from *oikos*, meaning "house," and *despotes*, meaning "ruler"). When this master of the house asks, "is it not lawful for me to do what I wish with my own things?" he indicates that the money paid to the laborers belongs to him (Matt. 20:15). Verse 8 calls him "the owner of the vineyard"—and it was a sizable estate to require so many workers to help with the harvest. So this was a man of great influence and wealth.

The multitudes listening to Jesus were very familiar with vineyards.

Vast parts of Israel were covered with neatly arranged grapevines growing in terraced vineyards. The land of Israel has two kinds of agricultural land: plains and mountain slopes. The plateaus and flat, expansive areas were used for farming grain or grazing livestock, and the steeper mountainsides were skillfully terraced for the planting of vineyards. This was difficult work because the terraces had to be supported with stones, which were carried up and put in place by hand. Any topsoil that was required also had to be carried up the steep slopes on men's shoulders or with beasts of burden.

Grapes were planted in the spring and pruned during summer. Harvest was a very short season near the end of September. The rainy season began immediately after that. So harvest time was hectic, because the crop had to be brought in before the rains came. The owner needed extra help during the harvest. Therefore he went to the marketplace to hire day laborers. That was the most public place in the village, and it served as a gathering place for workers whose only hope for employment was temporary unskilled labor.

Verse 1 says the landowner went out early in the morning—no doubt prior to 6:00 a.m., when the twelve-hour workday began.

Wages for day laborers were notoriously lower than the standard pay for a full-time employee or household servant, which was about a denarius a day. The denarius was a silver Roman coin containing just under four grams of silver. It was a typical day's pay for a soldier serving in the Roman army, and it was a respectable living wage. (The name *denarius* derives from a Latin word signifying "ten," because the original value of the coin was equivalent to the worth of ten donkeys.) A common, unskilled day laborer could of course be hired for a small fraction of that, because he wasn't in any position to negotiate. If he didn't work, he might not eat that day. Plus, competition for temporary jobs was fierce.

The landowner in Jesus' parable was unusually generous to offer day laborers a full denarius for a day's work. It was an honorable wage, much more than temporary workers would normally receive for menial labor.

Naturally, the early-morning crew heartily agreed to those terms and went to work.

At the third hour (9:00 a.m.), the landowner went back to the market-place. The parable portrays him as a kind and generous man, not abusive or a profit-monger. So perhaps he didn't need these extra workers so much as he felt compassion for them because of *their* extreme need. There were still many in the marketplace who were out of work. They were standing idle—not because they didn't want to work, but because no one had hired them yet.

This time he negotiated no specific amount before hiring workers and sending them into his vineyard. All he said was, "whatever is right I will give you" (Matt. 20:4).

"So they went." They must have known him to be an honorable man, and they took him at his word, even though the terms were vague. Three hours into the workday with no job prospects yet, they weren't in a nego-tiating position. They needed to take whatever they could get.

"Again he went out about the sixth and the ninth hour, and did likewise" (v. 5). He continued to go back to the marketplace at regular intervals—noon and three o'clock—gathering all he could to work in his vineyard.

The workday was virtually spent when verse 6 says he went yet again "about the eleventh hour" (5:00 p.m.). Only an hour was left in the work-day, but still he found more workers waiting. These were persistent men who had been waiting all day but were so desperate for work that they had not yet given up. No doubt after a day of fruitless waiting these men were utterly discouraged, thinking they would not be able to provide any sustenance for their families that day.

Again, we must not mistake their idleness for indolence. When the owner said, "Why have you been standing here idle all day?" they replied, "Because no one hired us." Perhaps they were older, weaker, or otherwise less qualified for hard work in the field. The owner hired them on the spot with the same vague terms he had used with the 9:00 a.m. group: "You also go into the vineyard, and whatever is right you will receive" (Matt. 20:7).

Elsewhere, Jesus says, "The laborer is worthy of his wages" (Luke 10:7; 1 Tim. 5:18). This was a strict principle in Moses' law: "The wages of him who is hired shall not remain with you all night until morning" (Lev. 19:13). That rule applied particularly to the poor and day laborers: "You shall not oppress a hired servant who is poor and needy, whether one of your brethren or one of the aliens who is in your land within your gates. Each day you shall give him his wages, and not let the sun go down on it, for he is poor and has set his heart on it; lest he cry out against you to the LORD, and it be sin to you" (Deut. 24:14–15).

This landowner was an honorable man, faithful to the precepts of God's law, "so when evening had come, the owner of the vineyard said to his steward, 'Call the laborers and give them their wages, *beginning with the last to the first*'" (Matt. 20:8, emphasis added). It is significant that he instructed the steward to pay the workers in reverse order. The immediate context suggests that is the key to the meaning of this parable—and we'll see why shortly. But for now, notice that the men at the front of the line had worked only one hour. Those at the end of the line had worked twelve. Yet as the steward began to distribute pay, those who had worked the shortest amount of time "each received a denarius." They received a full day's wage at a soldier's pay scale in return for just one hour of unskilled labor! They must have been overflowing with gratitude for the generosity of the landowner.

No doubt the men at the end of the line were salivating. By their reckoning, he had now committed himself to paying a denarius an hour. They must have assumed that by the time he got to them, they would receive twelve days' wages.

There's an ellipsis in Jesus' telling of the story at this point. He doesn't actually describe how the three o'clock, noon, and nine o'clock groups were paid, but the clear implication is that they also each received one denarius.

Verses 10–12 continue: "When the first came, they supposed that they would receive more; and they likewise received each a denarius. And when they had received it, they complained against the landowner, saying, 'These last men have worked only one hour, and you made them equal to us who have borne the burden and the heat of the day.'"

*Is that fair?*

What had the landowner promised to give them? "A denarius a day" (20:2). Not only was that a fair wage; it was unusually generous for minimum-wage workers. It is what they happily agreed to.

Yet they resented the landowner. The word translated "complained" in the Greek text is *egogguzon*. It's onomatopoeic: the word itself forms a sound that evokes its meaning. It sounds like a grumble or muttered complaint. They were murmuring under their breath, bellyaching about the pay they received.

When the landowner heard the complaint, he answered one of them: "Friend, I am doing you no wrong. Did you not agree with me for a denarius? Take what is yours and go your way. I wish to give to this last man the same as to you. Is it not lawful for me to do what I wish with my own things? Or is your eye evil because I am good?" (20:13–15).

The expression "evil eye" speaks of jealousy. And let's face it: jealousy is an intrinsic aspect of fallen human nature. Almost anyone at the end of that pay line would probably have felt some welling up of resentment. After all, those men had worked the full twelve-hour day—most of it under the hot sun, while the workers hired at 5:00 p.m. began work under a cooling breeze at twilight and worked for only an hour.

But we must not lose sight of the fact that when the 6:00 a.m. crew were hired, they were quite happy with the offer of a denarius a day. They began the workday in high spirits, thrilled that the landowner was being supremely generous with them. He was offering more in wages than they could reasonably expect.

What changed their mood so drastically? Just that someone less deserving (or so they thought) was treated with even *more* generosity. Instantly they felt mistreated—envious of the other person's good fortune. Their whole attitude changed. They couldn't stand the thought that other workers would get the same pay without working as hard as they did. Suddenly their gratitude and admiration for the landowner's extreme generosity gave way to bitter resentment.

The eleventh-hour workers were of course ecstatic. They understood better than anyone how graciously they had been treated (cf. Luke 7:40–48).

## The Proverb

Now look at the immediate context of this parable, and notice that both the preface and the epilogue are a single, simple proverb: "Many who are first will be last, and the last first" (Matt. 19:30). (The chapter break between Matthew 19 and 20 is an artificial interruption. The last verse of chapter 19 actually introduces the parable that follows.) Then the same proverb is repeated at the end of the parable: "So the last will be first, and the first last" (20:16).* An echo of the proverb is also found in the parable itself—in that key phrase in Matthew 20:8 where the landowner instructs the steward how to pay the workers their wages: "Call the laborers and give them their wages, beginning with the last to the first."

Jesus used variations of that same proverb on other occasions. We find it, for example, in Luke 13:30: "Indeed there are last who will be first, and there are first who will be last"; and in Mark 10:31: "Many who are first will be last, and the last first."

The proverb is also something of a riddle. What does it mean? It's not saying precisely the same thing as Mark 9:35: "If anyone desires to be first, he shall be last of all and servant of all." Or Mark 10:43–44: "Whoever desires to become great among you shall be your servant. And whoever of you desires to be first shall be slave of all." Those verses elevate humility and self-sacrifice. Those are *imperatives:* commands instructing us to be humble servants rather than seeking prominence and power.

---

* The New King James Version adds, "For many are called, but few chosen." But the most ancient manuscripts don't include that phrase, and it doesn't seem to fit in this context. It seems to have been borrowed from Matthew 22:14.

But the proverb that goes with this parable is an *indicative*, a simple statement of fact: "The last will be first, and the first last." What does that mean, and how would it work? In a foot race, for example, the only way for the last to be first and the first to be last is for everyone to finish simultaneously. If everyone crosses the finish line at exactly the same instant, the first are last and the last are first. Everyone ends in a dead heat.

That, of course, is precisely the point Jesus was making in the parable. Those hired first and those hired last all got exactly the same pay. All of them, from the first to the last, got the full benefit of the landowner's generosity, in equal shares.

What spiritual lesson is woven into that story?

## The Point

The lesson is actually quite simple: the story is a precise picture of God's sovereign saving grace. Since sinners are all unworthy, and the riches of God's grace are inexhaustible, all believers receive an infinite and eternal share of His mercy and kindness, though no one really deserves it. "In Him we [all of us] have [complete] redemption through His blood, the forgiveness of sins, according to the riches of His grace" (Eph. 1:7). He "raised us up *together*, and made us sit *together* in the heavenly places in Christ Jesus, that in the ages to come He might show the exceeding riches of His grace in His kindness toward us in Christ Jesus" (2:6–7, emphasis added). That speaks of all who are redeemed. It is the Father's good pleasure to give them the kingdom (Luke 12:32)—all of them, and in equal abundance. The dying thief who repented in his final moments entered paradise, where he is enjoying eternal life and everlasting fellowship with Christ just the same as Peter, James, and John, who literally gave their lives in service to the Savior.

The landowner in the parable represents God. The vineyard is the kingdom, the sphere of God's rule. The laborers are believers, people who come into the service of the King. The day of work is their lifetime. The evening is eternity. The steward, perhaps, represents Jesus Christ, to whom has been committed all judgment. The denarius represents eternal life.

*Note: this pay is not something the workers have earned.* It is not given to them like a minimum wage in a fair exchange for labor done. It is far too much for that. Rather, this represents a gracious gift, a lavish endowment that exceeds the best reward any day worker could ever merit.

So this is the point: If you are a genuine believer, you receive the full benefits of God's immeasurable grace, just like everyone else in God's kingdom. Your place in heaven is not a timeshare where your access is determined by the length of time you spent doing the Lord's work. The blessings of redemption are not doled out in quotas based on one's personal achievements. Forgiveness is not measured by weighing our good deeds against our sins, nor is it partially withheld if we have sinned for too long or too badly. *Everyone* who enters the kingdom receives the full abundance of God's grace, mercy, and forgiveness. That's true no matter how long you have worked in God's kingdom. It's true no matter how hard or how easy your circumstances are. It's true whether your service was minimal or maximal; whether you die as a martyr in the prime of life or live a fairly peaceful life and die of old age. It's as true of those who come to Christ in adolescence as it is of those who genuinely repent of their sins at the end of a profligate life. When this earthly life is over, if you are a believer, you will go to be with Christ, just like that thief on the cross (Luke 23:43); just like the apostle Paul (2 Cor. 5:8); and just like every other saint who has died since.

Heaven is not a reward for long service or hard work. Some people serve Christ their entire lives, and some for a very short time. We all enter into the same eternal life. We all will receive the same spiritual blessings in heaven.

If that seems inequitable, remember that it is far more than any of us deserve. The benefits of the kingdom are the same for everyone, because we are redeemed in the first place only by God's grace, and nothing else. That's truly good news for you and me; we don't have to earn our way into the kingdom. Heaven is not based on our merit.

## The Purpose

Why did Jesus devise this parable in this context? The events Matthew relates before and after the parable answer that question.

Our Lord gave this analogy primarily for the benefit of His twelve disciples immediately after His conversation with the rich young ruler. This young man of great wealth and influence had come to Jesus asking, "Good Teacher, what good thing shall I do that I may have eternal life?" (Matt. 19:16). He may have been fishing for praise, because he clearly thought he had fulfilled every spiritual duty and that his life was well in order. He certainly looked like a promising evangelistic prospect.

But rather than simply giving him the good news of the gospel, Jesus challenged him on his obedience to the law. When the fellow insisted, "All these things I have kept from my youth. What do I still lack?" (19:20), Jesus told him to sell all his possessions, give the profits to the poor, and follow Him. That was a sacrifice the young man wasn't willing to make.

Jesus thus exposed the fact that the young ruler loved his possessions more than he loved either God or his neighbor. In other words, although he claimed to have kept the entire law of God, he was in violation of both the first and second great commandments (22:37–40). But the man still did not acknowledge that. Unwilling to face his sin and repent, he "went away sorrowful" (19:22).

The disciples were clearly stunned when Jesus seemed to put obstacles in the rich young ruler's way rather than encouraging him. They were baffled: "Who then can be saved?" (v. 25).

Jesus' answer stresses the fact that salvation is God's work, not something any sinner can accomplish for himself: "With men this is impossible, but with God all things are possible" (v. 26).

So the disciples were thinking about the impossibility of meriting God's favor. They were no doubt examining their own hearts. Unlike the rich ruler, they *had* in fact left all to follow Christ (v. 27). And they were looking for some assurance from Christ Himself that their sacrifice wasn't all for naught. That is what prompted this parable.

As the rich young ruler walked away, it was Peter who spoke up on behalf of all the disciples and said, "See, we have left all and followed You. Therefore what shall we have?" (v. 27). The Twelve were like the 6:00 a.m. group in the parable. They were the first ones Jesus called at the start of His ministry. They had been working through the heat of the day, for a lot longer than twelve hours. It had already been nearly three years. They had given up homes, jobs, and relationships to serve Christ. With the sole exception of Judas, they certainly loved Jesus. All of them would go on to give their lives for the gospel's sake. They wanted to know what they would receive for their sacrifice.

The disciples no doubt thought they were going to get special benefits. They believed they were going to inherit the kingdom very soon, and that excited them. They were well aware that Jesus was Israel's Messiah. They fully expected an earthly, political kingdom with all the glory and riches one might gain through world dominion. They were the first disciples, so it made perfect sense to them that one of them would sit at Jesus' right hand, in the highest place of honor.

This was a naive and immature view of Jesus' mission, and they retained it even after the resurrection. While the risen Christ was meeting with them as a group, preparing them for Pentecost, they asked, "Lord, will You at this time restore the kingdom to Israel?" (Acts 1:6). Now that Christ had shown Himself triumphant even over death, they were hoping finally to get their crowns and thrones and places of honor.

At the end of Matthew 19, when Peter asked, "What shall we have?" Jesus answered by addressing their thirst for special honor. He reassured them that they would indeed have places of honor in the kingdom. But He went on to say that *everyone* in the kingdom would be honored: "Assuredly I say to you, that in the regeneration, when the Son of Man sits on the throne of His glory, you who have followed Me will also sit on twelve thrones, judging the twelve tribes of Israel. *And everyone* who has left houses or brothers or sisters or father or mother or wife or children or lands, for My name's sake, shall receive a hundredfold, and inherit eternal life" (vv. 28–29).

It is intriguing how little effect the lesson of this parable had on the twelve disciples. They were so obsessed with the idea of *special* honor that even after they heard this parable, they continued scheming and jockeying for first place. In fact, the very next episode in Matthew's account records this: "Then the mother of Zebedee's sons came to Him with her sons, kneeling down and asking something from Him. And He said to her, 'What do you wish?' She said to Him, 'Grant that these two sons of mine may sit, one on Your right hand and the other on the left, in Your kingdom'" (20:20–21). Matthew (who of course was one of the Twelve himself) goes on to say, "When the ten heard it, they were greatly displeased with the two brothers" (v. 24). They were annoyed because they all craved the inside seats!

This became a constant source of bickering among the Twelve. Even in the Upper Room on the night of Jesus' betrayal, it was Jesus who washed the others' feet, because all of them desired to be considered "great," and foot washing was a duty of the lowest servant (John 13:4–17). Later that same evening, right after Jesus broke the bread and consecrated the wine, "There was . . . a dispute among them, as to which of them should be considered the greatest" (Luke 22:24).

So although the parable of the laborers was given to confront the selfish, envious, confused perceptions of the disciples, it took a while to sink in.

## The Principles

Still, the parable is full of vital principles, including some that are core gospel truths, and most of these are obvious on the face of it.

It teaches, first of all, that *salvation is not earned*. Eternal life is a gift that God gives purely by grace according to His sovereign will.

But the parable's most obvious lesson is that *God gives the same abundant grace to everyone who follows Christ*. Tax collectors, harlots, beggars, and blind people will share in the same eternal life as those who have served all their lives; those who have preached the gospel to thousands; and those who were martyred for Christ. Thankfully, He does not give any believer what we truly deserve.

When we get to heaven we'll all live in the Father's house (John 14:2). We are all "heirs of God and joint heirs with Christ," and we will all be glorified together (Rom. 8:17). We don't each receive a part of heaven; we all get the whole!

Elsewhere Scripture does indicate that in addition to full redemption from sin and everlasting life, there will be differing rewards the Lord is pleased to give His children for their faithfulness. At the judgment seat of Christ, "If anyone's work which he has built on it endures, he will receive a reward. If anyone's work is burned, he will suffer loss" (1 Cor. 3:15–15). So some will suffer loss and some will be rewarded, depending on the enduring quality of their work.

But Revelation 4:10–11 pictures what becomes of those rewards: "The twenty-four elders fall down before Him who sits on the throne and worship Him who lives forever and ever, and cast their crowns before the throne, saying:

> 'You are worthy, O Lord,
> To receive glory and honor and power;
> For You created all things,
> And by Your will they exist and were created.'"

Rewards, however, are not the issue in the parable of the laborers. Jesus is teaching a lesson about the abundant, eternal life that belongs to all who embrace Him as Lord and Savior. Heaven itself is not a reward to be earned by hard labor; it is a gracious gift, given in full abundance to all believers equally. God "shows no partiality" (Acts 10:34), and He makes no distinction between male and female, rich and poor, Jew and Gentile (Gal. 3:28).

Some important secondary principles are also illustrated in this parable. For example, we see in the imagery that *it is God who initiates salvation*. In the parable, the landowner went out to find the laborers in the marketplace of the world and brought them into his vineyard. God does the seeking and the saving. Our salvation is entirely His work, and that's the main reason we have no right to make demands or set limits on what He gives to someone else. It is God's prerogative and His alone to show mercy to whomever He chooses.

Meanwhile, *He continues to call workers into His kingdom.* All through human history and in every phase of the human lifespan, God is calling people into His kingdom. It's an ongoing work. Jesus said in John 9:4, "I must work the works of Him who sent Me while it is day; the night is coming when no one can work." Our parable illustrates what He meant. Redemption continues until the judgment comes. And that time *is* coming.

*God calls sinners, not the self-sufficient.* He brings into His vineyard those who know their own need, not people who think they are "'rich, have become wealthy, and have need of nothing'—and do not know that [they] are wretched, miserable, poor, blind, and naked" (Rev. 3:17). The men gathered in the marketplace looking for work were desperate, fully aware of their need. They were poor and meek, devoid of resources, begging for work—representing the poor in spirit. There was nothing complacent or self-satisfied about them—especially those who had come to the end of the day and still had nothing. That's exactly the kind of person Christ came to seek and to save. "Those who are well have no need of a physician, but those who are sick. [Christ] did not come to call the righteous, but sinners, to repentance" (Mark 2:17; cf. also 1 Cor. 1:26–31).

*God is sovereign in the outworking of salvation.* Why does He wait till the last hour to call some? Why didn't the landowner hire everyone in the marketplace on his first trip there? The parable doesn't reveal the reasons. Neither do we know why God saves people at different stages of life. He sovereignly determines both when and whom He will call. But all those who are called know they are needy and are willing to work. And their willingness is a result, not the cause, of God's grace to them. "For it is God who works in you both to will and to do for His good pleasure" (Phil. 2:13).

*God keeps His promise.* The landowner told the first group he would give each of them a denarius, and he did. He kept his promise to those he hired later too. He said he would give them what was right—and what he gave them was more than generous. Likewise, God never gives less than He promises, and often He gives "exceedingly abundantly above all that we ask or think" (Eph. 3:20).

*God always gives more than we deserve.* "Every good gift and every perfect gift is from above, and comes down from the Father" (James 1:17). And everything we receive other than eternal damnation is more than we deserve. So there is no place for Christians to resent God's grace toward others or to think He has somehow defrauded us. That very idea is full of blasphemy. In fact, that was the spirit of the elder brother in the parable of the prodigal son. He deeply resented his father's grace toward the prodigal.

*God is gracious, and we should always celebrate His grace.* The parable of the laborers wonderfully exalts the principle of grace. My own response to this parable is profound thankfulness, for there are many who have been more faithful than I, worked harder than I, labored longer than I, and suffered under greater trials. There are perhaps others who have worked less, fewer years, with less diligence. But grace abounds even to the chief of sinners, and God saves all of us to the uttermost (Heb. 7:25). That gives Him glory, and that certainly is a reason to praise Him—and rejoice along with *all* who have received such grace.

# 5

# A Lesson About Neighborly Love

*All the law is fulfilled in one word, even in this:*
*"You shall love your neighbor as yourself."*

—GALATIANS 5:14

The dramatic tale of the good Samaritan in Luke 10:30–37 is one of the most beloved and interesting of all Jesus' parables. It is so well known that it has become a common idiom for lavish, sacrificial kindness. To call someone a good Samaritan is a noble compliment. But our familiarity with this parable may cause us to think we know the story better than we really do. Lots of people assume they understand exactly what this story is about and what it was intended to convey, when in fact, most don't.

The lesson of the good Samaritan is not merely an exhortation to help those in need. It is far too simplistic to say that Jesus' main point is about showing kindness to strangers. Rather, He told this story to illustrate how far we all fall short of what God's law actually demands. He is explaining *why* all our good works and religious merit are never sufficient to gain favor with God. He is showing what the law really demands of us—and thereby He is systematically deflating the hopes of superfastidious religious people who think they can merit eternal life by meticulously following rabbinical traditions, obsessing over the minutiae in God's law, and inventing ways around all the truly important principles and hard parts of Scripture.

The real point of the parable becomes clear when we pay attention to the immediate context in Luke 10. In short, Jesus is telling this parable to a pedantic religious legalist who was trying to diminish the force of God's law with a hairsplitting analysis of the word *neighbor*.

## A Trick Question

During Jesus' ministry in Galilee (the region where He grew up), He met with relentless opposition from key religious leaders and their followers. In Luke 10, He sends seventy of His disciples on a final mission to take the gospel to the cities of Galilee. He knows that the disciples, too, will meet with much opposition, so He instructs them:

> Whatever city you enter, and they do not receive you, go out into its streets and say, "The very dust of your city which clings to us we wipe off against you. Nevertheless know this, that the kingdom of God has come near you." But I say to you that it will be more tolerable in that Day for Sodom than for that city. (10:10–12)

Jesus then continues with some curt words of condemnation for three specific towns where He had already spent a great deal of time during His early Galilean ministry: Chorazin, Bethsaida, and (most significantly) Capernaum, hometown to many of the disciples (Luke 10:13–16). His words of condemnation to those cities are some of the harshest words Jesus ever uttered.

Predictably, that short prophetic discourse further angered the religious leaders who already opposed Him. At that point, a legal expert (one of the hostile religious leaders, not a civil lawyer), stepped forward and asked Jesus a question about eternal life in an attempt to trap or embarrass Him.

Luke records the exchange: "A certain lawyer stood up and tested Him, saying, 'Teacher, what shall I do to inherit eternal life?'" (Luke 10:25). Scripture makes a point of noting the man's insincerity. This was not an honest question from someone seeking to learn; it was a test—a challenge, or a ruse to try to trap Jesus or confound Him by posing a moral dilemma or paradox that the lawyer believed had no clear answer. This was just the first in a series of questions the lawyer planned to ask, and (as we shall observe shortly), it's clear where he was going. He wanted to embarrass Jesus and impress the crowd with his own supposedly superior skills as a legal sophist and quibbler over theological fine points.

Despite the lawyer's evil motive, the first question he raised is a fine question. It is in fact the greatest question ever asked or answered, and it was frequently on the minds and the hearts of those who approached Jesus to learn from Him. It's what was on the heart of Nicodemus when he came to Jesus under cover of darkness in John 3. It is the very same question the rich young ruler raised in Matthew 19. In fact, that same question was posed frequently to Jesus and appears several places in the Gospels.

The Old Testament promised eternal life, a never-ending kingdom in which true believers would live, in the presence of God, in fulfillment of all the divine promises. Jesus Himself spoke about eternal life often, because that was the central promise of the gospel—the very message He came to proclaim—"that whoever believes in Him should not perish but have everlasting life" (John 3:16). He said things like, "I am the resurrection and the life. He who believes in Me, though he may die, he shall live. And whoever lives and believes in Me shall never die" (John 11:25–26). "Whoever drinks of the water that I shall give him will never thirst. But the water that I shall give him will become in him a fountain of water springing up into everlasting life" (John 4:14). "He who hears My word and believes in Him who sent Me has everlasting life, and shall not come into judgment, but has passed from death into life" (John 5:24)—and so on.

Most Jews had been taught by their rabbis that their lineage, their circumcision, their ceremonies, and their traditions were what qualified them for the eternal kingdom. But clearly there was still a nagging sense of uncertainty and guilt in many hearts, so people constantly raised this question with Jesus. Their own hearts accused them, and they feared that in spite of all their ethnic and religious qualifications, despite what it looked like on the surface, they were only superficially keeping the Law and maintaining a front. They knew by the light of conscience that they were not worthy to be a part of that kingdom.

This time, Jesus answered the question with a question of His own. "He said to him, 'What is written in the law? What is your reading of it?'" (Luke 10:26). Literally: How do you read it? Jesus was referring to the *Keri'at Shema*, the daily reading aloud of Deuteronomy 6:4–5: "Hear, O Israel: The LORD our God, the LORD is one! You shall love the LORD your God with all your heart, with all your soul, and with all your strength."

In reply, the lawyer quoted from that very passage, adding the last half of Leviticus 19:18 as well. "He answered and said, '"You shall love the LORD your God with all your heart, with all your soul, with all your strength, and with all your mind," and "your neighbor as yourself"'" (Luke 10:27). That was a perfect summary of the law's moral demands. It is precisely the same answer Jesus gave on another occasion in Matthew 22:37–40 when a different lawyer asked Him, "Which is the great commandment in the law?" (v. 36). In that context Jesus Himself said Deuteronomy 6:5 ("love . . . God with all your heart") is the first and greatest commandment and Leviticus 19:18 ("love your neighbor as yourself") ranks a close second. Then he added, "On these two commandments hang all the Law and the Prophets" (Matt. 22:40).

Of course, as discussed earlier, the Ten Commandments are divided into those same two categories. The first through fourth commandments spell out what is entailed in loving God and honoring Him properly. The fifth through tenth commandments outline what love for one's neighbor looks like. So the entire moral content of the law is summarized and comprised in those two simple commandments. The lawyer in Luke 10 got it exactly right: love God with all your heart, and love your neighbor as yourself. If we did those two things perfectly, we would not need any other rules. All the other commandments—all the moral precepts in the Mosaic covenant—simply explain in detail what is truly involved in loving God and loving one's neighbor.

So Jesus said to the lawyer, "You have answered rightly" (Luke 10:28). Then our Lord added, "Do this and you will live." *You want eternal life? Obey the law.*

That is reminiscent of Jesus' answer to the rich young ruler. It's not gospel, but law. Scripture elsewhere says, "By the deeds of the law no flesh will be justified in His sight, for by the law is the knowledge of sin" (Rom. 3:20). In fact, Jesus' reply would seem at first glance to contradict the very heart of gospel truth: "A man is not justified by the works of the law but by faith in Jesus Christ . . . we [are] justified by faith in Christ and not by the works of the law; for by the works of the law no flesh shall be justified" (Gal. 2:16).

What's going on here? Why did Jesus not preach the gospel rather than the law to this man?

## A Hard Heart

Jesus was simply holding the mirror of the law up to this legal "expert" to demonstrate how the law condemned him. If the lawyer were an honest man, he ought to have acknowledged that he did *not* love God as he should; he didn't even love his neighbors as he should. This man, steeped in the study of God's law, should have been broken by the law's message. He should have felt deep conviction. He should have been penitent, contrite, humble. His follow-up question ought to have been something like this: "I know from bitter experience that I cannot fulfill even the most basic commandments of the law; where can I find redemption?"

Instead, he doused the fire of his conscience with the water of self-righteous pride. "But he, *wanting to justify himself,* said to Jesus, 'And who is my neighbor?'" (Luke 10:29, emphasis added).

He wanted to convince people that he was righteous, although he knew he wasn't. He wanted to maintain the facade. This was the whole problem with the legalists, Pharisees, and other self-righteous religious bullies who constantly challenged Jesus. They "trusted in themselves that they were righteous, and despised others" (Luke 18:9). It was Jesus' central criticism of the Pharisees' brand of religion. He told them, "You are those who justify yourselves before men, but God knows your hearts" (Luke 16:15). In the words of the apostle Paul, "They being ignorant of God's righteousness, and seeking to establish their own righteousness, [did not submit] to the righteousness of God" (Rom. 10:3). This particular legalist was desperate to make himself look good in others' eyes, regardless of what God thought of him.

So instead of asking the question Jesus' reply ought to have prompted from him, he asked, "Who is my neighbor?" (Luke 10:29).

Notice, first of all, that he skipped right over the part about loving God with all his heart, soul, mind, and strength. Instead, he wants to discuss a technical point about the identity of one's neighbor. Because, as Jesus says elsewhere, the traditional rabbinical and popular interpretation of Leviticus 19:18 ("Love your neighbor as yourself") is "You shall love your neighbor and hate your enemy" (Matt. 5:43). That takes all the force out of the command, because if you're free to hate your enemy, then you're relieved from the duty of loving anyone whom you decide to regard as an enemy. Under that interpretation, you have no legal or moral obligation to love anyone you don't really want to.

It is obvious where this lawyer was going. He wanted to entangle Jesus in a pettifogging debate about who is a neighbor and who isn't. He figured he could "justify himself" if he could make a convincing defense of the traditional notion that one's enemy is not one's "neighbor."

At that point, Jesus could have just dismissed him. He could have said, "I can see that you are shut out from the kingdom of God," and resumed His teaching. He could have left him standing there in self-righteous pride. But Jesus shows gentle compassion to this stubborn, self-righteous man. Our Lord is actually modeling for us the very same principle He is about to illustrate with a parable. It is a precept He both taught and lived: "Love your enemies, bless those who curse you, do good to those who hate you, and pray for those who spitefully use you and persecute you" (Matt. 5:44).

And even though this lawyer has managed to rebuff Christ's attempt to bring conviction to his heart; even though the man's sole motive in the first place was to try to elevate himself while putting Jesus down, the Savior replies to him with tenderhearted, longsuffering kindness. It's not the harsh rebuke the man deserves. Jesus tells him a story.

And the story our Lord tells is one of His most poignant, powerful parables. It would certainly have been enough to shatter the pride of any sensitive, spiritually minded truth seeker. It is a crushing story that produces immense conviction. This is not a simple lesson in etiquette or a manual on how to help the less fortunate (though it certainly has implications for both charity and good manners). This is not a lesson for children about how to share their toys and be kind to the new kid in class. This was a story told to a religious nonbeliever, a self-righteous man, as an evangelistic effort to bring him to the true sense of his sinfulness and his need for mercy. It was Jesus' appeal to a doomed (but deeply religious) soul. Jesus was urging the man to wake up and see how lost he really was.

## A Gentle Answer with a Powerful Point

Here is the parable of the good Samaritan:

> A certain man went down from Jerusalem to Jericho, and fell among thieves, who stripped him of his clothing, wounded him, and departed, leaving him half dead. Now by chance a certain priest came down that road. And when he saw him, he passed by on the other side. Likewise a Levite, when he arrived at the place, came and looked, and passed by on the other side. But a certain Samaritan, as he journeyed, came where he was. And when he saw him, he had compassion. So he went to him and bandaged his wounds, pouring on oil and wine; and he set him on his own animal, brought him to an inn, and took care of him.

On the next day, when he departed, he took out two denarii, gave them
to the innkeeper, and said to him, "Take care of him; and whatever
more you spend, when I come again, I will repay you." (Luke 10:30–35)

Again, the fact that Jesus continued to answer this man was in itself,
an act of grace. The man's attempt to show Jesus up was obnoxious.
Religious leaders tried this many times with Jesus and *always* failed. His
ability to answer well all their hard questions only infuriated them. But
try as they might, they could not provoke Him.

On this occasion in particular, Jesus' reply stands out for its warm-
hearted, gracious, loving restraint. The man was deliberately trying to
goad Jesus, begging for a sharp answer that he planned to pursue with
a heated debate. But sometimes "a gentle tongue breaks a bone" (Prov.
25:15), and that's what happens here.

Jesus is not telling this account as if it were a true story. It's a parable,
a tale spun to dramatize, in an unforgettable way, the point He wanted
to drive into this legalist's heart—and ours as well. As in most of Jesus'
stories and parables, He has one simple point to make. There are lots
of details in this story, and plenty of secondary implications, but what's
important here is the central lesson, and that is what we need to focus on.

## The Dangerous Road and the Attack

The story begins with a journey on a very dangerous road. It is the road
"from Jerusalem to Jericho" (Luke 10:30). The road is real. I have traveled on that very road. Visitors to Israel can still take the same route used
by travelers in Jesus' time. From Jerusalem to Jericho is about a four-
thousand-foot drop in elevation across seventeen miles of winding road,
crossing barren mountains over very rough terrain. In places, a steep,
three-hundred-foot precipice, rather than any kind of shoulder, borders
the road. Much of the route is lined with caves and massive boulders,
which offer hideouts for robbers. It is still a dangerous road.

In Jesus' story, the predictable happens. A man traveling alone on that road was jumped by a band of thieves—particularly brutal ones. They didn't just rob him; they stripped him almost naked. They didn't just take his purse with his cash; they took everything he had. Then they brutally beat him and left him for dead. We would say today he was in critical condition, a dying man on a desert road.

That road saw a steady stream of travelers when people were coming and going from Jerusalem for the feasts. But in other seasons—especially during the peak heat of summer or the stifling windy season and cold of winter—traffic on the road could be meager. There were no homes and very few stopping points on that stretch of road. It was not a friendly place—especially for someone alone and desperate. It might be a very long time before help came along—if ever. There was no guarantee anyone would find him or help him.

## The Priest and the Levite

At this dramatic point in the story, Jesus introduces a bit of hope: "By chance a certain priest came down that road" (Luke 10:31). This appears on the surface to be the best of news. Here comes a servant of God, one who offers sacrifices for people in the temple, a spiritual man who should be a paragon of compassion (Heb. 5:2). He represents the best of men. A priest, of all people, would be familiar with the Mosaic law. He would know Leviticus 19:18 says, "You shall love your neighbor as yourself." He ought to know as well that verses 33 and 34 in that same chapter expound on the principle of neighborly love by applying it to strangers in particular: "If a stranger dwells with you in your land, you shall not mistreat him. The stranger who dwells among you shall be to you as one born among you, and you shall love him as yourself." A priest would know Micah 6:8:

> [W]hat does the LORD require of you
> But to do justly,
> To love mercy,
> And to walk humbly with your God?

He would be fully aware that "whoever shuts his ears to the cry of the poor will also cry himself and not be heard" (Prov. 21:13). The principle spelled out in James 2:13 was woven into the Old Testament as well: "Judgment is without mercy to the one who has shown no mercy."

The priest was surely familiar with Exodus 23:4–5: "If you meet your enemy's ox or his donkey going astray, you shall surely bring it back to him again. If you see the donkey of one who hates you lying under its burden, and you would refrain from helping it, you shall surely help him with it." So if a person found his enemy's donkey in a ditch, he was obliged to rescue the donkey, right? Of course he had a greater duty to help a man in critical condition.

But that flash of hope was short-lived. When the priest saw the injured man, "he passed by on the other side" (Luke 10:31). The Greek text uses a verb found nowhere in Scripture other than in that verse and the one that follows: *antiparerchomai*. The anti-prefix, of course, means "opposite." It's an active verb signifying that the priest deliberately re-located to the opposite side of the road. He went out of his way to avoid the injured traveler—purposely shunning the man in need.

The priest obviously had no compassion for people in dire distress. No other conclusion can be drawn from this. Jesus turned the lawyer's question on its head. The question the fellow asked was, "Who is my neighbor?" But that's not the right question. Jesus is showing him through this parable that righteous compassion is not narrow. It is not seeking for definitions of what sufferers are qualified to deserve help. The duties of the second great commandment are not defined by the question of who our neighbor is. In fact, the converse is true: genuine love compels us to be neighborly even to strangers and aliens. The full meaning of the second great commandment includes the principle Jesus made emphatic in Matthew 5:44: *We should love even our enemies.* They are our neighbors, too, and therefore we are obliged to bless them, do good to them, and pray for them.

The coldhearted priest in this parable is not necessarily included as an indictment of the priesthood in general. It was quite true that many of the priests and other religious leaders in Jesus' time lacked compassion. But that is not the point here. This priest represents anyone with full knowledge of the Scriptures and a familiarity with the duties of the law, who is expected to help. But he does not.

The next verse introduces a Levite. All priests were of course from the tribe of Levi. More specifically, those who served as priests were descendants of Aaron (one of the sons of Levi). The term *Levite* therefore referred to descendants of Levi who were not also descended from Aaron. They served in subordinate roles in the temple. Some were assistants to the priests; some were temple police; others worked in various behind-the-scenes roles maintaining and servicing the temple grounds. But their lives were devoted to religious service, so they were (like the priests) expected to have a good knowledge of the Hebrew Scriptures.

Nevertheless, when this Levite came to the place where the wounded man lay, he did the same thing the priest had done. As soon as he saw the helpless victim lying there, he moved to the opposite side of the road. Here was another man devoid of compassion and bereft of lovingkindness.

Earlier in Luke 10, Jesus had prayed, "I thank You, Father, Lord of heaven and earth, that You have hidden these things from the wise and prudent and revealed them to babes. Even so, Father, for so it seemed good in Your sight" (v. 21). These two religious characters in the parable, a priest and a Levite, embodied what Jesus meant by "the wise and prudent." They represented their culture's best-educated and most highly esteemed religious dignitaries. But they did not really know God.

Neither was truly fit for heaven; they were "sons of disobedience"— and therefore objects of God's wrath (Eph. 2:2, 5:6; Col. 3:6). They didn't truly love God, because if you love God, you keep His commandments. They also didn't love their neighbors, because when they faced a real and urgent need and had an opportunity to demonstrate love, they refused. They are striking illustrations of religious hypocrites, observing the ceremonial law, and even devoting their lives to the service of the temple but lacking any real virtue.

People sometimes cite the story of the good Samaritan, point to the priest and Levite as examples of utter inhumanity, and then close the book with a sense of moral superiority.

To do that is to miss Jesus' point.

It's right, of course, to condemn the callous disregard of these two men and look upon their deliberate heedlessness with utter scorn. But in doing so, we condemn ourselves as well. Their attitude is precisely what we see in human nature today, even within our own hearts. We think, *I don't want to get involved. I don't know what this man, or the people who beat him up, might do to me.* Without in any way justifying the cold-hearted apathy Jesus was condemning, we must confess that we, too, are guilty of similar blind indifference, wretched insensitivity, and careless disregard of people in dire need. Even if we don't turn away every time we see someone in need, we all fail in this duty enough to stand guilty before the law with its demand for utter perfection.

Jesus makes that point unmistakable by introducing us to the good Samaritan.

## Jews and Samaritans

The Samaritan comes as an unexpected twist in Jesus' story. Like the man who was beaten and robbed, the Samaritan was on a journey alone. Sometime after the priest and Levite had passed by, the Samaritan arrived on the scene. Unlike those two professional clergymen, the Samaritan "had compassion" when he saw the bloodied body of the poor traveler (Luke 10:33).

The robbery victim was a Jewish man. That would be perfectly clear to Jesus' listeners, because the setting of the story is in Israel, on a desert road heading out of Jerusalem. Gentiles rarely traveled there, much less Samaritans. In the minds of Jesus' original audience, a Samaritan would be the least likely source of help for a Jewish traveler in distress on the Jericho road. For one thing, Samaritans assiduously avoided that road. A Samaritan would travel there only if there was a dire emergency forcing him to do so. But more than that, Jews despised Samaritans and vice versa.

An acrimonious mutual hostility had divided the two peoples for centuries. Jewish travelers going to Galilee took the road from Jerusalem to Jericho precisely because they wanted to avoid Samaria. People on that road were not headed straight north in the direction of Galilee, but east, to Perea, on the other side of the Jordan River. It was an indirect route to Galilee, longer and more arduous—but it bypassed Samaria.

Jewish people considered the Samaritans ethnically and religiously unclean—and the Samaritans likewise resented and despised their Jewish cousins. The Samaritans were descendants of Israelites who had intermarried with pagans after the Assyrians forced most of the population of Israel's Northern Kingdom into exile in 722 BC (2 Kings 17:6). When the Assyrians conquered Israel's Northern Kingdom, they carried away much of the population into captivity, and they purposely populated the land with expatriate pagans from other Gentile lands. "The king of Assyria brought people from Babylon, Cuthah, Ava, Hamath, and from Sepharvaim, and placed them in the cities of Samaria instead of the children of Israel; and they took possession of Samaria and dwelt in its cities. And it was so, at the beginning of their dwelling there, that they did not fear the LORD" (vv. 24–25).

Some Israelite stragglers remained or returned to the land after most of their brethren were forced into exile, and these scattered Israelites mixed with and married the pagan settlers. They kept some traditions that were rooted in Old Testament doctrine, but they also blended enough pagan beliefs into the mix that Samaritan worship ultimately became something fundamentally different from either Judaism or paganism. It was a mongrel religion—the Old Testament equivalent of today's quasi-Christian cults. Of course, faithful Jews saw Samaritanism as corrupt, unclean, and treasonous to the God of Scripture.

During the time of Ezra, Jews from the Southern Kingdom began to return from the Babylonian captivity. As they began to rebuild the temple in Jerusalem, the Samaritans offered help. Unable to hide their righteous contempt for Samaritan syncretism, the Jews refused. So the Samaritans tried to sabotage the project (Ezra 4:1–5). Then a few years later, at the instigation of Sanballat, they also tried to halt the rebuilding of Jerusalem's wall (Neh. 4:2). From that era and for centuries afterward, Jews and Samaritans had remained the bitterest of enemies.

Jewish people regarded the Samaritans as apostate people who had sold their spiritual birthright. After all, the Samaritans had actively participated in the defilement of the land; they had polluted the bloodline; and they were guilty of idolatry. As far as the Jews were concerned, the Samaritans' very existence was evil fruit that stemmed from the "sins of Jeroboam" (1 Kings 14:16; 2 Kings 17:22). Like Jeroboam, the Samaritans ultimately built a temple of their own, with counterfeit priests and unlawful sacrifices. By the Jews' reckoning, they were worse than rank pagans because of the subtlety with which they had polluted their religion.

Samaritans' hatred for the Jews was at least equal to that. About 130 years before the time of Christ, John Hercanus, a Jewish king in the Hasmonean (Maccabean) dynasty, defeated the Samaritan nation. The Jews demolished the Samaritan temple on Mount Gerizim. And although that temple was never rebuilt, the Samaritans insisted that Gerizim was the only legitimate place of worship (John 4:20). Today there are fewer than a thousand Samaritans, but they still worship on Gerizim.

In Jesus' time, animosity between Jews and Samaritans was especially fierce. The depth of the Jews' contempt for their wayward cousins is seen not only in how they avoided traveling through Samaria, but perhaps even more in how they spoke about the Samaritans. At one point some exasperated Jewish leaders, losing a public debate with Jesus but trying desperately to discredit Him, spat out the worst insult they could imagine: "Do we not say rightly that You are a Samaritan and have a demon?" (John 8:48).

So here is a Samaritan man, whom the typical Jewish religious leader would assume is the blood enemy of the injured traveler. If the priest and Levi turned their backs, what will this Samaritan do when he sees a helpless Jew out in the middle of nowhere? Kill him and rob his corpse?

Not at all: "When he saw him, he had compassion" (Luke 10:33).

What was Jesus trying to say? It was a preliminary answer to the original question. And it was a tough reply with a subtle rebuke aimed at the lawyer who raised the question in the first place. Elite status as religious leaders did *nothing* to make the priest and Levite fit for the kingdom. "Pure and undefiled religion before God" does not consist in birthrights and bloodlines, or rituals and rote confessions of faith (cf. James 1:27). Pure religion is something else entirely.

## How the Samaritan Loved

The Samaritan now takes center stage in the story, and here comes the main point: notice *how* this man loves. "He saw him," (Luke 10:33). Nothing remarkable there. The priest and the Levite got that far, but they showed no love. This man, a heretic and outcast, was moved by compassion. Something in his heart went out to the man—a sense of sadness, grief, tenderhearted empathy. He saw and embraced the urgent need to rescue and recover the man. *He bore the injured man's burden as if it were his own.*

"So he went to him" (v. 34). That's the polar opposite of what the priest and Levite did. He "bandaged his wounds, pouring on oil and wine." Remember that everything of value had been taken from the injured man. So whatever the Samaritan used for bandages came out of his own bag or from his own clothes. The wine was antiseptic and the oil was a balm and an anodyne. This would both sanitize and seal wounds in a way that would help prevent infection. The oil would also moisturize, soothe, and soften the tissue. (Olive oil was the chief emollient used in the medicine of that time, and it was effective for bringing quick relief from the stinging pain of abrasions and bleeding wounds.)

Where did the oil and wine come from? Travelers on a long journey would carry oil for cooking and wine for drinking (water along the way wasn't safe). The Samaritan was using his own provisions. The expression used tells us that he was not stingy with the wine and oil. He wasn't using an eyedropper or dabbing at the injured places. He washed the man's wounds thoroughly. Jesus is purposely stressing the lavishness of the Samaritan's generosity.

Then Jesus says, "he set him on his own animal"—probably a donkey or a mule (v. 34). It's *the Samaritan's* "own animal." So the Samaritan walks, with the injured man riding. What Jesus aims to underscore here is that this is not minimal care; the Samaritan was making an extraordinary sacrifice for someone he didn't even know.

He "brought him to an inn, and took care of him" (v. 34). He didn't leave him alone there; the Samaritan stayed with the wounded traveler. He acquired a room, got the man settled, and then stayed with him to help nurse him back to health. He continued to treat his wounds, providing food, sleep, comfort, water, and whatever care the injured man needed. He stayed with him through the night, because verse 35 says, *"On the next day* when he departed, he took out two denarii, gave them to the innkeeper, and said to him, 'Take care of him; and whatever more you spend, when I come again, I will repay you'" (emphasis added).

Two denarii constituted two full days' wages—and from what we know of the rates at the time, that was enough for two months' room and board in a wayside inn like that. Again, this was remarkable charity, especially considering the men were strangers to one another and would have been deemed by most as enemies. Yet the Samaritan gave up his own clothes, his supplies, his time, a night's sleep, and a significant sum of cash. He even promised to pay more if necessary. Someone might scold him for naively exposing himself to the possibility of being taken advantage of. But he was more concerned about the needs of his neighbor. So he left an open account on behalf of the wounded man.

The Samaritan had never met the other man. He didn't know how the traveler got in the condition he found him in, and in Jesus' telling of the story, he didn't even stop to investigate or subject the man to any kind of cross-examination. His heart was so full of love that when someone came across his path with a desperate need he was able to meet, he did everything he could possibly do. There was never a question or hesitation.

In other words, the Samaritan never stopped to ask what the lawyer had asked: "And who is my neighbor?" The far more important question is, "Whose neighbor am I?" And the answer is anyone in need.

But let's be honest with ourselves. If we encountered a scenario like this in real life, most of us would probably think the Samaritan's generosity toward a stranger seems excessive. Did you ever set aside everything to help a total stranger in a desperate situation? More to the point, have you ever done that for someone who was your enemy? Did you risk defilement in order to minister to all his needs? Did you singlehandedly provide everything he needed—dress his wounds, feed him, stay with him through a long night of pain, pay his bills, provide him with several weeks' room, board, and medical care—and then leave him with a blank check to pay everything he might need in the meantime?

No?

## Limitless Love

Actually, there *is* someone you have done all those things for: yourself. That is precisely how we look after our own needs, isn't it? *Give me whatever I need. Call the best doctor. Get me to the best medical facility. Arrange the best care I can get. Take care of me as long as I need it. Pamper me. Don't skimp on the amenities.* We might get closest to true self-sacrifice with a family member or a very close friend. But who would do this for a stranger—and an enemy to boot? This kind of thing is simply not done.

No doubt you have done something wonderfully generous at some point in your life. But do you truly love strangers like this all the time?

Of course not. Jesus is describing a rare love that has no limits. Keep in mind that this also a sort of backhanded reply to the lawyer's original question in Luke 10:25: "What shall I do to inherit eternal life?" The answer goes like this:

*What does the law say?*

"Love . . . your neighbor as yourself" (v. 27).

"You have answered rightly; do this and you will live" (v. 28).

Jesus told the parable of the good Samaritan in order to show what an impossibly high standard the law sets for us. And it is a rebuke not just to the lawyer, but to all of us. If we always truly loved our neighbors the way we love and care for ourselves, the Samaritan's generosity would not seem so remarkable.

Whatever polemical trap the lawyer was planning to lay for Jesus was defeated by the parable. At the end of the story, Jesus turned the lawyer's own question right back to him: "So which of these three do you think was neighbor to him who fell among the thieves?" (v. 36).

With the powerful lesson of that parable still hanging in the air, the lawyer had only one possible reply: "He who showed mercy on him" (v. 37).

Jesus' next reply ought to have provoked deep conviction and a humble confession of the man's own inability: "Go and do likewise" (v. 37).

Because here's the catch: the law demands that you love like that *all the time*. As a lawyer, the man should have known that he couldn't perform a single act of extravagant altruism and imagine that he had fulfilled the demands of the law forever. The law demands perfection *all the time*. "Cursed is the one who does not confirm *all* the words of this law" (Deut. 27:26). "Whoever shall keep the whole law, and yet stumble in one point, he is guilty of all" (James 2:10).

So Jesus' final reply to the man, "Go and do likewise," should have moved the lawyer to plead for grace and forgiveness. If that is what the law means when it promises life to those who obey (Lev. 18:5), we have no hope at all under the law. The only thing the law can do for us is doom us. "The commandment, which was to bring life, [is thus instead] found to bring death" (Rom. 7:10). Because the law demands absolute and utter godlike perfection (Matt. 5:48), no one who has ever sinned can be fit for eternal life on the law's terms. That's what the lawyer should have realized. So should we. The full truth is that even Christians, into whose hearts "the love of God has been poured out" (Rom. 5:5), do not consistently love like the law demands.

But there's a deeper lesson here. The way the good Samaritan cared for the traveler is the way God loves sinners. In fact, God's love is infinitely more profound and more amazing than that. The Samaritan sacrificed his time and money to care for a wounded enemy. God gave His own eternal Son to die for sinners who deserve nothing more than eternal damnation. "When we were still without strength, in due time Christ died for the ungodly. For scarcely for a righteous man will one die; yet perhaps for a good man someone would even dare to die. But God demonstrates His own love toward us, in that while we were still sinners, Christ died for us" (Rom. 5:6–8). Indeed, "when we were *enemies* we were reconciled to God through the death of His Son" (v. 10, emphasis added).

What Christ did to redeem His people far exceeds the lavish act of benevolence pictured in the parable. Christ is the living embodiment of divine love in all its perfection. He is spotless, sinless—"holy, harmless, undefiled, separate from sinners" (Heb. 7:26). During His earthly life, He *did* literally fulfill every jot and tittle of the law to absolute perfection. And then in dying, He even bore the penalty of sin for others. Moreover, His unblemished righteousness—including the full merit of that perfect love—is imputed to those who trust Him as Lord and Savior. Their sins are forgiven, and they are clothed in the perfect righteousness the law requires. They inherit eternal life—not as a reward for their own good works, but purely by grace, because of Christ's work on their behalf.

If that lawyer had only confessed his own guilt and admitted his inability to do what the law demands, Jesus would have been ready to offer him an eternity of mercy, grace, forgiveness, and true love. If he had simply sensed his need, the straightforward, plain-language answer to his question was already on the lips of Jesus, who repeatedly said things like, "He who hears My word and believes in Him who sent Me has everlasting life, and shall not come into judgment, but has passed from death into life" (John 5:24). "He who believes in the Son has everlasting life" (3:36). "My sheep hear My voice, and I know them, and they follow Me. And I give them eternal life, and they shall never perish" (10:27–28). "Whoever lives and believes in Me shall never die" (11:26).

Jesus never made such a promise to smug and self-righteous souls. Both this man and the rich young ruler asked Him specific questions about how to inherit eternal life, and He answered by confronting them with the law's demands. But for those with ears to hear, He constantly made it perfectly clear that eternal life is not earned through legal merit; rather, it is the gracious inheritance of all who truly put their faith in Christ as Lord and Savior.

Did the man embrace the lesson Jesus was teaching him? Did he confess his inability when Jesus told him "Go and do likewise"? Did he acknowledge his need for grace and repent?

Apparently not. That is the end of the story. Luke turns immediately to a different incident from the ministry of Jesus. Publicly disgraced in his failed attempt to win a verbal sparring match with Jesus, the anonymous lawyer simply disappears from the narrative and we never hear about him again. Like the typical proud, self-sufficient religious person, he might have made a resolution to double down on doing good works in order to prove himself worthy of divine favor and eternal life. Such people are oblivious to (or else they refuse to believe) what the righteousness of God really demands of them. They seek to establish their own righteousness without submitting to the righteousness God has revealed in Christ (cf. Rom. 10:3). They read the parable of the good Samaritan as if it were nothing more than a mandate for humanitarianism.

It's fine to be motivated by the parable to perfect our love for our neighbors. I hope you are motivated that way. But if that is your *only* response to this parable, it is practically the worst response anyone could have to the lesson Jesus was teaching. This parable is meant to constrain us to confess our sinful weakness (revealed in our lack of compassionate, sacrificial love) and seek grace and mercy by turning with repentant faith to Jesus Christ—the only One who truly and perfectly fulfilled what the law demands of us. He alone is "able to save to the uttermost those who come to God through Him" (Heb. 7:25). He is the only true source of eternal life.

If that lawyer had truly looked into the law of God (as he himself recited the commandments) and recognized his sin rather than turning away "and immediately [forgetting] what kind of man he was" (James 1:24)—he would have found a Savior whose yoke is easy and whose burden is light. But as we see, the story ends without a hint of his repentance.

That *must not* be our response to this parable.

# 6

# A Lesson About
# Justification by Faith

*The kindness and the love of God our Savior toward man appeared,
not by works of righteousness which we have done, but according
to His mercy He saved us, through the washing of regeneration and
renewing of the Holy Spirit, whom He poured out on us abundantly
through Jesus Christ our Savior, that having been justified by His
grace we should become heirs according to the hope of eternal life.*

—TITUS 3:4–7

The Pharisees of Jesus' time were the strictest and most influential religious sect in all of Israel. The New Testament does not paint them in
a positive light. One of the key moments in the ministry of John the
Baptist was his shocking rebuke of some Pharisees who came to be baptized. John refused them, saying, "Brood of vipers! Who warned you to
flee from the wrath to come? Therefore bear fruits worthy of repentance"
(Matt. 3:7–8; Luke 3:7–8).

Not long after that, John the Baptist singled out Jesus as the true

Lamb of God (John 1:29–30)—and as you might expect, John's endorsement immediately put Jesus on the wrong side of the Pharisees. As soon as it became clear that Jesus was gaining an even larger following than John, the Pharisees opposed Him (John 4:1–3). Throughout Jesus' earthly ministry, they were His most vocal and relentless opponents. Leading Pharisees were the ones who ultimately initiated and masterminded the conspiracy to put Him to death (John 11:46–53).

The Pharisees' contempt for Christ continued even after His resurrection, especially while the early church was beginning to take root. In Acts 7:58–8:1, we are told that Saul of Tarsus oversaw the stoning of the first Christian martyr, Stephen. Acts 26:10 suggests that Stephen's stoning was only the start of a brutal campaign of terror Saul waged against believers. Saul was "a Pharisee, a son of Pharisees" (Acts 23:6 NASB). In other words, he came from a line of Pharisees and was trained from birth in the doctrines of Pharisaism—striving to observe Moses' law all his life. He was the ideal Pharisee, "circumcised the eighth day, of the stock of Israel, of the tribe of Benjamin, a Hebrew of the Hebrews; concerning the law, a Pharisee; concerning zeal, persecuting the church; concerning the righteousness which is in the law, blameless" (Phil. 3:5–6).

Thus born and bred into Pharisaism, Saul became a leading figure in the sect while he was still a very young man. He was personally appointed by the chief priests to harass and imprison early Christians for their faith. Whenever followers of Jesus were on trial for their lives before the Jewish ruling council, Saul cast his vote in favor of stoning (Acts 26:10). The fact that he had a vote in the matter suggests that Saul himself was at that time a member of the Sanhedrin. He had reached the pinnacle of influence in the sect and devotion to its teachings. His unusual zeal for Pharisaism was clearly reflected in his hatred of Christianity.

All of that, of course, preceded his famous encounter with Christ on the road to Damascus, when Saul of Tarsus was instantly and utterly transformed into the apostle Paul. Giving his testimony years later, Paul said he counted all his efforts to be righteous as a Pharisee nothing but "rubbish" (Phil. 3:8). The King James Version translates the word more literally and more vividly as "dung." That was Paul's candid assessment of Pharisaism, writing as a seasoned saint and mature apostle.

From beginning to end, the New Testament makes it clear that Pharisaism and Christianity don't mix. Indeed, certain core principles of the Pharisees' religion and worldview are hostile to the fundamental message of the gospel.

That is not to suggest that Pharisaism is the most extreme possible perversion of religion. Far from it. The Pharisees taught much that was true, because their beliefs were closely tied to Scripture. Jesus Himself said of them, "Whatever they tell you to observe, that observe and do" (Matt. 23:3). Unlike so many cults and false religions that are grossly unorthodox, overtly diabolical, or blithely indifferent to the law of God, the Pharisees were traditionalists and idealists well known for their punctilious obsession with the smallest details of the law. Pharisaism is singled out in the New Testament not because it was some far-fetched brand of extreme human superstition, but because it represents the most slight and subtle departure from biblical truth. The spiritual dangers embodied in Pharisaism can be a temptation and a snare even to the most devoted student of Scripture.

Why was this particular brand of Judaism so deadly? After all, the Pharisees gave every *appearance* of being champions of righteousness. In fact, external appearances were what concerned them the most. Their idea of righteousness was mostly cosmetic. They excelled at hiding their own unrighteousness and papering over their secret sins with works of religion—while they declaimed passionately against the more visible sins of others. Far from being careless with respect to the law, they made a great show of obeying the law's fine points in an exaggerated, ostentatious way (Matt. 23:5). Their use of the law as a cloak for their sin therefore turned the whole purpose of the law on its head. Whereas the law is supposed to reveal sin and show its exceeding sinfulness, they used the law to disguise what was really in their hearts—and they salved their own guilt by self-righteously comparing themselves with others. The subtlety of their error, obscured by the pretense that they were strongly committed to the law of God, is what made their brand of religion so dangerous.

Nevertheless, the Pharisees were indeed rigorous students of the biblical text. Quite a few noble and praiseworthy elements stand out in their beliefs and teachings. For example, they opposed all pagan forms of idolatry and were determined not to allow their nation to fall into the kind of compromise and backsliding that colored the history of Old Testament Israel. They were in many ways the very best of all the first-century sects of Judaism.

Specifically, the Pharisees were less mystical and more committed to practicing their faith in the real world than the Essenes—ascetics who lived in communal groups. They were much more doctrinally sound than the Sadducees, who were skeptical about everything supernatural (Matt. 22:23; Acts 23:8). They did not produce political extremists, ruffians, outlaws, and even wanton murderers the way the party of the Zealots did.

By contrast, the Pharisees were so meticulous in their compliance with legal minutiae that they would carefully strain any drink while pouring it to make sure no gnat had got into the wine while it was aerating. (Gnats are insects and therefore ceremonially defiling.) They would painstakingly count tiny seeds in order to make sure their tithe was accurate (Luke 11:42). After all, Leviticus 27:30 says, "Every tithe of the land, whether of the seed of the land or of the fruit of the trees, is the LORD's; it is holy to the LORD" (ESV).

Jesus did not chide them for their overparticular obsession with seed counts, gnat straining, and other trifling observances. Rather, Jesus said, "These you ought to have done"—but without leaving the law's larger moral principles undone (Matt. 23:23). Despite all their attention to the law's external details, they were utterly oblivious to the law's central message. The law ought to have humbled them by showing them the magnitude of their guilt. Instead, it became a point of extreme pride for them.

Jesus called the Pharisees "Blind guides, who strain out a gnat and swallow a camel!" (v. 24). Gnats, of course, are the tiniest unclean creatures described in Moses' law; camels are the largest. Jesus' word picture makes a humorous mental image, but His point was totally serious: All their exacting efforts to keep up appearances had not diminished their guilt in the smallest measure. Much less had it curtailed the expression of sin in their own hearts. He told them, "You are like whitewashed tombs which indeed appear beautiful outwardly, but inside are full of dead men's bones and all uncleanness. Even so you also outwardly appear righteous to men, but inside you are full of hypocrisy and lawlessness" (Matt. 23:27–28). They were guilty sinners. They were as lost, depraved, and spiritually blind as the outcasts and unclean people whom they treated with extreme contempt. Although their well-honed legalism obscured their wickedness from human eyes, it did not fool God. The Pharisees' hypocrisy was itself a damnable sin.

## Two Men at the Temple

Despite what they thought, there was absolutely no justifying value in the Pharisees' preoccupation with legal minutiae. On the contrary, their pious ostentation actually magnified their guilt while producing a false trust in themselves. That precise lesson was the central point of the parable Jesus tells in Luke 18:9–14. This parable also stands as clear, succinct affirmation from our Lord's own lips regarding the Reformation principle of *sola fide*—the truth that faith is the sole instrument of justification:

> He spoke this parable to some who trusted in themselves that they were righteous, and despised others: "Two men went up to the temple to pray, one a Pharisee and the other a tax collector. The Pharisee stood and prayed thus with himself, 'God, I thank You that I am not like other men—extortioners, unjust, adulterers, or even as this tax collector. I fast twice a week; I give tithes of all that I possess.' And the

tax collector, standing afar off, would not so much as raise his eyes to heaven, but beat his breast, saying, 'God, be merciful to me a sinner!' I tell you, this man went down to his house justified rather than the other; for everyone who exalts himself will be humbled, and he who humbles himself will be exalted."

As is true of so many of our Lord's stories, that parable was not only counterintuitive but also shocking and shameful by every religious standard of the time. By saying that a self-confessed sinner left the temple justified while essentially dismissing as utterly worthless the many good works of a fastidious Pharisee, Jesus put Himself 180 degrees opposite the prevailing Jewish theology of salvation. More than that, He set His gospel against the teaching of every major world religion, against every doctrine that stems from natural theology, and against every innate notion of the fallen human heart.

This parable was a poignant lesson about grace toward the humble, carefully calculated to puncture the self-righteous pride of the Pharisees. As such, it provided the Jewish leaders who heard Jesus with one more reason to reject Him. It stepped on the toes of their pretension and demeaned their whole religion. People today who are more concerned with being polite and politically correct than they are with speaking the truth might even deem this a form of hate speech. Followers of the Pharisees in Jesus' original audience probably regarded the story as sacrilegious. They certainly would have seen it as a lowering of the divine standard. To suggest that the lowest of sinners can be justified while a devout religious leader is rejected sounded to them like an all-out attack on divine justice, the Mosaic law, and every rule of righteousness and piety. How can God be just if He justifies the ungodly?

That, of course, is the very question the gospel answers. Because God has graciously provided an atonement through the death of Christ, He is *both* "just and the justifier of the one who has faith in Jesus" (Rom. 3:26). "He is faithful *and just* to forgive us our sins and to cleanse us from all unrighteousness" (1 John 1:9, emphasis added).

## The Problem for Sinners

Nevertheless, it is easy to see why the justification of sinners posed an impossible dilemma for people prior to the death and resurrection of Christ. They had no notion what a perfect atonement for sin might look like. They could not conceive how full pardon for a lifetime of sin might even be possible. Indeed, on the terms of the law alone, forgiveness might seem to be completely out of reach.

The difficulty starts with an understanding of the law's righteous requirement. In Leviticus 19:2, God Himself says, "You shall be holy, for I the LORD your God am holy." God's own perfect holiness therefore establishes the legal standard and the moral requirement for a right standing with God. Jesus reiterates that same standard in the New Testament, this time with language clearly designed to stress the sheer impossibility of attaining such a high standard. In His Sermon on the Mount, he said, "Unless your righteousness exceeds the righteousness of the scribes and Pharisees, you will by no means enter the kingdom of heaven" (Matt. 5:20).

That was undoubtedly a major shock to everyone who heard it. Say what you will about the Pharisees' hypocrisy and hidden wickedness, they had nevertheless elevated obedience to the law's external commands to an unprecedented level. If God graded human behavior on a curve, the Pharisees would have been at the head of the class. But Jesus was pointing out that God doesn't adjust the scale of righteousness to accommodate human failure. His own righteousness is flawlessly perfect, and to lower that standard even slightly in order to accommodate our sin would make Him unholy.

So the righteousness God demands must exceed even the apparently superior righteousness of the Pharisees. What, precisely, does this require of us? Jesus answers that question, too, and in unequivocal terms: "You shall be perfect, just as your Father in heaven is perfect" (Matt. 5:48). True righteousness, as defined by the character of God Himself, demands absolute, uncompromising perfection. He Himself is the standard and only true measure of the perfection He requires from us.

In that same context, Jesus taught that it is simply not enough to obey the obvious, external demands of the law—even the minutiae like seed counting and gnat straining. Our attitudes and desires must also at all times conform perfectly to the requirements of the law. A lustful look violates the same moral principle as an act of adultery (Matt. 5:27–28). To be angry without cause, to insult someone, or to hate another person is to breach the same commandment that forbids us to commit murder (Matt. 5:21–22).

To make matters worse, James 2:10 says, "Whoever shall keep the whole law, and yet stumble in one point, he is guilty of all." There are no loopholes or escape clauses in the law. It can only condemn those who break it.

On top of all that, God abominates anyone who would justify an evildoer: "He who justifies the wicked, and he who condemns the just, both of them alike are an abomination to the LORD" (Prov. 17:15). We know, of course, that "the LORD is slow to anger and great in power" (Nah. 1:3). But the same verse that makes that promise also goes on to say that God "will not at all acquit the wicked." God warned the Israelites, "Keep yourself far from a false matter; do not kill the innocent and righteous. For *I will not justify the wicked*" (Ex. 23:7, emphasis added).

Who, then, can be right with God? If God says it is evil to justify anyone who is guilty, and He states emphatically that He will not justify the wicked, how can anyone who has ever sinned be granted entry into the heavenly kingdom? The answer is hinted at in the Genesis record of Abraham: "He believed in the LORD; and He reckoned it to him as righteousness" (Gen. 15:6 NASB). Righteousness was *imputed* to Abraham. A righteousness that did not belong to him was credited to his account (Rom. 4:1–12). He did not earn righteousness by his works; he laid hold of it by faith. Furthermore, "[all] those who are of faith are blessed with Abraham, the believer" (Gal. 3:9 NASB). That is the doctrine of justification by faith.

But on what grounds is such justification possible, given that God says He will not simply acquit sinners or declare them righteous by divine fiat alone?

The full answer to that question is seen in the sacrifice offered by Jesus Christ. God does not dismiss the guilt of sinners by pretending their sin never happened. He doesn't ignore evil, sweep it aside by sheer edict, or acquit sinners capriciously on a whim. Rather, He provided a full and perfect atonement for sin in the Person of His own Son, "whom God set forth as a propitiation by His blood, through faith, to demonstrate His righteousness" (Rom. 3:25). Christ also provides the perfect righteousness that is imputed to those who believe: "[God the Father] made Him who knew no sin to be sin on our behalf, so that we might become the righteousness of God in Him" (2 Cor. 5:21 NASB).

There were hints of this truth in the Old Testament. In Isaiah 53, God, speaking prophetically, says, "My righteous Servant shall justify many, for He shall bear their iniquities" (v. 11). The theme of that whole chapter is substitutionary atonement:

> *He has borne our griefs*
> *And carried our sorrows;*
> *Yet we esteemed Him stricken,*
> *Smitten by God, and afflicted.*
> *But He was wounded for our transgressions,*
> *He was bruised for our iniquities;*
> *The chastisement for our peace was upon Him. . . .*
> *The LORD has laid on Him the iniquity of us all. (vv. 4–6)*

But full understanding of that passage was elusive until Jesus fulfilled the prophecy in His death on the cross. That, of course, had not occurred yet when Jesus gave this parable. But the parable itself is nevertheless full of lessons about human depravity, divine grace, redemption from sin, and the doctrine of justification by faith.

## "Justified"

The closing line of the parable is the key to Jesus' point. He says of the hated tax collector, "I tell you, this man went down to his house justified" (Luke 18:14). That's what the parable is about: justification.

Here is the most abject type of sinner—a tax collector. He is a traitor to his people who has sold out for money. Yet he gains a right standing with God, apart from any religious ritual, absent any kind of self-atonement, and without performing any deeds of merit. Every detail of the doctrine of justification by faith is either expressly set forth, implied, illustrated, or otherwise affirmed in this parable.

Not only did Jesus say God accepted the tax collector; He also made it clear that the Pharisee was rejected. "This man went down to his house justified *rather than* the other" (Luke 18:14). That was stunning. How was such a thing possible?

That question is relevant to every one of us: *How can a sinner be made right with God?* In fact, there is no more important question. How can we be redeemed from our fallenness? In the words of Bildad in Job 25:4, "How then can man be righteous before God?" Or as the Philippian jailer put it in Acts 16:30, "What must I do to be saved?" It is ultimately the same question raised by the rich young ruler in Matthew 19:16— "What good thing shall I do that I may have eternal life?"—and by the lawyer in Luke 10:25: "What shall I do to inherit eternal life?"

Bear in mind that Jesus responded to both the rich young ruler and the lawyer by citing the demands of the law. The rich young ruler claimed he had kept the law from the earliest age. He seemed stunned when Jesus did not commend him (Matt. 19:20). The lawyer's agenda likewise was "to justify himself" (Luke 10:29). Both of them were precisely like the Pharisee in the Luke 18 parable—confident that they deserved the praise and acceptance of God, unaware of the magnitude of their own guilt, oblivious to the real message of the law, and contemptuous toward people they deemed sinners.

Did you ever wonder why Jesus preached law instead of grace to them? In neither case did He go on to give the gospel's answer to the eternally important question those men raised. Why? Because the law was what they needed to hear. Neither man had ever truly felt the weight of the law. They did not believe themselves to be lost. "Those who are well have no need of a physician, but those who are sick. [Jesus] did not come to call the righteous, but sinners, to repentance" (Mark 2:17).

The gospel has nothing to say to people who are satisfied with their own righteousness. There is no truly good news for someone in that state of mind.

The parable of the Pharisee and the tax collector illustrates that point with vivid precision. In veiled story form, this parable *does* give the true gospel answer to the question of how sinners can be made right with God. What is the answer? In a word: *grace.* God freely "justifies the ungodly" (Rom. 4:5). He "imputes righteousness apart from works" (v. 6). The whole doctrine of justification by faith is here put on display with amazing profundity, simplicity, and clarity.

Jesus' message is simple: all who are determined to establish a righteousness of their own will fail and thus condemn themselves; but those who submit to the righteousness of God are graciously justified by Him (cf. Rom. 10:3–4). No one can justify himself before God; God alone is "the justifier of the one who has faith in Jesus" (Rom. 3:26).

This principle is the simple dividing line between the gospel of Jesus Christ and every erroneous or demonic belief system. Stripped down to its bare essence, every false religion ever devised by reprobate minds is a merit system. All of them teach that justification is earned or achieved by something the worshiper does for God—some kind of good work, sacrament, or religious ceremony; an act of charity or altruism; an austere lifestyle; or (lately) devotion to some political cause, environmental campaign, or alternative value system. The religious zeal that fallen people cultivate for their chosen cause or credo is never truly selfless or sacrificial. The cause becomes a platform from which they look down on others. Most people think exactly like the Pharisee in Jesus' parable: *I'm not as bad as other people; I should be okay.* Nothing is more natural to the unregenerate human heart.

One needn't be a full-fledged Pharisee to think like that. Even the most impassioned atheists tell themselves they are decent, honorable, generous, or otherwise good enough. They rarely follow their unbelief to its obvious moral conclusion (just in case some karmic principle or natural force exists to keep the universe balanced by making paybacks). Like everyone else, they cannot live up to whatever moral standard they think they must meet—but they have a seemingly irresistible urge to justify themselves anyway. Every survey that has ever raised the question reveals that most people assume they are good enough to go to heaven—or at least too good for God to send them to hell.

The underlying error in all of that—the belief that people can gain God's favor by being good enough—is the central lie that dominates all false religion.

Jesus' parable exposes the folly of that idea. The parable draws a clear line of distinction between the only two types of religion that exist: the false religion of *human achievement*, versus the true gospel of *divine accomplishment*. The Pharisee in the parable is smug, self-righteous, contemptuous, with a massive superiority complex. He stands as near as he can to the holy place without touching anyone he deems beneath him. By his way of thinking, contact with sinners would contaminate him. He seeks no mercy, no grace, no forgiveness, no sympathy for himself. He asks God for absolutely nothing, because he can think of nothing he needs. He is simply thankful that he is not unrighteous. Self-exalted, he goes away unjustified.

The other character is the tax collector—a sinful outcast, the object of everyone's contempt (including, now, his own). He knows he is guilty. He stands far away from the holy place, because he feels unclean and unwanted. He cannot even lift his eyes to heaven. He is clearly distraught over his own sin. He beats his breast in shame. He is at the lowest possible point of desperation—without any hope of redeeming himself. All he can do is humbly ask God for mercy and grace. Jesus said he went home that very day, justified.

## Analyzing the Parable

Luke is clear about Jesus' target audience for this parable: "He spoke this parable to some who trusted in themselves that they were righteous, and despised others" (Luke 18:9). The Greek text uses an indefinite pronoun (*tis*, translated "some") meaning "everyone, anyone, or whosoever." This was not directed at a specific Pharisee (or even the Pharisees in particular) like the parable of the good Samaritan. It is a message for all and sundry "who trusted in themselves that they were righteous, and despised others." As we've just seen, that includes every unregenerate person. There's a deliberate evangelistic point to this parable. This is a lesson for all those who trust in themselves that they are righteous—instead of looking to Christ for His own righteousness (perfect righteousness) to be imputed.

There's no question, however, that the point of this parable was especially significant for the Pharisees. It was a direct blow to the very heart of their belief system. They were not only self-righteous; they were obnoxiously so. They constantly viewed others with contempt (Luke 7:39; 15:2; John 7:47–49; 9:34). And we know that Pharisees were constantly present whenever Jesus taught publicly because they were desperately looking for reasons to accuse Him. Just two chapters earlier, in Luke 16:14, we read, "The Pharisees . . . heard all these things, and they derided Him." Jesus' reply to them in that text strikes the same note as our parable: "You are those who justify yourselves before men, but God knows your hearts. For what is highly esteemed among men is an abomination in the sight of God" (v. 15).

So although Jesus intended the lesson of this parable for all of us, it clearly applies to the Pharisees and their misled followers in a particular way. The character who embodies self-righteousness in the parable is himself a Pharisee, and he perfectly fits the description of Luke 18:9. He was clearly someone who trusted in himself while despising others.

The Greek word translated "despised" in verse 9 is *exoutheneō*, a word used only one other time in the Gospels—in Luke 23:11, where

"Herod, with his men of war, treated [Jesus] with contempt and mocked Him, arrayed Him in a gorgeous robe." The word speaks of the most low-brow, biting kind of derision—open scorn, ridicule, mockery, sarcasm. The Pharisees tended to treat others that way. They were so steeped in their distinctive style of holier-than-thou piety that they actually viewed their utter contempt for others as a symbol of their own righteousness. That Greek word, *exoutheneō*, is formed by combining the preposition *ex* ("out of") with the word *outhen* ("nothing" or "worthless"). The Pharisees viewed anyone outside their circle of disciples as good for nothing. The more notorious a person's sin, the more the Pharisees despised that person.

Their name for their own disciples—people who followed their strict interpretation of the law—was *haberim* ("associates"). People who did not follow the Pharisees' rules were *am ha'aretz* (literally, "people of the land"). The expression signified someone who was unclean—a lowlife.

Commenting on this distinction, Kenneth Bailey writes,

> In the eyes of a strict Pharisee the most obvious candidate for the classification of *am-haaretz* would be a tax collector. . . . If [the Pharisee] accidentally brushes against the tax collector (or any other *am-haaretz* who might be among the worshipers), he would sustain *midras*—uncleanness. His state of cleanliness is too important. It must not be compromised for any reason. Physical isolation, from his point of view, would be a statement and an important one at that. Thus the Pharisee carefully stands aloof from the others gathered around the altar.[1]

So these two characters in Jesus' parable represent opposite extremes.

## The Contrasts

Here are two men, poles apart in every way. The stark differences between them are seen in their social status, their posture at prayer, the content of their prayers, and their final standing before God.

## Their Position

The Pharisee was a social and religious insider, occupying one of the top rungs on Jewish high society's ladder. Pharisees were guests of honor in any social gathering. Because of the exclusivity of their fellowship (the name *Pharisee* meant "separatist"), to have a Pharisee attend a meal or a gathering was a mark of high status.

At the opposite end of the social scale were the tax collectors—the most universally despised people in all Israel. They were basically turncoats and criminals—morally and ethically bankrupt, patsies of Rome, and enemies of everything holy. In fact, tax collectors belonged to the same social category as harlots (Matt. 21:31–32) and drunkards (Luke 7:34)—and most tax collectors surrounded themselves with such people. They had a reputation for being not only dishonest and cruel, but also morally debased in every conceivable way.

Tax collectors purchased franchises from the Roman occupiers. The agreement required them to pay a fixed amount to the Romans each year. Anything they collected over that was theirs to keep. They accumulated their wealth by taking unfair advantage of their own people. Wretched traitors to their religion and to their nation, they were excluded from all religious activity and normal social relationships. They were, in the eyes of their countrymen, the furthest creatures from God—the lowest of the low—utterly without social standing, no matter how much wealth they might accumulate through thievery and extortion.

## Their Posture

The contrast in physical demeanor between these two men is significant as well. The Pharisee "stood and prayed . . . with himself" (Luke 18:11). It was fine—even normal—for him to stand erect. Jesus told His disciples, "Whenever you stand praying . . . forgive" (Mark 11:25). Standing upright was and still is the normal posture for prayer at or near the temple mount in Jerusalem. Men in Israel would typically have their eyes and hands lifted toward heaven when they prayed. They stood thus open-faced, ready to receive from the Lord. It was a posture that signified both praise and compliance.

So in and of itself, the fact that the Pharisee was standing was not a problem. What is significant about his posture is the way he chose to position himself in some distinctive place where he would surely stand out—and stand apart—from everyone else. Jesus mentioned this practice of the Pharisees in His Sermon on the Mount: "When you pray, you shall not be like the hypocrites. For they love to pray standing in the synagogues and on the corners of the streets, that they may be seen by men" (Matt. 6:5).

This Pharisee was no doubt in some prominent place in the inner court, as close as he could get to the Holy of Holies—because in his own mind, he belonged there. That transformed what should have been a worshipful posture into an ostentatious sign of self-promoting pride.

The tax collector also positioned himself in a place apart—not conspicuously in the center of the traffic pattern or on some pedestal in the inner court, but "afar off, [and he] would not so much as raise his eyes to heaven" (Luke 18:13). In other words, the tax collector stayed at the outer edge of the temple grounds. Why? Because he knew he didn't deserve to be in the presence of God or even the presence of other worshipers. He was a pariah not only to society, but more significantly to God. He knew that, and it was reflected in his posture. Unlike the Pharisee, this man could not even lift up his eyes. He was overwhelmed with profound guilt, intense shame, and an utter sense of disgrace. He knew he was unworthy, and he confessed it without any excuse or proviso. There's not even a hint of self-justification. He clearly felt the full weight of his alienation from God. Everything about his posture said so.

Jesus says the man "beat his breast" (v. 13). To pray with eyes down and with one's hands over the chest was a posture of humility. This man went even beyond that. His hands became fists, and he was pounding his own chest. The meaning of such a gesture hardly needs explanation. The man was clearly in a state of extreme anguish—mourning over his sin, filled with remorse, sadness, shame, and every related emotion. There is no parallel for this in the Old Testament, and there is only one other place in the New Testament where this gesture is mentioned. We see it around the cross, just after Jesus died. Luke 23:48 says "the whole crowd who came together to that sight, seeing what had been done, beat their breasts and returned." This gesture is mentioned in ancient extrabiblical literature, but mostly associated with the grief of women.

So here is a man doing a very unusual gesture that demonstrates extreme anguish. And why his chest? Why not pound somewhere else on the body? Proverbs 4:23 says, "Keep your heart with all diligence, for out of it spring the issues of life." Our true character is defined by what is on the inside, in the inner person—the seat of our thoughts, desires, and affections. Scripture speaks of that as the heart. Jesus Himself said, "From within, out of the heart of men, proceed evil thoughts, adulteries, fornications, murders, thefts, covetousness, wickedness, deceit, lewdness, an evil eye, blasphemy, pride, foolishness. All these evil things come from within and defile a man" (Mark 7:21–23). Jesus wasn't speaking of the literal organ in one's chest, of course. That is figurative language. But beating the breast nevertheless symbolized this man's remorse over the evil he had treasured up in his own heart. He understood that the "heart is deceitful above all things, and desperately wicked" (Jer. 17:9), and smiting his own breast was a vivid way of acknowledging that.

## Their Prayer

Jesus makes this interesting statement about the Pharisee's prayer: he "prayed . . . with himself" (Luke 18:11). That can have two possible meanings. He might have been praying inaudibly (as Hannah did in 1 Samuel 1:13). But this was a Pharisee, so silent prayers in a public place were not his style. Furthermore, Jesus' choice of words as well as the context in Luke 18 seem to indicate that the Pharisee was praying loudly, in a self-congratulatory fashion, because he took pleasure in hearing himself recite his own virtues in public this way. In effect, he was praying to himself, to stroke his own ego, rather than truly speaking to God. As a matter of fact, in the span of two verses (vv. 11–12) he uses the first-person pronoun five times. Though he thanks God that he is better than others, the Pharisee gives God no actual praise. He asks nothing from God—no mercy, no grace, no forgiveness, no help. He seems to refer to God only because that's the way prayers are supposed to begin: "God, I thank You that I am not like other men . . ."

The man's only unequivocal confession to God was this assertion about his own merit, buttressed by a recitation of other people's sins. That was then followed by a verbal catalogue of his own good deeds. Remember, he was standing in a prominent place. He was surely praying audibly—probably as loudly as he could pray without yelling.

And to make sure God and everyone else within earshot got the message, the Pharisee was as specific as possible. As self-righteous people invariably do, he compared himself with the worst of the worst. He specifically mentioned people who steal, people who cheat, and people who commit fornication: "extortioners, unjust, adulterers" (v. 11). Remember, those categories of sin were all associated with tax collectors.

And as he was giving that rundown of notorious moral failures, his eyes were on the tax collector. So he pointed to the man as the living epitome of what he, the Pharisee, was proud not to be like.

That is obnoxious self-righteousness. The Pharisee was praying to himself, putting on a demonstration for people, forgetting God. He asked nothing from God. Why should he? He couldn't think of anything he lacked. He just wanted people to take note of how different he was from the *am ha'aretz*.

That wasn't the end of the Pharisee's prayer, though. He also wanted to announce his positive virtues. "I fast twice a week; I give tithes of all that I possess" (v. 12). He was doubtless one of those who counted seeds to make sure his tithe was precise. And as for his fasting, Old Testament law required only one fast annually, in preparation for the Day of Atonement (Lev. 16:29–31). But the Pharisees fasted every Monday and Thursday. They believed they could acquire surplus merit by padding the actual law of God with lots of man-made rules, rites, and religious rituals. Many false religions do the same thing, thinking they can actually do *more* than God Himself requires and thereby earn extra credit. Roman Catholics refer to this as "works of supererogation."

But the only thing the Pharisee really had in great abundance was a surplus of self-esteem. He clearly thought more highly of himself than he ought to think. This is where the contrast between him and the tax collector is most clearly evident.

The tax collector's prayer was short and earnest. It is a genuine and urgent plea to God for mercy. It is not an exhibition of artificial religious passion for the benefit of passersby. The man's utter shame is evident in his words as much as in his posture. These are the words of a true penitent: "God, be merciful to me a sinner!" (Luke 18:13). The original Greek text employs the definite article: "Me, *the* sinner!" The expression is reminiscent of what the apostle Paul said in 1 Timothy 1:15, "sinners, of whom I am chief." This man is concerned with his own guilt, not someone else's. And he confesses his need for grace—something the Pharisee made no reference to.

## The Similarities

The Pharisee and the tax collector actually held many of their core beliefs in common. Both of them understood that the Old Testament Scriptures reveal the one true God—YHWH. Both believed in Him as the God of Abraham, Isaac, and Jacob; the God who gave His Word through Moses, David, and all the prophets. They believed in the Old Testament priesthood and sacrificial system. Their belief in those things is what brought them both to the Temple.

That means the Pharisee *did* believe in the need for atonement. No one with a Pharisee's knowledge of the law could possibly believe he was totally sinless. But he thought he had earned the right to be forgiven. In other words, he believed he had effectively atoned for his own sins. He apparently thought his good works outweighed and nullified his failures. He had offered the requisite sacrifices. He had performed so much better than most. Surely if good works and religious devotion could tip the scales of divine justice in one's own favor, this Pharisee of all people deserved a place of high honor. That's the way most religious people think. Most aren't the least bit reluctant to confess that they have sinned; they just can't seem to come to grips with the fact that their good works cannot earn them any merit. They think God is going to forgive the bad things they have done because they have earned His favor with good works.

The tax collector may have thought that way once, too, but life had brought him to the realization that he had nothing with which to bargain for God's favor. His very best deeds were defiled by the now obvious truth of who he really was at heart. The lesson of Isaiah 64:6 had been thrust upon him in living color: "We are all like an unclean thing, And all our righteousnesses are like filthy rags."

The misery he must have felt on coming to that understanding was actually a gracious gift from God—the necessary precursor to the man's redemption. "Godly sorrow produces repentance leading to salvation, not to be regretted" (2 Cor. 7:10).

## The Chief Difference

The pivotal difference between the Pharisee and the tax collector boils down to that one very clear and obvious distinction between the two men. The Pharisee thought he could please God on his own; the tax collector knew he couldn't. The tax collector was truly repentant; the Pharisee seemed not to sense any need for repentance. That same distinction divides everyone on the planet into two clear categories.

Several key lessons emerge from the vivid contrast Jesus makes between these two men. For one thing, we see that true gospel ministry should point sinners to repentance. It's not sufficient to tell sinners that God loves them and has a wonderful plan for their lives. Before the gospel can come as truly good news, the sinner must have come to grips with the bad news of the law.

There is no shortage of religious people who believe many things that are biblical. They profess faith in Jesus Christ. They sing hymns about the cross and the resurrection. Most of them will freely confess that they have sinned. But too many people (even in solid evangelical churches) do not see the true gravity of their sin. They think they are good enough, charitable enough, or religious enough to nullify whatever guilt they incur by sinning. That is what the Pharisee believed.

But notice how the tax collector prayed: "God, be merciful to me." That is a very important phrase. The language he used is not a general plea for leniency; he was using the language of atonement. In the Greek text, the expression is *hilaskoti moi*, "be propitious to me." It does not mean "show me forbearance"; that would have been a different word. But the word Jesus used in this parable is a form of the Greek verb *hilaskomai*, which means "be appeased." Knowing that he could never atone for his own sin, the tax collector was essentially asking God to make atonement on his behalf. He didn't ask God to overlook his sin or ignore it; he was pleading with God to make whatever satisfaction might be required to deliver him from sin's condemnation.

He knew that the wages of sin is death (Rom. 6:23), and that "the soul who sins shall die" (Ezek. 18:20). Perhaps he thought of Abraham's words to Isaac: "God will provide for Himself the lamb for a burnt offering" (Gen. 22:8). He understood the central lesson of the sacrificial system, that "without shedding of blood there is no remission" (Heb. 9:22). "For the life of the flesh is in the blood, and [blood is therefore required on an altar] to make atonement for [our] souls; for it is the blood that makes atonement for the soul" (Lev. 17:11).

The tax collector confessed that he was a hopeless sinner. His very posture acknowledged that he was unworthy to stand near the Holy Place. He sensed that he was unworthy even to look heavenward. He was in profound anguish over his wretchedness. All he could do was plead for a full and efficacious atonement to be applied to him.

The Pharisee's attitude would have been, "Take that guy and throw him out the eastern gate with the rest of the riffraff who don't belong on the temple mount."

But that was not the heart of God at all.

# Right with God

Jesus must have drawn loud gasps of amazement and indignation from His audience when He said, "I tell you, this man went down to his house justified rather than the other" (Luke 18:14). The word *justified* in the Greek text is a perfect passive participle: "having been justified." He is describing a past-tense, already-completed reality, just like Romans 5:1: "Therefore, having been justified by faith, we have peace with God through our Lord Jesus Christ." The result is a present-tense possession, just like Romans 8:1: "There is therefore now no condemnation to those who are in Christ Jesus." The tax collector was now permanently right with God.

That would have shattered the Pharisees' theological sensibilities. But when Jesus said, "I tell you . . ." He was making it clear that He did not need to quote some eminent rabbi or scribe. He wasn't drawing doctrine from Jewish tradition; He was speaking with absolute, divine authority. God incarnate, the holy one of Israel, the spotless, sinless Lamb of God, was teaching that in one gracious moment the most extreme sinner can be pronounced instantly righteous without performing any work, without earning any merit, without following any ritual, and with absolutely no righteousness of his own to bring to the table.

Jesus' point is crystal clear. He was teaching that justification is by faith alone. All the theology of justification is there. But without delving into abstract theology, Jesus has clearly painted the picture for us with a parable.

## A Forensic Decree of God

This tax gatherer's justification was an instantaneous reality. God declared him just in the same way a judge passes the verdict on a defendant: by a forensic decree. There was no process, no time lapse, no fear of purgatory. He "went down to his house justified" (Luke 18:14)—not because of anything he had done, but because of what had been done on his behalf.

Remember, the tax collector fully understood his own helplessness.

He owed an impossible debt he knew he could not pay. All he could do was repent and plead for God to provide atonement. He did not offer to do anything for God. He was looking for God to do for him what he could not do for himself. That is the very nature of the penitence Jesus called for.

## By Faith Alone

The tax collector went away fully justified without performing any works of penance, without doing any sacrament or ritual, without any meritorious works whatsoever. His justification was complete without *any* of those things, because it was solely on the basis of faith. Everything necessary to atone for his sin and provide forgiveness was done on his behalf. He was justified by faith on the spot.

Again, this makes a stark contrast with how the smug Pharisee was thinking. He was *certain* that all his fasting and tithing and other works made him acceptable to God. But the Pharisee was dead wrong. The righteousness that truly justifies is not acquired by legal obedience or works of any kind; it must be laid hold of by faith.

## An Imputed Righteousness

Christ's declaration that this man was justified was no fiction. This was not a trick or a word game. God cannot lie. So where did the tax collector obtain a righteousness that exceeded that of the Pharisee (Matt. 5:20)? How could a traitorous tax collector ever become just in God's eyes?

The only possible answer is that he received a righteousness that was not his own (cf. Phil. 3:9). Righteousness was imputed to him by faith (Rom. 4:9–11).

Whose righteousness was reckoned to him? It could only be the perfect righteousness of a flawless Substitute, who in turn must bear the tax gatherer's sins and suffer the penalty of God's wrath in his place. And the gospel tells us that is precisely what Jesus did.

That's the only way a tax gatherer could be justified. God must declare him righteous, imputing to him the full and perfect righteousness of Christ, forgiving him of all *un*righteousness, and delivering him from all condemnation. Forever thereafter the justified sinner stands before God on the ground of a perfect righteousness that has been reckoned to his account.

*That* is what justification means. It is the only true gospel. Every other point in the biblical doctrine of salvation emanates from that key truth. As J. I. Packer once wrote, "The doctrine of justification by faith is like Atlas: it bears a world on its shoulders, the entire evangelical knowledge of saving grace."[2] A right understanding of justification by faith is the very foundation of the gospel. Go wrong on this point and you will eventually corrupt every other doctrine as well.

What this parable illustrates is the *true* gospel. All any sinner can possibly do is receive the gift by penitent faith, believing that a perfect atonement must be made—and has been made by Christ—that satisfies the wrath of God against sin. The One who told this story is the One who made the atonement: Jesus Christ. There is no salvation in any other name.

## A Short Coda

Our Lord ends this amazing story with a simple proverb: "for everyone who exalts himself will be humbled, and he who humbles himself will be exalted" (Luke 18:14). The word *exalted* in this context is a synonym for justification. The one who humbles himself in repentant faith will be obtain righteousness.

Strictly speaking, only God is truly exalted, and therefore only God can exalt men. He does this by conferring on them the perfect righteousness of Christ. So the exaltation referred to here includes salvation from sin and damnation; reconciliation with God; full justification; and membership in Christ's eternal kingdom.

All efforts at achieving that on your own will leave you humiliated. So "everyone who exalts himself"—meaning those who think they can save themselves, acquire a righteousness of their own, or merit favor with God by their own works—"will be humbled." They will be "humbled" in the severest sense of that word: crushed under divine judgment, suffering eternal loss and everlasting punishment. The path of self-exaltation *always* ends in eternal judgment, because "God resists the proud, but gives grace to the humble" (1 Peter 5:5; James 4:6).

To say it another way: The damned think they are good. The saved know they are wicked. The damned believe the kingdom of God is for those worthy of it. The saved know the kingdom of God is for those who realize how unworthy they are. The damned believe eternal life is earned. The saved know it's a gift. The damned seek God's commendation. The saved seek His forgiveness.

And He grants forgiveness through the work of Christ. "For by grace you have been saved through faith, and that not of yourselves; it is the gift of God, not of works, lest anyone should boast" (Eph. 2:8–9).

# 7

# A Lesson About Faithfulness

*Of that day and hour no one knows, not even the angels in heaven, nor
the Son, but only the Father. Take heed, watch and pray; for you do
not know when the time is. It is like a man going to a far country, who
left his house and gave authority to his servants, and to each his work,
and commanded the doorkeeper to watch. Watch therefore, for you do
not know when the master of the house is coming—in the evening, at
midnight, at the crowing of the rooster, or in the morning—lest, coming
suddenly, he find you sleeping. And what I say to you, I say to all: Watch!*

—MARK 13:32–37

Matthew's gospel is neatly structured so that his detailed account of
Jesus' public ministry is bracketed between two of our Lord's longest
discourses—the Sermon on the Mount and the Olivet Discourse.

Matthew 5 launches Matthew's record of Jesus' teaching with the
Sermon on the Mount.* That sermon, covering three chapters, is the

---

\* The first four chapters of Matthew's gospel are introductory, describing the birth, baptism, and temptation
of Jesus. Chapter 4 culminates with the calling of the disciples. With the Sermon on the Mount, then,
Matthew begins to recount events from the public ministry of Christ.

longest uninterrupted record of Jesus' words anywhere in Scripture. This was by no means the first event in Jesus' earthly ministry. The best chronologies place it about a year and a half after Jesus' baptism (in other words, around the halfway point of His three-year ministry). But it is a fitting place for Matthew to start, because it wonderfully summarizes the content of Jesus' teaching and helps us view everything else He said and did in a clearer light.

Matthew then arranges the various events of Jesus' life and ministry somewhat thematically. He punctuates the key lessons with major discourses—five of them in total. There's an extended commission from Jesus that accompanies the sending of the Twelve in chapter 10; a lengthy series of parables about the kingdom in chapter 13; and a protracted lesson about childlike faith in chapter 18.

Finally, toward the end of his gospel, just before describing Jesus' arrest and crucifixion, Matthew brings his account of Jesus' formal teaching ministry to a close with the Olivet Discourse (Matt. 24–25). Here Jesus, seated atop the Mount of Olives (24:3), speaks privately to His closest disciples about His second coming—answering their questions about "the sign of [His] coming, and of the end of the age" (v. 3).

As we observed in the introduction to this book, Matthew's record of the Sermon on the Mount contains only one very short parable, comprising the closing four verses (7:24–27). That parable (the wise and foolish builders) illustrates the folly of hearing Jesus' words without believing.

By contrast, the Olivet Discourse contains many parables, some very short and some more complex. These include the carcass and the vultures (24:28); the fig tree (vv. 32–34); the master of the house (vv. 43–44); the wise and evil servants (vv. 45–51); the wise and foolish bridesmaids (25:1–13); the talents (vv. 14–30); and the sheep and goats (vv. 32–33).

In this chapter we'll examine three of the longer parables in that series: the wise and evil servants, the wise and foolish bridesmaids, and the talents. Those three stories tie Matthew 24 and 25 together. They are deliberately told in close sequence, and together they make a single, simple point about the importance of faithfulness in the light of Jesus' return.

The Olivet Discourse is one of the most abused passages anywhere in Scripture. Some interpreters relegate the whole discourse to virtual irrelevance by claiming that all the prophetic words in this section of Scripture were completely fulfilled in AD 70 when Roman armies sacked Jerusalem and destroyed the Jewish temple. (That view is known as *preterism*.) At the opposite extreme there are those who seem to think today's newspaper is key to understanding the Olivet Discourse. They scour the daily news for "wars and rumors of wars" (Matt. 24:6); "famines, pestilences, and earthquakes in various places" (v. 7); heavenly signs and wonders (v. 29)—or other echoes of this passage. Of course, they never fail to discover fresh reports that seem to fit the passage. Some seem to think the whole discourse is an extended puzzle containing a code that gives a hidden answer to the disciples' question, "When will these things be?" (v. 3). Almost every decade some false prophet comes along who claims to have figured out precisely when the Lord will return.

But Jesus emphatically denies the possibility of such knowledge: "Of that day and hour no one knows, not even the angels of heaven, but My Father only" (v. 36). In fact, Jesus makes this point *repeatedly* in the Olivet Discourse: "You do not know what hour your Lord is coming" (v. 42). "The Son of Man is coming at an hour you do not expect" (v. 44). "The master of that servant will come on a day when he is not looking for him" (v. 50). "You know neither the day nor the hour in which the Son of Man is coming" (25:13). The three parables we will be looking at *all* stress the impossibility of knowing the day or the hour of His return.

In other words, Jesus purposely left unanswered the disciples' question about the timing of events surrounding His coming. He left no room for speculation or sensationalism.

Furthermore, in the process of outlining the extreme woes of the last days, He told His disciples, "See that you are not troubled" (Matt. 24:6).

Clearly Jesus is not giving us a way to figure out precisely when to look for His return; nor is He trying to frighten us regarding the terrible time of tribulation that will precede His coming. What, then, is the main point of this discourse? The answer is simple and obvious: it is an extended exhortation from Christ to His disciples, urging them to remain faithful until He returns. Rather than answering their question about the timing of His return, He tells three parables that cover every possibility.

## A Tale of Two Servants

First in this trio is a story that contrasts two servants—one who is "faithful and wise"; the other, evil (Matt. 24:45, 48). The true character of the evil servant is quickly manifest when the master is called away for a season. He tells himself that the master is not going to return anytime soon. That belief removes any sense of accountability from his mind, and he runs amok:

> Who then is a faithful and wise servant, whom his master made ruler over his household, to give them food in due season? Blessed is that servant whom his master, when he comes, will find so doing. Assuredly, I say to you that he will make him ruler over all his goods.
>
> But if that evil servant says in his heart, "My master is delaying his coming," and begins to beat his fellow servants, and to eat and drink with the drunkards, the master of that servant will come on a day when he is not looking for him and at an hour that he is not aware of, and will cut him in two and appoint him his portion with the hypocrites. There shall be weeping and gnashing of teeth. (Matt. 24:45–51)

The contrast between the two servants is deliberately extreme. The wise and faithful servant understood that the master's absence actually increased the burden of responsibility for him. He needed to work harder and be more conscientious than ever because he knew in the end he would have to give an account. Whether the master returned early or late, this wise servant wanted to be found patiently fulfilling his duties.

But the evil servant saw the master's absence as an opportunity to party. He threw off all constraint and shirked every responsibility. He did whatever his evil heart inclined him to do, just because there was no one to watch him and he had no sense of accountability.

When the master suddenly returns, the faithful servant is rewarded beyond any expectation. He is immediately promoted to the highest position of authority and honor. He is given privileges that mirror the prerogatives of the master himself. That pictures the eternal reward for all faithful Christians. They will reign with Christ in the kingdom (2 Tim. 2:12; Rev. 20:6). They are joint heirs with Him, and they will be glorified together with Him (Rom. 8:17). Their place in heaven will be a position of unfathomably high honor and reward. They will sit with Him on His throne (Rev. 3:21).

The evil servant, however, represents a self-deluded unbeliever who has nevertheless identified with the church and who pretends to be serving the Master. In reality, he does not really love the Master or look forward to His return. In fact, he doesn't really seem to believe the Master will return at all—or at least not any time soon. He "says in his heart, 'My master is *delaying* his coming'" (Matt. 24:48, emphasis added). His lack of faith emboldens his evil conduct.

When the master *does* return—suddenly, and much sooner than expected—the evil servant is instantly exposed for what he is. His punishment is as severe as the reward of the first servant was lavish. He is "cut . . . in two" (v. 51)—which of course would be fatal. But that is not the end of him. His portion (his lot in the afterlife) is appointed "with the hypocrites. There shall be weeping and gnashing of teeth." Such language, of course, denotes hell—so we know this man pictures an unbeliever.

In fact, the expression "weeping and gnashing of teeth" was familiar to the disciples, because Jesus had used it many times to describe the endless sorrow and agonizing regret of souls in hell (Matt. 8:12; 22:13; Luke 13:28). That's the meaning here as well. The evil servant's cynical attitude about his master's return is emblematic of rank unbelief, and "he who does not believe is condemned already" (John 3:18). This shows what a grave sin it is to scoff at the promise of Christ's return (2 Peter 3:3–4).

The same grace that saves us teaches us that "we should live soberly, righteously, and godly in the present age, looking for the blessed hope and glorious appearing of our great God and Savior Jesus Christ" (Titus 2:12–13). "For yet a little while, And He who is coming will come and will not tarry" (Heb. 10:37). In the book of Revelation, Christ repeatedly says, "Behold, I am coming quickly!" (Rev. 3:11; 22:7, 12, 20).

That is the lesson underscored by this parable. Christ's return is *imminent*. That means it could happen at any time. "The Lord is at hand" (Phil. 4:5). "The coming of the Lord is at hand . . . the Judge is standing at the door!" (James 5:8–9). Nothing stands in the way of our Lord's immediate return, and we are taught repeatedly in Scripture that we should be ready, expectant, busy, obedient, loyal, fully prepared, like the wise and faithful servant in this parable—"for you do not know what hour your Lord is coming" (Matt. 24:42).

## The Ten Bridesmaids

The chapter division between Matthew 24 and 25 makes an artificial interruption in the flow of the narrative. (The chapter and verse divisions, of course, are not part of the inspired text; they were added around the thirteenth century for convenience's sake.) There is no interruption or interlude between the parable of the servants and the story that follows—and it is important to read it that way. The two parables go hand in hand, emphasizing different aspects of one key lesson.

The parable of the two servants makes the point that we must not assume Christ will delay His coming, but be ready for Him to return at any time. The parable of the wise and foolish bridesmaids follows immediately and simply reverses the point. Being "ready for Him to return at any time" also means we must not be caught off guard if He *does* delay. True readiness requires that balance in our expectations.

Church history is full of stories about date setters and their cults who, thinking they had figured out a specific time frame for the Second Coming, quit their jobs, sold off their assets, and moved to a mountaintop or desert somewhere to await the sounding of the last trumpet. The past few decades especially have seen an upsurge in self-styled prophets and amateur numerologists who have been certain they have the date and chronology of the end times all figured out. All of them have been disappointed, discredited, disillusioned, or otherwise brought into disrepute—and deservedly so.

Jesus expressly forbids that kind of presumption. As noted, that's one of the main points of the entire Olivet Discourse, and it is the very point these three parables illustrate.

Of course we *do* believe without qualification that the return of Christ is fast approaching. "It is high time to awake out of sleep; for now our salvation is nearer than when we first believed" (Rom. 13:11). "The time is short. . . . For the form of this world is passing away" (1 Cor. 7:29, 31). "The end of all things is at hand; therefore be serious and watchful in your prayers" (1 Peter 4:7). Nothing stands in the way of the Lord's return, and it is imperative that we be ready if He should return today.

But our ignorance about the timing of Christ's return has another implication as well: we need to remain patient, diligent, faithful—no matter how long our Lord may seem to delay His return. Time *is* short, but "with the Lord one day is as a thousand years, and a thousand years as one day. The Lord is not slack concerning His promise, as some count slackness, but is longsuffering toward us, not willing that any should perish but that all should come to repentance. But the day of the Lord *will* come as a thief in the night" (2 Peter 3:8–10, emphasis added). Meanwhile, we must be ready, whether He returns right away or waits another thousand years. And while we wait, we must stay faithful to our responsibilities. That's what real readiness looks like. It is diametrically opposed to the escapism of those who drop out, move to the top of a mountain, and sit there idly waiting for the last trumpet to sound.

In order to illustrate why we must be prepared in case His coming is delayed, Jesus tells a parable about "ten virgins." These are ten bridesmaids in a wedding. (By custom only unmarried girls served as bridesmaids.) That is an unusually large wedding party, so what Jesus is describing here is a grand wedding feast, suggesting that these are eminent families, and it is a highly important occasion.

But the wedding is fraught with a set of problems no bride would ever want. It's getting very late. The bridegroom hasn't arrived yet. The bridesmaids have fallen asleep, and their ceremonial lamps are burning out. Half of the girls came without extra oil, making it impossible for them to refill their lamps. Without proper lamps, they cannot perform the one simple task they are supposed to do.

Here's the parable in Jesus' words.

> Then the kingdom of heaven shall be likened to ten virgins who took their lamps and went out to meet the bridegroom. Now five of them were wise, and five were foolish. Those who were foolish took their lamps and took no oil with them, but the wise took oil in their vessels with their lamps. But while the bridegroom was delayed, they all slumbered and slept. And at midnight a cry was heard: "Behold, the bridegroom is coming; go out to meet him!" Then all those virgins arose and trimmed their lamps. And the foolish said to the wise, "Give us some of your oil, for our lamps are going out." But the wise answered, saying, "No, lest there should not be enough for us and you; but go rather to those who sell, and buy for yourselves." And while they went to buy, the bridegroom came, and those who were ready went in with him to the wedding; and the door was shut. Afterward the other virgins came also, saying, "Lord, Lord, open to us!" But he answered and said, "Assuredly, I say to you, I do not know you."
>
> Watch therefore, for you know neither the day nor the hour in which the Son of Man is coming. (Matt. 25:1–13)

A midnight wedding punctuated by the late arrival of the bridegroom will sound bizarre and utterly disastrous in most twenty-first-century cultures. But the scenario Jesus describes would not have sounded terribly odd or far-fetched at all to the disciples.

The process of engagement and marriage in first-century Judaism had three phases. The first phase was the *promise* of marriage, usually formalized by contract. This arrangement was usually made between the two sets of parents and sealed with a payment made by the bride-groom's father to the father of the bride. Phase two was *betrothal*. This began with the public exchange of vows and gifts between the couple. A betrothed couple were then legally committed to marry one another; the union could not be severed except by divorce (cf. Matt. 1:19). But the marriage was not fully consummated until after phase three—*the wedding feast*. This might come as late as a year after betrothal. It marked the completion of the betrothal period with a large celebra-tion—often lasting several days. Only after the wedding banquet did the couple live together.

What the parable describes is day one of the wedding feast. The bride-groom's arrival would signal the start of the festivities, and the bridesmaids would come out to meet him and escort him through the streets of the city or village to his destination with oil-fueled lamps or torches. A nighttime start would be common in that culture. (It was scheduled after sunset for the convenience of people who traveled to get there.)

But in this case the bridegroom was late—very late. We're not told the reason for the long delay, but it must have been something signifi-cant and unavoidable. It clearly was not because the bridegroom was indifferent about the wedding or aloof toward his bride—because when he finally arrived at midnight, he was not willing to wait another minute to start the ceremony. The guests had stayed despite the delay. All was ready except for the five foolish bridesmaids who had left the premises to try to buy more oil.

Their absence was an understandable annoyance to the bridegroom. It was inexcusably thoughtless of them not to bring oil in the first place. Keeping a burning lamp was their one duty. Their irresponsibility was similar to (maybe even worse than) the negligence of the man in Matthew

22:11–14 who showed up at a royal wedding without being dressed for such an occasion. It was a thoughtless insult to the bridegroom.

As soon as it was known that the bridegroom was coming, the irresponsible girls woke from their slumber and went out to try to buy oil (surely a difficult quest at that hour of the night). "And while they went to buy, the bridegroom came, and those who were ready went in with him to the wedding; and the door was shut" (Matt. 25:10). They missed his coming, so they were excluded from the wedding feast. They ought to have been prepared for a possible delay.

They finally returned and begged to be admitted to the feast, but the bridegroom was resolute. They had bungled their one duty as bridesmaids; now they were a disruption to the celebration. The bridegroom's reply to them is chilling: "Assuredly, I say to you, I do not know you" (v. 12). That's an eerie echo of what Jesus will say to the religious hypocrites in the final judgment: "I never knew you; depart from Me, you who practice lawlessness!" (Matt. 7:23). It is also reminiscent of His words in Luke 13:24–28:

> Strive to enter through the narrow gate, for many, I say to you, will seek to enter and will not be able. When once the Master of the house has risen up and shut the door, and you begin to stand outside and knock at the door, saying, "Lord, Lord, open for us," and He will answer and say to you, "I do not know you, where you are from," then you will begin to say, "We ate and drank in Your presence, and You taught in our streets." But He will say, "I tell you I do not know you, where you are from. Depart from Me, all you workers of iniquity." There will be weeping and gnashing of teeth, when you see Abraham and Isaac and Jacob and all the prophets in the kingdom of God, and yourselves thrust out.

The point of the parable is simple: Christ (the bridegroom) is coming. He may arrive later than we expect, and we must be prepared for that possibility. That means remaining awake, staying at the watch, and being ready for Him no matter how late the hour. In fact, as time passes and His arrival grows closer, the need for watchfulness is greater, not less. The *only* time we can prepare for Him is now, because His sudden arrival will signal the end of all such opportunity. Those not ready for Him when He arrives will be completely and permanently shut out of the wedding feast.

## The Talents

The parable of the wise and foolish bridesmaids is followed without interruption by the third and final parable in this chain of lessons. This is the parable of the talents, and the respective lessons of these three parables are purposely braided together to give us a complete understanding of what it means to be faithful as we await the return of Christ. The parable of the two servants commends the virtue of *expectantly watching* for Christ's return. The parable of the virgins is a lesson about *patiently waiting* for Him. The parable of the talents is a reminder that we must keep *diligently working* while we look for Him.

In contrast to those inclined to drop out of life and wait on a hilltop, the faithful believer must continue to work and plan with an eye to the future. Careful, prudent planning is not antithetical to living by faith. In fact, a failure to plan for the future is not faith at all; it's sheer foolishness. In Jesus' words, "Which of you, intending to build a tower, does not sit down first and count the cost, whether he has enough to finish it—lest, after he has laid the foundation, and is not able to finish, all who see it begin to mock him, saying, 'This man began to build and was not able to finish'" (Luke 14:28–30).

The parable of the talents commends faithful work and prudent planning. In this story, a rich man travels to some faraway place. He appoints three servants as managers over specific allotments of his wealth until he returns. Two of them put the money to work and were able to double their portions. The third buried his treasure and thus gained nothing for the master:

The kingdom of heaven is like a man traveling to a far country, who called his own servants and delivered his goods to them. And to one he gave five talents, to another two, and to another one, to each according to his own ability; and immediately he went on a journey. Then he who had received the five talents went and traded with them, and made another five talents. And likewise he who had received two gained two more also. But he who had received one went and dug in the ground, and hid his lord's money. After a long time the lord of those servants came and settled accounts with them.

So he who had received five talents came and brought five other talents, saying, "Lord, you delivered to me five talents; look, I have gained five more talents besides them." His lord said to him, "Well done, good and faithful servant; you were faithful over a few things, I will make you ruler over many things. Enter into the joy of your lord." He also who had received two talents came and said, "Lord, you delivered to me two talents; look, I have gained two more talents besides them." His lord said to him, "Well done, good and faithful servant; you have been faithful over a few things, I will make you ruler over many things. Enter into the joy of your lord."

Then he who had received the one talent came and said, "Lord, I knew you to be a hard man, reaping where you have not sown, and gathering where you have not scattered seed. And I was afraid, and went and hid your talent in the ground. Look, there you have what is yours."

But his lord answered and said to him, "You wicked and lazy servant, you knew that I reap where I have not sown, and gather where I have not scattered seed. So you ought to have deposited my money with the bankers, and at my coming I would have received back my own with interest. Therefore take the talent from him, and give it to him who has ten talents.

"For to everyone who has, more will be given, and he will have abundance; but from him who does not have, even what he has will be taken away. And cast the unprofitable servant into the outer darkness. There will be weeping and gnashing of teeth." (Matt. 25:14–30)

That parable is not to be confused with the parable of the minas in Luke 19:11–27. The gist of the two stories and the lessons they teach are very similar, but the details and the context are clearly different. Both parables gently correct the expectation of disciples who "thought the kingdom of God would appear immediately" (Luke 19:11).

Whenever the subject of the Lord's return is raised, Scripture encourages us to be watchful and expectant. This parable is a pointed reminder that while we wait, we are to prepare for that day by working faithfully for the Master. The two previous parables showed that expectation must be tempered with patience. This parable reminds us that whether Christ returns early or late, He should find us busy for Him. This parable rounds out the necessary threefold balance: watching, waiting, and working.

The story is about a wealthy man who goes on a long journey. He clearly represents Christ. He appoints servants to take charge of his affairs, and they of course are expected to act as faithful stewards of their master's resources. They are in effect given full power of attorney to manage the allotments of wealth he leaves in their care.

These three servants were entrusted with immense responsibility. The first servant received "five talents" (Matt. 25:15). The others received two talents and one talent respectively. A *talent* is not coin or currency, but a unit of weight—quite a heavy amount.** The large gold menorah in the tabernacle weighed a talent (Ex. 25:39). A Greek talent weighed about sixty pounds; a Roman talent about seventy; a Babylonian talent slightly less than seventy. These would have been talents of gold or silver, so a talent was no small sum. Even a single talent would be an immense fortune.

Each man was given responsibility in keeping with his character and ability. The first servant was clearly the most skilled and trustworthy of the three, so he was entrusted with the most—and the master's assessment of his character proved precisely accurate.

---

** The English word *talent,* signifying a special skill or ability, is actually derived from this parable. It is a fitting connection to draw, because all our aptitudes and faculties are given to us as a stewardship from the Lord, and we have a duty to put them to profitable use for His glory.

Two of the three men faithfully set to work and fulfilled their duty. The adverb *immediately* in Matthew 25:15 ("immediately he went on a journey") probably belongs instead to verse 16, describing the action of the servants rather than their master's departure. The master leaves on his journey, "Then he who had received the five talents *[immediately]* went and traded with them, and made another five talents. And likewise he who had received two gained two more also" (vv. 16–17). The stress is on the vigor with which the two faithful servants undertook the responsibility that had been given them. Not knowing how much time they would have, they quickly set to work, trading and investing. Both servants doubled the value of the resources that had been put in their care.

But the third literally did nothing but bury his master's money in the ground (v. 18). He took advantage of the boss's absence to do whatever he wished to do for himself. Perhaps he salved his conscience with the reassurance that he was avoiding financial risk. He may have even envisioned a scenario where the market would take a downward turn, and he would look like a hero for having preserved his allotment of cash while everyone else lost money. In reality, he was simply shirking his duty. His lack of responsibility guaranteed that the resources given to him in trust would never earn any profit.

The master's journey was a long one "to a far country" (v. 14). In that culture it was impossible to travel long distances on a definite timetable. The servants therefore did not know precisely when their master would return, and it seems the trip lasted longer than anyone expected. The delay no doubt reinforced and emboldened the unfaithful servant's complacency. He was clearly not prepared to give an account when the time came.

But the time for settling accounts did finally arrive: "After a long time the lord of those servants came" (Matt. 25:19). The faithful servants were commended and rewarded equally. In fact, the master's words to the two faithful servants were identical: "Well done, good and faithful servant; you were faithful over a few things, I will make you ruler over many things. Enter into the joy of your lord" (vv. 21, 24). They were honored for their faithfulness—not proportionally based on the size of the profit they earned. That is precisely how Scripture describes the judgment seat of Christ: "Each one will receive his own reward *according to his own labor*"—not according to results (1 Cor. 3:8, emphasis added).

The master's response shows him to be a gracious and generous man. He rewarded the faithful stewards with expanded authority, increased opportunity, and a place of joy and favor. Their reward clearly pictures heaven. Heaven is not a place of eternal boredom and tedious inactivity; it is filled with exaltation and honor, expanded opportunities for service, and the greatest joy of all—endless fellowship with Christ Himself. The promises and parables of Jesus are full of similar imagery signifying heaven (cf. Luke 12:35–37, 44; 19:17–19; 22:29–30; John 12:26).

Notice how the unfaithful servant attempted to deflect the judgment he deserved by claiming that he was paralyzed with terror because the master's own character and reputation revealed him to be a ruthless, demanding, and unethical man, reaping profits from the labors of others (Matt. 25:24–25). It was a classic case of blame shifting and an ungodly slander against the kindness of the master. None of it was true. But even if it had been entirely true, it was no excuse for inactivity. As the master pointed out, if this shiftless servant really believed the master was so severe and demanding, the *worst* thing he could possibly do was bury his talent in the ground, where it was guaranteed not to earn anything. Had that really been what he was thinking, he could have put the money in a bank, where it could at least earn interest. Clearly, the claim that he was stymied by fear was a total lie. The real problem was the faithless servant's own wicked laziness (vv. 26–27). In reality, this man lacked both fear and respect for his master.

The punishment of the unprofitable servant is reminiscent of what the profligate man in Matthew 24:51 received. Again, Jesus employs language that clearly evokes the imagery of hell: "Cast the unprofitable servant into the outer darkness. There will be weeping and gnashing of teeth" (Matt. 25:30).

It is clear, therefore, that the unprofitable servant pictures an unbeliever. He belongs to the same category as the wicked servant and the foolish bridesmaids in the two previous parables. He provides us with yet another picture of the typical careless worldling—arrogant in his utter indifference, disobedient to his master, self-willed in his behavior, and unfaithful in every moral duty. From the point where the master returns, the story line follows the same basic pattern as the previous two. The man is caught unprepared; his unfaithfulness is exposed; his guilt cannot be covered up or explained away; and his punishment is frightfully severe.

## What Links These Parables Together?

The collective impact of these three parables is a profound exhortation regarding how we should think about the Lord's return. On the surface, the three parables seem completely different. They paint contrasting scenarios. One parable shows the folly of thinking the Lord will not return soon; the next shows the folly of presuming that He *will* come soon; and the third shows the importance of remaining faithful regardless of when He returns.

But there are clear similarities that tie the three parables together. All three stories speak of the inevitability of the Lord's return and the impending judgment. All three stories exhort us to be ready. And all three stories contrast faithfulness and unbelief; wisdom and folly; preparedness and indifference.

In fact, those features are shown to be the defining characteristics that set authentic Christians apart from unbelievers. No one in any of these parables pictures a halfhearted or lukewarm "carnal Christian." That's because Jesus Himself ruled out the possibility that such people exist. In His own words, "He who is not with Me is against Me, and he who does not gather with Me scatters abroad" (Matt. 12:30). A person is no true believer at all if he has no real expectation of Christ's return, no eagerness to meet Him, no love for His appearing. In fact, the lessons of these parables are the very same lessons saving grace teaches every true believer: "That, denying ungodliness and worldly lusts, we should live soberly, righteously, and godly in the present age, looking for the blessed hope and glorious appearing of our great God and Savior Jesus Christ" (Titus 2:12–13).

So the three parables combined give us one clear and powerful message: "You do not know when the master of the house is coming—in the evening, at midnight, at the crowing of the rooster, or in the morning" (Mark 13:35). "Therefore you also be ready, for the Son of Man is coming at an hour you do not expect" (Matt. 24:44). Meanwhile, keep watching, waiting, and working faithfully.

# 8

# A Lesson About
# Serpentine Wisdom

*Be wise as serpents and harmless as doves.*

—MATTHEW 10:16

Money is a common theme in Jesus' parables. Roughly a third of the forty or so parables Jesus told have something to do with earthly riches, treasure, coins, or currency of some kind. That fact is often cited by today's false prophets and prosperity preachers. They use it to justify their own obsession with all the tokens of temporal wealth. Listening to them, you might get the impression Jesus Himself was a lover of money, or that the main (or only) way God blesses faithful people is by making them rich.

But Jesus' actual point (and the consistent theme of His teaching) was precisely the opposite: "How hard it is for those who trust in riches to enter the kingdom of God!" (Mark 10:24). "You cannot serve God and mammon" (Matt. 6:24). "Seek first the kingdom of God and His righteousness" (v. 33). In no instance did Jesus ever do or say anything that

141

would encourage His disciples to fix their hearts and hopes on material prosperity or earthly possessions. In fact, all the parables that mention money make the opposite point.

For example, the rich man and Lazarus as well as the story of the rich fool in Luke 12:16–21 illustrate how riches can be an impediment to entering the kingdom of heaven (Matt. 19:23–24). Or consider the parable of the talents, the parable of the minas (Luke 19:12–27), and the parable of the vinedressers (Luke 20:9–16). Those stories all remind us that we are merely stewards of whatever earthly resources the Lord entrusts to our care—and we need to be wise and faithful in how we use whatever assets and opportunities God places at our disposal. The hidden treasure and the pearl of great price (Matt. 13:44–46) are not about seeking or hoarding earthly wealth. Just the opposite; they illustrate the infinite value of the heavenly kingdom.

Scripture emphatically condemns the love of money. "For the love of money is a root of all kinds of evil, for which some have strayed from the faith in their greediness, and pierced themselves through with many sorrows. But you, O man of God, flee these things and pursue righteousness, godliness, faith, love, patience, gentleness" (1 Tim. 6:10–11).

Jesus summed up His teaching on the matter in one clear exhortation in His Sermon on the Mount: "Do not lay up for yourselves treasures on earth, where moth and rust destroy and where thieves break in and steal; but lay up for yourselves treasures in heaven, where neither moth nor rust destroys and where thieves do not break in and steal. For where your treasure is, there your heart will be also" (Matt. 6:19–21).

In Luke 16, our Lord tells a parable that both echoes and illustrates that admonition in a very unusual way. It is the story of a lying, cheating, unfaithful servant who is found out and put on notice that he will be fired. He then cunningly uses his master's wealth to buy friendships that will be useful for cushioning his fall from grace:

> There was a certain rich man who had a steward, and an accusation
> was brought to him that this man was wasting his goods. So he called

him and said to him, "What is this I hear about you? Give an account of your stewardship, for you can no longer be steward."

Then the steward said within himself, "What shall I do? For my master is taking the stewardship away from me. I cannot dig; I am ashamed to beg. I have resolved what to do, that when I am put out of the stewardship, they may receive me into their houses."

So he called every one of his master's debtors to him, and said to the first, "How much do you owe my master?" And he said, "A hundred measures of oil." So he said to him, "Take your bill, and sit down quickly and write fifty." Then he said to another, "And how much do you owe?" So he said, "A hundred measures of wheat." And he said to him, "Take your bill, and write eighty." So the master commended the unjust steward because he had dealt shrewdly. For the sons of this world are more shrewd in their generation than the sons of light. (v. 8)

What a strange thing for which to praise someone! This is one of the most astonishing and enigmatic of all Jesus' parables. The stories our Lord told often contained profoundly shocking twists and turns, but none is more baffling than this. How is it possible to build any kind of positive spiritual principle on the unethical actions of an unrighteous steward? Can any good teaching come from such a patently bad example?

But this is no mistake. Jesus was very adept at illustrating His points by parables.

## The Story

The main character in this parable is a man whom Jesus refers to as an "unjust steward" (Luke 16:8). So there's no question about his crooked character. The steward's own actions reveal that he was wicked, conniving, totally unprincipled, and shamelessly brazen in his evildoing.

But he apparently got to that point by a progression of compromises that probably seemed petty at first. His downfall began because he handled his master's assets in a way that was wasteful—overspending, or perhaps using company resources to pay for personal expenses. He must have figured he was free to spend extravagantly because the master would never check up on him. But a credible accusation against him reached the ears of his wealthy boss, who subsequently gave him his termination notice and ordered a full audit.

The steward now knew it would be impossible to cover up his malfeasance. His wasteful mismanagement would be fully documented, and he would be disgraced and discredited. By his own admission, he was not cut out for a ditch-digging job and he was too proud to beg. So he opted instead to cheat the rich man even more. He cooked the books in favor of people who owed his master money. He gratuitously forgave large debts—in effect, stealing from the master in order to win friends and purchase favors, thereby insuring that when the rich man finally threw him out, he would be received by people who would now be in his debt.

There is no way to put a nice spin on the man's wantonly unscrupulous behavior or tiptoe around the fact that Jesus is using the behavior of a scoundrel to make His point. Remember, Jesus Himself refers to the man as an "unjust steward." There are no mitigating facts or hidden details that would put this man's immoral and unethical actions in a better light. Had Jesus Himself wished to be exonerated from the accusation that He commends an evil man's shrewdness, He could have used a different story line. And there's no need to imagine a context that might make the man's behavior seem less dastardly. This is a parable, after all. It's not real life. Jesus made this story up. The only facts on record anywhere are the ones He gave. If we are shocked at the surprise ending, that's what He intended. His original audience would have been scandalized too.

The main audience here was the disciples ("He also said *to His disciples* . . ." [Luke 16:1, emphasis added]). So this is not the same genre as the parable of the prodigal son. That story is an evangelistic message calling the Pharisees and scribes to repent, believe the gospel, be granted admission to the heavenly kingdom, and enter into the joy of the Lord. Our parable immediately follows the prodigal son in Luke's gospel, but it is addressed to people who are already committed to following Jesus—men and women who love righteousness, turn from evil, and live their lives with a concern for the glory of Christ. This is a discipleship message. This is for believers.

The rich man in the parable is an impressively wealthy magnate, not a small businessman. He is so rich that he does not even deign to be involved in the hands-on, day-to-day operation of his business affairs. Instead, he pays a manager, a steward, to run his enterprise by proxy. It's clearly an enormous operation, because the debts owed to this man by just two of his debtors are sizable—"a hundred measures of oil" and "a hundred measures of wheat" (vv. 6–7). The rich man probably lived on an estate some distance from the actual headquarters of his business, because he clearly did not have firsthand knowledge of what his steward was doing.

It is likewise clear that the steward was himself a skilled and resourceful manager and a man of refinement. (By his own testimony he was not someone accustomed to manual labor.) He no doubt had most people's respect. He would not have been put in such a role in the first place if he did not have the rich man's full, unconditional confidence. The two men probably had a long-standing relationship of mutual trust and affection. (Stewards were often trusted servants who had been born and raised in the master's household—treated like part of the family.) In any case, the rich man's faith in the steward's skill and integrity was such that he had entrusted the man with full control over his affairs and assets. The steward was entitled to act on his own authority without close oversight or interference. The landowner might never have discovered the steward's mismanagement if word had not come to him from some other source.

It must therefore have come as very bad news to the rich man when "an accusation was brought to him that this man was wasting his goods" (v. 1). Judging from both the rich man's response and the steward's subsequent actions, there was plenty of truth in the report. This once-trusted steward had indeed violated the implicit trust that had been placed in him—and there was no denying the fact.

The rich man acted immediately. He summoned his steward and said, "What is this I hear about you? Give an account of your stewardship, for you can no longer be steward" (v. 2). This suggests, again, that the owner lived some distance from the center of business, because he did not step in immediately and take over the affairs of the company. Instead, he demanded a full accounting from the steward and gave him notice that once he had finished making his report, his employment would be terminated. The steward just needed to wrap up his remaining business and prepare to leave the company.

Frankly, this was a bad decision on the owner's part. If the report charging the man with financial impropriety was credible, why give him extra time to do more damage? When clear signs indicate that someone is guilty of mismanagement, it is a good idea to relieve that person of all responsibility immediately. Because if a steward would squander his master's possessions when he is accountable and there's a price to pay for wrongdoing, he clearly cannot be trusted when the last incentive for him to deal honestly has been removed.

Evidently there was no way to cover his guilt, so while the steward was preparing his final accounting, he concocted an audacious scheme to insure that when he lost his job, he would not end up homeless. The business evidently provided him with housing, because that was one of his main concerns (v. 4). Once he was released from this job he would literally have no income and no place to live. He faced a dismal future with an indelible blot on his employment record. His situation seemed dire.

All these thoughts came out in his soliloquy: "I cannot dig; I am ashamed to beg" (v. 3). He was a white-collar man. Not only is digging hard work; he thought it was below his status. He *certainly* did not want to be reduced to begging.

But then he had a *eureka!* moment, a kind of epiphany. "I have resolved what to do" (v. 4). The verb in the Greek text is *egnon*—literally, "I know!" It has the sense of a bright idea that dawned on him suddenly. It occurred to him that he still had at his disposal the means to ingratiate himself to the rich man's debtors. Judging from the size of their debts, they too were men of substantial means. The steward would use the waning remnants of his delegated authority to reduce their debts so that they would owe him great favors.

Here was his scheme: Debts in that agricultural economy were normally paid in kind at harvest time. The oil in verse 6 refers to olive oil, a staple in every Mediterranean culture. Wheat, of course, is likewise an essential commodity. It was not unheard of then (as now) for a creditor to renegotiate debts on commodities such as these—and thereby avoid foreclosures in times of drought, crop damage, or other financial troubles. For example, if bad weather or locusts caused widespread destruction to crops, the value of wheat and oil would rise anyway. A single bushel of wheat in hard times might be worth more than five bushels in times of abundance. A creditor might actually find it advantageous to accept a reduced payback in hard times rather than driving borrowers out of business.

But in this case there was no hint of price fluctuations or crop failures. This was all about the unjust steward working a deal for himself. So before the debtors even learned that the steward was being fired, he called them in, one by one, and struck deals to discount their debts by amounts ranging from 20 to 50 percent. When harvest arrived and the debt came due, they would owe much less than what they originally agreed to. This was a huge favor to the debtors, and the steward thus made his master's borrowers indebted to him personally. In that society reciprocation was deemed essential, so this guaranteed that when he was no longer employed as a steward, he would still be well taken care of.

Strictly speaking, the man still had legal authority to agree to discounts like those. Morally and ethically, however, his actions were reprehensible. He was already being fired for wasting his master's resources. This discounting scheme was tantamount to embezzlement. It was a deliberate misappropriation of the master's resources. The unjust steward would never be able to hide what he was doing, of course. But this man had neither conscience nor compunction. He was shameless. He was concerned about only one person on the planet:

himself. If he couldn't make a living honestly, he would do it any other way he could.

After all, he had nothing to lose. If he had been someone who stood on principle or cared about integrity, he would not have been in this situation in the first place. His reputation would soon be severely and permanently tarnished. But for a very short time, he still had legal authority to bargain for those discounts. The master had no means of punishing him further. What are scruples to a man in that position?

These were deep and costly discounts. A hundred measures of oil was 875 gallons. The price for that much oil would be about a thousand denarii. A 50 percent discount on one deal like that was equal to a workman's average salary for more than a year and a half. A hundred measures of wheat was a thousand bushels. A hundred acres were required to produce that much wheat. Its full value equaled eight to ten years' labor for the typical farmer. That means a 20 percent reduction amounted to about two years' pay. And those two debtors were merely a representative sample. Verse 5 says the steward "called every one of his master's debtors to him," giving similar discounts to all of them. A dozen or more discounts at rates like those would represent a massive fortune—buying favors enough to set the steward up for life.

The debtors, of course, were happy to sign ("quickly," as the steward says in verse 6). They probably assumed he was acting in good faith for his master.

But he had just conned the rich man out of a fortune.

## The Shocker

Here is where the story takes a startling turn. We might expect this parable to end like the story of the other wicked steward in Matthew 24:50–51: "The master of that servant will come on a day when he is not looking for him and at an hour that he is not aware of, and will cut him in two and appoint him his portion with the hypocrites. There shall be weeping and gnashing of teeth."

But no. "The master commended the unjust steward because he had dealt shrewdly" (Luke 16:8).

Until that point in the story, it was pretty easy to sympathize with the rich man. He seemed merely a victim of the unjust steward's chicanery. But the fact that he admired his employee's unethical stratagem suggests that the rich man himself was hardly a paragon of pure integrity.

It's important to understand that unlike the master in Matthew 24:45–51 or the lord in Matthew 25:14–30, the rich man in this story is not a figure of Christ. Jesus deliberately set this story in the realm of secular business, where this sort of sinful, self-protective, Machiavellian maneuvering is not only common but is often deemed part of the game. Even in today's world, rich businessmen often voice admiration for the shrewd but underhanded tactics of both rivals and partners. Such is the nature of business as usual in a godless realm.

But notice also that the language in the text is very specific. It's not the steward's villainy *per se* that the master admires. Remember that the rich man in this parable meant to punish the steward for being wasteful. He certainly did not approve of the man's disloyalty or think highly of his despicable character. He doesn't applaud the steward's lack of honor. What he commended was the man's forward-looking ingenuity. "The master commended the unjust steward *because he had dealt shrewdly*" (Luke 16:8, emphasis added).

The Greek word translated "shrewdly" is *phronimos*, meaning "prudently," or "cannily." The word has the idea of being cautious, keen witted, and circumspect. The steward's plan, though underhanded, was wickedly ingenious. The sheer cleverness of the scheme was what elicited the master's admiration. The steward took careful advantage of a brief and fleeting opportunity. He manipulated what resources were temporarily in his power to achieve ends that were to his long-term advantage. He used the master's resources to do those debtors immense good. He won their friendship with lavish generosity. And it was not just one debtor whose friendship he bought, but all of them. Thus he maximized his options, because now he had a claim on the kindness of many influential businessmen—and he would desperately need it.

The steward showed amazing foresight because he wasn't thinking about how to cover or excuse his past transgressions. He was just trying to secure his future.

## The Explanation

Then Jesus plainly states His whole point. "The sons of this world are more shrewd in their generation than the sons of light" (Luke 16:8). Sinners tend to be more clever and forward thinking and diligent with regard to their short-term temporal well-being than saints are in the work of laying up treasure for eternity. That's the whole point as stated succinctly by Jesus Himself. "Sons of this world" are those who have no part and no interest in the kingdom of God. They have nothing to look forward to except the remaining years of their earthly lives. But they are more concerned and more clever when it comes to securing an advantageous future for their retirement years than the "sons of light," who have an eternal future to prepare for. It's true. Ungodly people bring amazing energy, skill, and focus to the task of acquiring earthly comforts for the remaining years of this life. Mainly because that's all they really have to look forward to.

The expression "sons of light," is a common New Testament phrase that designates true disciples of Christ—redeemed people (John 12:36; Eph. 5:8; 1 Thess. 5:5). After all, "our citizenship is in heaven, from which we also eagerly wait for the Savior, the Lord Jesus Christ" (Phil. 3:20). It is therefore right that we should have our minds "set . . . on things above, not on things on the earth" (Col. 3:2). Yet compared to all the strategizing, maneuvering, twisting, and turning unbelievers go through to secure their future in this world, "the sons of light" display a distinct lack of wisdom.

Consider how absurd that is. People preparing for retirement probably have (at most) three decades to plan for—usually much less. Life is short and "the world is passing away, and the lust of it" (1 John 2:17). Yet "the sons of this world" will go to almost any length to gain whatever advantage they can for the waning years of their lives. Their worldliness and their lack of scruples are not what Jesus commends. Their shrewd resourcefulness is. Surely "sons of light," bound for eternity, ought to be more active, more zealous, more mindful, and more wise about redeeming the time, preparing for the future, and laying up treasure in heaven.

Starting with that point, Jesus makes three practical exhortations regarding the believer's attitude toward "unrighteous mammon"— money. He is outlining for His disciples how their perspective on money should shape their thoughts and behavior toward others, self, and God (in that order). Here are the key points of wisdom Jesus draws from His parable about the unjust steward.

## Lesson 1: Money is a resource to be used for the good of others.

Immediately after commending the shrewdness of the sons of this world for their forward-thinking resourcefulness, Jesus adds this word of advice for His disciples: "And I say to you, make friends for yourselves by unrighteous mammon, that when [it fails], they may receive you into an everlasting home" (Luke 16:9). Use your money to make friends— not earthly friends, but friends who will welcome you into your eternal home. In other words, be generous with the people of God. Put your money to work for others; help the truly needy among God's people; "and you will have treasure in heaven" (Matt. 19:21). Remember the words of Jesus in Matthew 25:35–40: "I was hungry and you gave Me food; I was thirsty and you gave Me drink; I was a stranger and you took Me in; I was naked and you clothed Me; I was sick and you visited Me; I was in prison and you came to Me. . . . Inasmuch as you did it to one of the least of *these My brethren,* you did it to Me" (emphasis added).

This also underscores our duty to use our money to support the ministry of the gospel. Will people be standing on the edge of glory when you arrive, eager to embrace you, because through your investment in gospel ministry and the extension of the kingdom they heard and believed and gained eternal life in Christ? That's the imagery Jesus' exhortation evokes.

The unjust steward was liberal with his master's money in an unethical way. His actions, though unjust, nevertheless won him friends and secured his future. Jesus is reminding His disciples that we are stewards too. Unlike the unjust steward, we have our Lord's explicit permission—nay, we are under express orders—to be generous with the Master's resources in order to make friends for eternity.

The Lord is making a simple argument from the lesser to the greater. This was a typical form of rabbinical teaching. The point is that if a scheming, dishonest, earthly reprobate is shrewd enough to use his stewardship to make friends for such a brief, temporal future, how much more should we use our Master's resources to make friends for eternity? This is one key way Jesus wants us to be "wise as serpents and harmless as doves" (Matt. 10:16).

*Mammon* is the Aramaic word for "riches." Jesus refers to money as "the unrighteous mammon" because earthly riches belong to this fallen, transient world. All earthly wealth will one day be burned up. "Riches are not forever" (Prov. 27:24). "The form of this world is passing away" (1 Cor. 7:31). "The end of all things is at hand" (1 Peter 4:7). "The heavens will pass away with a great noise, and the elements will melt with fervent heat; both the earth and the works that are in it will be burned up" (2 Peter 3:10).

That is the failure referred to in Luke 16:9. The proper translation is not "when *you* fail" (NKJV), but "when *it* fails": "Make friends for yourselves by unrighteous mammon, that when it [the mammon fails], they [the friends] may receive you into an everlasting home." The clear implication is that it is every believer's duty to invest the temporary value of unrighteous mammon in an enterprise that will reap far greater, eternal value—by putting our money to work for ministry to the people of God, and especially for the spread of gospel truth. The relationships gained through such investments will enrich heaven for eternity. Nothing else we do with our money will last forever.

Jesus wants His disciples to think in those terms. Endless personal accumulation is sinful and wasteful, and it robs us of eternal blessing. Give to the Lord, "and it will be given to you: good measure, pressed down, shaken together, and running over will be put into your bosom. For with the same measure that you use, it will be measured back to you" (Luke 6:38). The ultimate fulfillment of that promise is everlasting treasure in heaven (Matt. 6:19–20). And "where your treasure is, there your heart will be also" (v. 21).

## Lesson 2: Everything we have belongs to God, and we should always think of ourselves as stewards.

Jesus' first exhortation highlighted the needs of *others*. The second one is an encouragement to examine *ourselves*. It is an echo of one of the lessons we saw in the parable of the talents, namely, that the believer who receives little is ultimately accountable to God just like the person who is given much. Both will give an account for what they do with the resources they are given. In fact, true character is seen in how a person handles the small things. "He who is faithful in what is least is faithful also in much; and he who is unjust in what is least is unjust also in much" (Luke 16:10).

I have heard people say, "If I had more I would give more." No you wouldn't. Truly faithful people are generous because of their character, not because of their circumstances. The widow who had virtually nothing gave everything she had. Lots of people who have everything give nothing. A person with meager resources who spends everything he has on himself is not going to become selfless if he suddenly becomes rich. More money will only exacerbate the self-indulgent impulse and compound the unfaithful steward's judgment.

So it is crucial for believers to have a proper perspective on their duty as stewards, regardless of whether they have little or much. In fact, Jesus' statement in this text seems to suggest that wise stewardship is best learned and committed to practice in small ways first. It's folly to wish for wealth if you haven't been a true and faithful steward with what God has already given.

But the real point is that praiseworthy stewardship is not about large sums and lavish gifts. It's about integrity and spiritual character. If you truly see the immense value of investing in eternity, you will do it with whatever resources are available to you. What makes a good steward is the understanding that *everything* we have is a gracious gift from God (1 Cor. 4:7). "'The silver is Mine, and the gold is Mine,' says the LORD of hosts" (Hag. 2:8). "The earth is the LORD's, and all its fullness, the world and those who dwell therein" (Ps. 24:1). The psalmist acknowledged this truth with a prayer to God: "The earth is full of Your possessions" (Ps. 104:24).

The things we call our own are ultimately *God's* possessions, not ours. They are not private property to be used chiefly for our personal benefit. They are divine blessings held in trust, to be invested as wisely as possible for the good of others and the glory of God. That's true whether you have little or much. "Where your treasure is, there your heart will be also" (Luke 12:34). The converse is true as well. Whatever your interest and affections are set on will determine where you invest your treasure. "If then you were raised with Christ, seek those things which are above, where Christ is, sitting at the right hand of God" (Col. 3:1).

In other words, what we do with our money reveals the true state of our heart. Therefore, "If you have not been faithful in the unrighteous mammon, who will commit to your trust the true riches?" (Luke 16:11). Those who are not investing in the work of redemption are shirking their duty to be faithful stewards, wasting this passing moment of opportunity, and impoverishing themselves in eternity. God doesn't reward people for frittering away His resources. To spend money on unnecessary luxuries and status symbols—or even cheap trinkets, trifles, creature comforts, and worthless, time-wasting diversions—is to rob oneself of true, eternal riches.

Verse 12 adds another stinging indictment: "And if you have not been faithful in what is another man's, who will give you what is your own?" That is a reminder of the first principle of stewardship: *We don't currently own anything as a permanent possession.* "We brought nothing into this world, and it is certain we can carry nothing out" (1 Tim. 6:7).

Everything we have is a stewardship—not just the money we give to the church, or to charity. All that we have is God's, and it is all to be used for His glory. "Therefore, whether you eat or drink, or whatever you do, do all to the glory of God" (1 Cor. 10:31).

The tragic irony of sinful self-indulgence is that the more you waste on yourself—the more stuff you accumulate in this life—the less treasure you will have in heaven. The true riches are over there. "We do not look at the things which are seen, but at the things which are not seen. For the things which are seen are temporary, but the things which are not seen are eternal" (2 Cor. 4:18).

## Lesson 3: Do not let money usurp the place of God in your heart.

This story ends with one final exhortation. The first one (Luke 16:9) emphasized our duty to use our earthly resources for ministry to *others*. In verses 10–12, Jesus urged us to examine *ourselves*. This final exhortation focuses our hearts on *God:* "No servant can serve two masters; for either he will hate the one and love the other, or else he will be loyal to the one and despise the other. You cannot serve God and mammon" (v. 13).

Stewardship of God's resources is an all-consuming obligation. It is not a part-time calling (or even a forty-hour-per-week occupation). It's not a once-a-week duty that we can discharge by putting an offering in the church collection. It's not a casual custodianship. In biblical terms, a steward is a slave. Believers are the property of a Master who has purchased us. He has exclusive and absolute control over us, by divine right. We cannot have such a relationship with anyone or anything else. No slave can serve two masters.

Jesus is suggesting that the way we manage our stewardship is important evidence revealing whether we are genuine believers or mere pretenders. Those who truly belong to God cannot serve money and material things. People who squander all their resources on things that cannot last, plowing their wealth right back into "unrighteous mammon" are not true stewards of the living God. What they do with their treasure reveals where their heart really is.

On the other hand, if you "honor the LORD with your possessions, and with the firstfruits of all your increase" (Prov. 3:9), you demonstrate by your stewardship that you have repudiated all other gods, starting with "unrighteous mammon," filthy lucre—the love of money.

There is no middle way. "You cannot serve God and mammon."

The leading Pharisees were walking, talking, real-life illustrations of that principle. They pretended to serve God, but their real god was mammon. Some of them must have wandered by and stopped to eavesdrop while Jesus was telling this parable to His disciples. Luke tells us, "The Pharisees, who were lovers of money, also heard all these things, and they derided Him" (Luke 16:14).

That launched Jesus into another parable, told for their benefit. It is a story about Lazarus and a very wealthy man in the afterlife. It is by far the most grim and disturbing of all Jesus' parables, and it will be our subject in the chapter that follows.

# 9

# A Lesson About Heaven and Hell

*If your hand causes you to sin, cut it off. It is better for you to enter into life maimed, rather than having two hands, to go to hell, into the fire that shall never be quenched—where*

> *"Their worm does not die*
> *And the fire is not quenched."*

*And if your foot causes you to sin, cut it off. It is better for you to enter life lame, rather than having two feet, to be cast into hell, into the fire that shall never be quenched—where*

> *"Their worm does not die*
> *And the fire is not quenched."*

*And if your eye causes you to sin, pluck it out. It is better for you to enter the kingdom of God with one eye, rather than having two eyes, to be cast into hell fire—where*

> *"Their worm does not die*
> *And the fire is not quenched."*

—MARK 9:43–48

No one in the Bible had more to say about hell than the Savior of sinners, the Lord Jesus Christ. The most vivid and detailed biblical descriptions of hell appear in the four gospels, and they come from Jesus. Other New Testament authors allude to the reality of hell, but the substance of what we know about it comes mainly from Jesus' public discourses (with occasional references drawn from the private instruction He gave to the Twelve). Our Lord had much more to say about hell than the average person might think—and a lot of what He taught about hell is profoundly shocking.

He indicated, for example, that hell will be full of religious people. According to Scripture, multitudes of seemingly devout and philanthropic people (including some self-styled miracle workers) will be astonished when they are turned away at the throne of judgment.

Jesus made that point emphatically: "Not everyone who says to Me, 'Lord, Lord,' shall enter the kingdom of heaven, but he who does the will of My Father in heaven. *Many* will say to Me in that day, 'Lord, Lord, have we not prophesied in Your name, cast out demons in Your name, and done many wonders in Your name?' And then I will declare to them, 'I never knew you; depart from Me, you who practice lawlessness!'" (Matt. 7:21–23, emphasis added). Those turned away will include not only people who are ensnared in cults and false religions, but also confessionally orthodox people who don't truly believe what they profess. Such people cover their unbelief and secret sins with a veneer of hypocritical religiosity.

Jesus furthermore indicated that *most* of this world's religious activity is nothing more than a highway to hell: "Wide is the gate and broad is the way that leads to destruction, and there are many who go in by it" (v. 13). But "narrow is the gate and difficult is the way which leads to life, and there are few who find it" (v. 14).

## Jesus v. the Pharisees

The Pharisees were perhaps the most biblically oriented religious leaders of their time, and yet they epitomized what Jesus was warning about. He said so publicly and repeatedly: "Beware of the leaven of the Pharisees, which is hypocrisy" (Luke 12:1; Matt. 16:6, 11–12). "Woe to you, scribes and Pharisees, hypocrites!" (Matt. 23:13–15, 23, 25, 27, 29).

Our Lord's obvious contempt for the Pharisees' religion must have sent major shockwaves through every region where He ministered. As we have noted in previous chapters, the Pharisees were obsessively meticulous in their observance of the fine points of Old Testament ceremonial and dietary laws. They were the most respectable, seemingly upright, ardently devoted holy men in the whole Roman empire. Most of the Pharisees themselves were quite confident that they deserved heaven. After all, no one in the history of Judaism had ever worked harder to enforce the statutes and ceremonies commanded in Moses' law. As we have seen, the Pharisees even added extra rules and restrictions of their own meant to safeguard ceremonial purity. And they literally wore their religion on their sleeves, in the form of enlarged phylacteries—leather boxes (containing little scrolls with portions of the written law) bound to their left arms and foreheads with elaborate leather straps. They wore tassels on their robes as commanded in Numbers 15:38–39 to be a reminder of the Lord's commandments, but they made their tassels extra large so that no one could miss seeing them. They were walking billboards for ceremonial law. Their religion defined who they were, dictated what they looked like, and dominated all their waking thoughts.

But Jesus never once saluted their efforts, congratulated them on their achievements, or sought to emphasize any "common ground" between His teaching and theirs. Every time He addressed the issue of their religion, He bluntly made it clear that their righteousness was not sufficient to merit heaven (Matt. 5:20) and their religion was the fast lane on the broad road to eternal condemnation (Matt. 23:32; Luke 20:47). They were obsessed with what others could see in them and how they wanted other people to act—but they neglected weightier issues like the pride, lust, greed, and covetousness that festered in their own hearts (Matt. 15:19–20; 23:23). Jesus outspokenly denounced their hypocrisy (Matt. 23:25–28). He fully knew their hearts (Matt. 12:25) and said plainly and publicly that the Pharisees were inwardly corrupt and self-condemned (vv. 33–37).

When Jesus reached the end of the parable of the unjust steward in Luke 16, some Pharisees overheard Him warning His disciples against making an idol of money: "You cannot serve God and mammon" (Luke 16:13).

Luke says, "Now the Pharisees, who were lovers of money, also heard all these things, and they derided Him" (v. 14).

Jesus replied with yet another forceful condemnation of their religion. He pointed out that although the Pharisees labored nonstop to make it look as though they were serious, diligent, and single-minded in their devotion to the law, the reality was that their religion was too superficial. God was not impressed. Their best-looking good works were of no more value in the eyes of God than a pile of nasty rags soiled and stained with bodily fluids. I realize that imagery is revolting in the extreme, but it faithfully conveys the literal meaning of Isaiah 64:6. It reflects God's utter contempt for self-righteousness and human religion. Jesus told them: "You are those who justify yourselves before men, but God knows your hearts. For what is highly esteemed among men is *an abomination* in the sight of God" (Luke 16:15, emphasis added).

## Some Context for This Parable

At this point in Luke's narrative (16:16–18), Jesus sums up in a few words everything He ever preached about the Pharisees, the law, the gospel, and true righteousness. He does so by making three quick points. *One*, the old covenant is giving way to the new. "The law and the prophets were until John. Since that time the kingdom of God has been preached, and everyone is pressing into it" (v. 16). The threats and punishments of the law were being answered by the promises of the gospel and the sacrifice of Christ. So the way was wide open for sinners to enter the kingdom, and they were already pressing in. But for those arrogant enough to insist on measuring their own performance by the law, the case remained hopeless. Although they thought they were sufficiently righteous, they would find themselves condemned forever.

Why? That's Jesus' point *two*: "It is easier for heaven and earth to pass away than for one tittle of the law to fail" (v. 17). The law's demands and threats are relentless. "Whoever shall keep the whole law, and yet stumble in one point, he is guilty of all" (James 2:10).

And *three*, all the Pharisaical interpretations of the law that were designed to make its standard seem easier or more attainable were wrong and misleading. For example, the Pharisees taught that men were entitled to divorce their wives for practically any reason. But "the LORD God of Israel says that He hates divorce, for it covers one's garment with violence" (Mal. 2:16). So Jesus says, "Whoever divorces his wife and marries another commits adultery; and whoever marries her who is divorced from her husband commits adultery" (Luke 16:18).

The Pharisees, with all their exacting obsessions, had not even begun to grasp how demanding and inflexible the law really is. Furthermore, the law governs not merely what others can see, but the secret thoughts of the heart as well. The Pharisees' assumption that they were earning merit with God under the law was a damning delusion.

Jesus launches from that point immediately into a tragic parable that highlights the hopeless horror of hell and the infinite regret that will eternally haunt well-to-do and self-righteous people whose wealth or religion or other earthly advantages have insulated them from the reality of their need for divine grace. This is by far the most disturbing and frightful of all Jesus' parables. It confronts us with truths about eternity and the afterlife that we don't like to think about but desperately need to take seriously.

There was a certain rich man who was clothed in purple and fine linen and fared sumptuously every day. But there was a certain beggar named Lazarus, full of sores, who was laid at his gate, desiring to be fed with the crumbs which fell from the rich man's table. Moreover the dogs came and licked his sores. So it was that the beggar died, and was carried by the angels to Abraham's bosom. The rich man also died and was buried. And being in torments in Hades, he lifted up his eyes and saw Abraham afar off, and Lazarus in his bosom.

Then he cried and said, "Father Abraham, have mercy on me, and send Lazarus that he may dip the tip of his finger in water and cool my tongue; for I am tormented in this flame." But Abraham said, "Son, remember that in your lifetime you received your good things, and likewise Lazarus evil things; but now he is comforted and you are tormented. And besides all this, between us and you there is a great gulf fixed, so that those who want to pass from here to you cannot, nor can those from there pass to us."

Then he said, "I beg you therefore, father, that you would send him to my father's house, for I have five brothers, that he may testify to them, lest they also come to this place of torment." Abraham said to him, "They have Moses and the prophets; let them hear them." And he said, "No, father Abraham; but if one goes to them from the dead, they will repent." But he said to him, "If they do not hear Moses and the prophets, neither will they be persuaded though one rise from the dead." (Luke 16:19–31)

The parable deals with several extreme opposites: torment and comfort; death and life; hell and heaven. The characters are an extravagantly wealthy man and a beggar who lived in extreme poverty; but their fortunes are reversed in the afterlife. Because the focus is on the misery of the man in hell, it is a deeply disturbing story, and yet Jesus had a gracious purpose in telling it to the Pharisees. He was warning them not to follow their own instincts, traditions, and religious convictions. He was urging them to repent.

## Knowing the Terror of the Lord

Obviously, Jesus was not telling this story for anyone's amusement. This is a solemn, earnest word of warning—precisely the kind of testimony the rich man in the parable was begging to be delivered to his five brothers. If the story slams you with a feeling of shock or dismay, that was precisely Jesus' intent. The severity of the subject matter is exceeded only by the urgency of the point our Lord was making. This is hard-edged teaching—on purpose. Jesus is not concerned here with academic nuance or diplomatic finesse. But don't think for a moment that He has overstepped the bounds of propriety. Those who are put off by the shrillness of the parable or the unpleasantness of the subject matter need to adjust their own thinking and gain a higher esteem for the truth. Truth is not judged by how it makes people feel.

Of course, hell has always stirred negative passions. That was true even in Jesus' time. But today the subject is virtually taboo—even in supposedly evangelical circles. Hell is an embarrassment to those who want Christianity to fit the modern dogmas of universal goodwill and broad-minded tolerance. It is an inconvenience to those who want the biblical message to always sound cheerful to unchurched people. It is an irritant to those who want a religion that makes people always feel good about themselves. And it is an offense to those who care little about righteousness and don't really fear God—but want to maintain some pretense of piety anyway.

Because opinions such as those are so widespread, countless church leaders today think they need to downplay what the Bible says about hell (or totally ignore it). Most of the popular tracts and evangelism programs produced over the past hundred years intentionally sidestep any mention of the horrors of hell. The goal, supposedly, is to give greater emphasis to the love of God—as if to exonerate Him from the reproach of what He Himself says in His own Word.

In recent years a few popular quasi-evangelical authors and church leaders have gone further yet. They have vocally waged war against hell and all its related doctrines. They oppose any emphasis on negative biblical truths like sin, hell, the wrath of God, human depravity, the impossibility of human merit, and the true cost of atonement. Some have even argued that negative themes like those need to be totally eliminated from the evangelical repertoire. Such ideas have an unwholesome, primitive sound, they say—especially in an enlightened postmodern generation where self-esteem, inclusivism, and positive thinking are embraced as high virtues.

Even a few otherwise sound Christian leaders and Bible commentators have sometimes complained that the idea of hell seems cruel or unfair.* They wonder how a truly loving God could ever send people into everlasting punishment.

Those are shortsighted, untenable objections. To make such an argument is to elevate human reason (or raw emotion) above God Himself. God by definition is not subject to judgment from any higher authority than Himself. (There *is* no higher authority, of course.) The Lord defines righteousness by His own nature. Question whether God has a right to do what He says He will do, and you might as well deny the very existence of God.

The Word of God *does* say often and categorically that He will punish evildoers with "everlasting punishment" (Matt. 25:46) by "everlasting fire" (v. 41). The Bible describes hell repeatedly as a place "where 'Their worm does not die and the fire is not quenched'" (Mark 9:48, quoting Isa. 66:24). Revelation 14:10–11 says any person who receives the mark of the Beast during the Great Tribulation "shall be tormented with fire and brimstone in the presence of the holy angels and in the presence of the Lamb. And the smoke of their torment ascends forever and ever; and they have no rest day or night."

So hell is consistently described as a place of never-ending affliction: "These will go away into everlasting punishment, but the righteous into

---

* John Stott, for example, famously wrote, "Emotionally, I find the concept [of hell] intolerable and do not understand how people can live with it without either cauterising their feelings or cracking under the strain." David L. Edwards and John Stott: *Evangelical Essentials: A Liberal-Evangelical Dialogue* (London: Hodder & Stoughton, 1988), 313. Stott's position on the question appeared somewhat ambivalent. He added immediately, "But our emotions are a fluctuating, unreliable guide to truth and must not be exalted to the place of supreme authority in determining it. As a committed Evangelical, my question must be—and is— not what does my heart tell me, but what does God's word say?" (Ibid.). That's quite true. But Stott himself did not stop there. He went on to argue for a severely strained interpretation of Scripture that demonstrated his preference for the view that the wicked will ultimately be annihilated.

eternal life" (Matt. 25:46). The word translated "everlasting" is *aiōnios*. It is exactly the same Greek word translated "eternal" near the end of that same verse. In other words, the "everlasting punishment" of the wicked lasts precisely as long as the "eternal life" of the redeemed. *Aiōnios* is also the word used of God's glory in 1 Peter 5:10 ("His eternal glory by Christ Jesus"). And it is used of God Himself in Romans 16:26 ("the everlasting God"). The way that word is consistently used in the Bible means it simply cannot be redefined or reinterpreted to accommodate the notion of a finite time span.

The parable of the rich man and Lazarus is the Bible's most vivid description of what hell entails. It *is* a horrific and deeply unsettling story. Again, we are supposed to be troubled and grieved by it. But if we confess Jesus as Lord, it is nevertheless our duty to believe what He taught, including His many graphic warnings about the eternal punishment of unbelievers.

Lest there be any confusion: I don't like the thought of hell either. I don't enjoy teaching or writing about it. We are certainly not supposed to imagine that Jesus Himself found some kind of perverse glee in describing the horrors of hell. No sane person could possibly relish the thought of it. On one occasion I heard a conference speaker teaching about hell in an almost joking manner, with a frivolous, impertinent tone. Such an approach to this topic is unthinkable. No one who takes Jesus seriously could have such a flippant attitude toward hell. Much less should we ever think of the subject without a deep sense of our responsibility to proclaim the gospel to the lost.

Western secular culture has gone the opposite direction, reducing hell to a meaningless swear word, a trivial epithet to express anger. People today casually tell one another to go to hell. The result, ironically, is that the word *hell* is frequently on the lips of unbelievers, and they sometimes use it in the most lighthearted manner. Meanwhile, many believers who know and believe the hard truth Jesus taught in this parable remain totally silent about it.

That is obviously how Satan wants it. But that's not how it should be.

The parable makes clear that even people in hell right now *want* their loved ones to be warned about the terrors of a very real hell. Christians must not remain silent. After all, the whole point of this parable (and the rest of Jesus' teaching about hell) is to sound a clear warning about the fearsomeness of hell, its horrors, and the very real threat it poses to those who live in unbelief and unrepentant sin. Jesus' primary intent is to produce in sinners a terror of eternal hell—a fear that would drive them toward repentance and faith in the gospel. Knowledge of that fear should motivate believers as well: "Knowing, therefore, the terror of the Lord, we persuade men" (2 Cor. 5:11).

## The Characters

Some have argued that Jesus' account of Lazarus and the rich man is not a parable at all, but an account of a real event. They point out that in every other parable Jesus ever told, human characters were always kept anonymous: "a certain man" (Luke 13:6; 14:16; 15:11; 20:9); "a certain king" (Matt. 18:23; 22:2); "a certain landowner" (Matt. 21:33); "a certain creditor" (Luke 7:41); "a certain priest" (Luke 10:31); and so on. Here, the beggar has a name: "a certain beggar *named Lazarus*" (Luke 16:20, emphasis added). And an Old Testament character, Abraham, even plays a central role.

As we shall see, there are important reasons why the Lazarus character is given a name. But this is indeed a parable, not a true story about something that literally happened. We are not expected to interpret every detail of the story in a rigidly literal way. Both the context and the content of the story clearly confirm this.

How? Well, we know from other clear statements of Scripture that people in hell cannot see into heaven and observe or recognize people there, much less have conversations with them. Hell is repeatedly described as "outer darkness" (Matt. 8:12; 22:13; 25:30)—a place of total isolation and alienation from heaven; "the blackness of darkness forever" (2 Peter 2:17; Jude 13). The apostle Paul referred to hell as "everlasting destruction from the presence of the Lord and from the glory of His power" (2 Thess. 1:9). And in the parable itself, Abraham says, "between us and you there is a great gulf fixed, so that those who want to pass from here to you cannot, nor can those from there pass to us" (Luke 16:26). The Greek word translated "gulf" is *chasma*, signifying a vast, yawning chasm—a distance of cosmic proportions. The very notion of a great gulf too vast to traverse rules out the idea that one could literally see people, recognize them, and have a conversation with them across such an impassible distance.

So this is quite clearly not supposed to be thought of as a true story. It is an imaginary narrative told with a clear didactic purpose, like all the other parables. No time or place or specific details (other than the beggar's name) are given. The story has one purpose: to warn the hearers that hell will be full of people who never expected to be there. And as we shall see, Jesus had good reasons for giving the Lazarus character a name.

In this sobering story, Jesus illustrates what it is like to be in hell. The parable makes it clear that hell is an agonizing existence, full of regret, anguish, and relentless, burning torment—with full consciousness and without hope, forever and ever. There is no possibility of escape and no rest. Not one fingertip's drop of relief will ever ease the suffering or diminish the pain of a soul eternally tormented in hell. It is a horrific, heartbreaking picture of absolute damnation.

But the story is not merely a warning about hell. It portrays a shocking reversal that shattered the sensibilities of Jesus' listeners because it destroyed their carefully crafted theology.

Luke 16:19 introduces us to the rich man, and every phrase in that verse lets us know that he was lavishly, outlandishly, over-the-top wealthy. "Clothed in purple and fine linen," he lived it up "every day." His life was a perpetual feast of pleasures (he "fared sumptuously"). Such great wealth, then, as now, assured that he was highly influential. In whatever synagogue he belonged to, people would naturally defer to him. He was precisely the kind of person the average Israelite, under the teaching of the Pharisees, believed to be most assured of heaven. He was Jewish, and a religious man, not an utter pagan. We know that, because he addresses Abraham as "Father" (and Abraham replies to him as "son"). He must have therefore had a working knowledge of "the adoption, the glory, the covenants, the giving of the law, the service of God, and the promises" (Rom. 9:4). Most of those listening to Jesus would have concluded that this man was greatly blessed by God.

As for the poor man, Lazarus, he was beyond destitute, paralyzed, unable to move or care for himself. Luke 16:20 says he "was laid at" the rich man's gate. The verb is passive, indicating that someone basically discarded him in front of the rich man's mansion. Whoever left him there probably assumed he would receive charity from a man who lived in such luxury—a man who wore purple robes like royalty. But Lazarus was "full of sores." (These were probably bedsores associated with paralysis—ulcers caused by pressure from lying too long in one position.) The ruined and emaciated condition of his body must have made him repulsive to passersby, because he received no help whatsoever. He had to endure being licked by filthy street mongrels, as if he were already dead. He longed for a crumb of the dirty bread the dogs would eat from the floor under the rich man's table.

The Pharisees and their disciples would regard such suffering as proof that Lazarus was cursed by God. Of these two characters, he was the one whom they would have regarded as worthy of hell. In their view, he was as abominable as the circumstances of his life.

The shock of Jesus' story is the great reversal. "The beggar died, and was carried by the angels to Abraham's bosom. The rich man also died and was buried. And being in torments in Hades . . . " (vv. 22–23). "Abraham's bosom" signifies a place of honor at Abraham's table. Guests at a lavish banquet in that culture would recline on cushions around the table. (That's the literal meaning of the word in Luke 13:29: "They will come from the east and the west, from the north and the south, and [recline at the table] in the kingdom of God.") The guest of honor, placed next to Abraham, would therefore have his head next to Abraham's breast (cf. John 13:25). In other words, the beggar who longed for a bread crumb and seemed so loathsome to the refined Pharisees receives a place of high honor in heaven. The rich man who enjoyed every earthly advantage—whom the Pharisees wanted so much to emulate—goes to hell, where he is humiliated, abandoned, without hope, and reduced to begging for a drop of water.

There's irony at every point of this unexpected twist. Lazarus is named in this parable precisely to mark him out with honor. His name (a form of the name *Eleazar*) means, "whom the Lord has helped." It's a name that evokes the idea of divine favor, and by naming him, Jesus graciously lifts him out of the disgrace and anonymity so typical of beggars in that position. The rich man, by contrast, isn't given a name, to underscore the fact that he is no longer important.** He has been stripped of all the badges of prominence, including his name, while the poor beggar (whose desperate need the rich man once failed even to notice) has been given all the privileges of God's eternal blessing.

## The Rich Man's Plea and Abraham's Reply

Why is the rich man in hell? After all, he was apparently a religious man. Jesus does not charge him with any gross or notorious sin. In fact, the story doesn't expressly mention any specific evil deed he had committed. He was a typical leading citizen in that society. It's clear, of course, that he was selfish, uncaring, and stunningly oblivious to the needs of his neighbors, because he did nothing to help poor Lazarus. But we don't see him throwing Lazarus off his property or abusing him in any way. Jesus purposely does not paint the rich man as an uncommonly cruel man or a heinous evildoer, as if hell were only for the monstrously abominable. That is not the point.

Notice also that when the rich man finds himself in hell, he does not ask for reconsideration or release on the grounds of pity or mercy.

** The rich man is sometimes referred to as Dives (pronounced DIVE-ees), which is a Latin adjective meaning "rich," but Jesus gave him no name.

He doesn't say, "Someone made a mistake!" He doesn't ask, "Why am I here?" All pretense has now been stripped away and he is under the full weight of his own guilt. He knows he deserves to be in hell. All he asks for is the smallest hint of relief.

He's never going to get that. There is no hope of a moment's pause in the grinding, eternal, bitter accusations of his own guilty conscience. The only concern he has left is for his brothers, because he knows they are exactly like him—respectable, complacent, comfortably wealthy pillars of society, doing whatever they want, going through the motions of enough religious activity to maintain an honorable reputation, but headed directly for hell.

So he says to Abraham, "I beg you therefore, father, that you would send [Lazarus] to my father's house, for I have five brothers, that he may testify to them, lest they also come to this place of torment" (Luke 16:27–28). He's pleading on the basis of his Jewish heritage. He was one of the covenant people, a descendant of Abraham. *That ought to be worth something.* Many among the Pharisees and their disciples assumed that their genealogical connection through the line of Abraham, Isaac, and Jacob was the main basis of their eternal hope (cf. Phil. 3:5). This man now knows from experience that genealogical connections don't get anyone into heaven. Perhaps his relationship to Abraham will get him a drop of water. If not, how about a warning to his brothers from a man who comes back from the dead?

The request he makes suggests that the five remaining siblings would recognize the beggar who used to lie in filth and pain at their brother's gate. They also must have known that Lazarus had died; otherwise, a message from him wouldn't really carry any extra weight with the brothers.

But notice that even in hell, the rich man saw Lazarus as beneath him, a nobody who could be given orders and sent where he pleases. Hell is punitive, not remedial. People in hell don't get better. And Scripture is emphatic about that. "He who is unjust, let him be unjust still; he who is filthy, let him be filthy still" (Rev. 22:11). Hell fixes the destiny and the character of the reprobate forever.

Here, the rich man not only still views Lazarus as someone he can pass commands to; his priorities and concerns are still too narrowly self-centered. Like anyone steeped in Pharisaical religion, his only concern is about a few people in his immediate family. It's normal, of course, to care for one's own siblings. But as we saw in the parable of the good Samaritan, the love required by the Second Great Commandment is much broader than that. Why order Lazarus back from heaven with a private warning for five brothers?

Abraham's response is firm: "They have Moses and the prophets; let them hear them" (Luke 16:29). "Moses and the prophets" was a common way of designating the Old Testament Scriptures (cf. Luke 24:44; 28:23). Abraham is saying, *Let them read with understanding what it says in the thirty-nine books of Scripture they already have in their possession.*

This is a powerful affirmation of the sufficiency of Scripture. Abraham's point is that the reason the rich man's brothers were unregenerate, unbelieving reprobates in danger of hell was not owing to any deficiency in the methodology that brought them God's Word in the first place. There is no better method or more effective messenger with special power to give sight to the blind or life to the dead. There is no new style of ministry or strategy for evangelism that has superior power to overcome depravity and awaken a spiritually dead, self-centered, self-willed, hypocritical, religious sinner (or any other kind of sinner, for that matter). The power is in the Word of God.

The redeemed have been "born again, not of corruptible seed but incorruptible, through the word of God which lives and abides forever" (1 Peter 1:23). "Faith comes by hearing, and hearing by the word of God" (Rom. 10:17). The rich man was in hell forever not because he lacked information, but because he ignored the message he had received through the Word of God. The only way his brothers would ever escape hell would be by listening to that message and believing it.

The rich man's request was an echo of what Jesus heard all the time. The Pharisees were always asking Him for signs. In Matthew 12:38, for example, immediately after Jesus had performed a string of miracles, healings, and demonic deliverances, "Some of the scribes and Pharisees answered, saying, 'Teacher, we want to see a sign from You.'" Jesus' everyday miracles weren't enough for them; they were asking for a heavenly sign of cosmic proportions. Jesus' reply was, "An evil and adulterous generation seeks after a sign, and no sign will be given to it except the sign of the prophet Jonah. For as Jonah was three days and three nights in the belly of the great fish, so will the Son of Man be three days and three nights in the heart of the earth" (vv. 39–40). In other words, *I'll give you a sign—the sign of all signs—a resurrection.*

Would even that be enough to convince the Pharisees? Abraham answers that question in our parable: "If they do not hear Moses and the prophets, neither will they be persuaded though one rise from the dead" (Luke 16:31).

That embodies the main point of this parable. It is not merely a warning about what hell will be like. It is a lesson about the sufficiency of Scripture, and a plea for all who hear to take the message of the Bible seriously.

## Though One Rise from the Dead

A few months after Jesus told this parable, His good friend Lazarus, a real man, died. By the time Jesus arrived in Lazarus's hometown, Bethany, the corpse had already lain in the grave four days. But Jesus raised him from the dead—merely by speaking the word: "Lazarus, come forth!" (John 11:43). Scripture says, "He who had died came out bound hand and foot with graveclothes, and his face was wrapped with a cloth. Jesus said to them, 'Loose him, and let him go'" (v. 44).

So this real Lazarus was indeed an eyewitness who came back from the dead. It was a well-attested miracle, because the graveyard was crowded with mourners when Lazarus came to the mouth of the grave, still bound in the burial shroud. Scripture says, "Many of the Jews who had come to Mary [Lazarus's sister], and had seen the things Jesus did, believed in Him" (v. 45). It was an amazing miracle. There was no denying the reality of it, and there was no way to keep it silent. Some of the eyewitnesses reported to the Pharisees what had happened (v. 46).

How do you think the Pharisees responded? Surely if someone came back from the dead, they would believe, right?

Wrong. They convened a council to plot how to put Jesus to death:

> The chief priests and the Pharisees gathered a council and said, "What shall we do? For this Man works many signs. If we let Him alone like this, everyone will believe in Him, and the Romans will come and take away both our place and nation."
>
> And one of them, Caiaphas, being high priest that year, said to them, "You know nothing at all, nor do you consider that it is expedient for us that one man should die for the people, and not that the whole nation should perish." Now this he did not say on his own authority; but being high priest that year he prophesied that Jesus would die for the nation, and not for that nation only, but also that He would gather together in one the children of God who were scattered abroad.
>
> Then, from that day on, they plotted to put Him to death. (vv. 47–53)

In fact, we're told a chapter later that "the chief priests plotted to put Lazarus to death also" (12:10). Rather than heeding the message of Jesus, they resolved to eradicate the messenger. When He gave them greater signs, they only grew more determined to destroy Him.

Miracles have no special power to convince those who reject the message of Scripture. The message itself "is the power of God to salvation for everyone who believes" (Rom. 1:16).

What was the Pharisees' reaction when Jesus rose from the dead by His own power? Immediately after the resurrection, according to Matthew 28:11, "Some of the guard came into the city and reported to the chief priests all that had happened." Were they finally convinced by that?

Not at all. "When they had assembled with the elders and consulted together, they gave a large sum of money to the soldiers, saying, 'Tell them, "His disciples came by night and stole Him away while we slept." And if this comes to the governor's ears, we will appease him and make you secure'" (vv. 12–14). They conspired with the Roman guard to cover it up and deny the resurrection with a lie.

No miracle of any magnitude will convince someone who hears and understands the message of Scripture but rejects it anyway. Only the Holy Spirit can open blind eyes and melt hardened hearts to receive the Word. And the truth of God's Word is the only message with the power to save. If you reject the Word of God but believe in some miracle, religious experience, or private revelation, your faith is not saving faith at all.

And those the Word of God will be judged by the very truth they reject. In John 12:46–48 Jesus said, "I have come as a light into the world, that whoever believes in Me should not abide in darkness. And if anyone hears My words and does not believe, I do not judge him; for I did not come to judge the world but to save the world. He who rejects Me, and does not receive My words, has that which judges him—the word that I have spoken will judge him in the last day."

# A Lesson About Persistence in Prayer

*As for me, I will call upon God,*
*And the Lord shall save me.*
*Evening and morning and at noon*
*I will pray, and cry aloud,*
*And He shall hear my voice.*

—Psalm 55:16–17

Scripture is full of exhortations to pray, often paired with promises that the Lord will surely hear and answer our prayers.

The effective, fervent prayer of a righteous man avails much. (James 5:16)

Ask, and it will be given to you; seek, and you will find; knock, and it will be opened to you. For everyone who asks receives, and he who seeks finds, and to him who knocks it will be opened. Or what man is there among you who, if his son asks for bread, will give him a stone?

Or if he asks for a fish, will he give him a serpent? If you then, being evil, know how to give good gifts to your children, how much more will your Father who is in heaven give good things to those who ask Him! (Matt. 7:7–11)

Whatever things you ask in prayer, believing, you will receive. (Matt. 21:22)

This is the confidence that we have in Him, that if we ask anything according to His will, He hears us. And if we know that He hears us, whatever we ask, we know that we have the petitions that we have asked of Him. (1 John 5:14–15)

Yet our prayers are not always answered speedily, on our preferred timetable. For reasons that are supremely wise, and gracious, and right—but often unknown and unexplained to us—God sometimes delays answering our prayers. Yet He encourages us to keep praying with persistence and passion, never losing faith and not growing faint.

Luke 18 begins with a parable illustrating that principle. It is the story of a woman who simply will not give up seeking justice, even though her case is trapped in a corrupt judicial system before the bench of a crooked and apathetic judge.

Jesus is speaking here to a group of His closest disciples (cf. Luke 17:22):

He spoke a parable to them, that men always ought to pray and not lose heart, saying: "There was in a certain city a judge who did not fear God nor regard man. Now there was a widow in that city; and she came to him, saying, 'Get justice for me from my adversary.' And he would not for a while; but afterward he said within himself, 'Though I do not fear God nor regard man, yet because this widow troubles me I will avenge her, lest by her continual coming she weary me.'"

Then the Lord said, "Hear what the unjust judge said. And shall God not avenge His own elect who cry out day and night to Him, though He bears long with them? I tell you that He will avenge them speedily. Nevertheless, when the Son of Man comes, will He really find faith on the earth?" (Luke 18:1–8)

That is the penultimate story in a special series of parables that are highlighted in Luke 13–18. They are ordered somewhat thematically, and all of them are unique to Luke's gospel. In fact, they are part of a lengthy narrative that has no parallel in any of the other gospels—beginning in Luke 13:22 and ending with the parable of the Pharisee and tax collector in 18:14. Several of Jesus' best-known stories, including the three famous parables in Luke 15 (the lost sheep, the lost coin, and the prodigal son), appear only in this singular portion of Luke's gospel.[1]

Of course, this poignant tale about an unjust judge and a persistent widow is likewise unique to Luke. The story comes immediately after a short discourse on the Second Coming (describing what it will be like on "the day when the Son of Man is revealed" [17:30]). The closing sixteen verses of Luke 17 (vv. 22–37) are reminiscent of the Olivet Discourse.* But this is actually a much shorter message with noticeably different content, and it belongs to an earlier time in Jesus' ministry. The Luke 17 discourse is dominated by warnings of doom and sudden disaster, culminating in a gruesome image of death and corruption: "Where the body is, there also the vultures will be gathered" (v. 37 NASB).

Our parable begins immediately after that, its point being "that men always ought to pray and not lose heart" (Luke 18:1). No matter how bleak the times; even if all the world seems to be barreling toward doom and eternal judgment, righteous men and women must persist in prayer— and they can be confident that God will hear and answer His people.

This is an encouragement for believers living in evil times, seeing the world grow more hostile, sensing the approach of judgment, feeling alone and isolated "as it was in the days of Noah" (17:26) and "as it was

---

* Cf. verse 26 ("as it was in the days of Noah") with Matthew 24:37 ("But as the days of Noah were, so also will the coming of the Son of Man be").

also in the days of Lot" (v. 28). In other words, this story has a particular application in times like ours. The days are evil. The need is critical. Our praying should be urgent, passionate, and persistent. We must not lose heart.

## The Judge

The scenario described in the parable would likely be all too familiar to anyone in first-century Israel. Jesus sets the scene in "a certain city" (Luke 18:2) without naming the place. He didn't need to. Widows and corrupt judges were familiar characters throughout the culture of that time. Justice was often hard to come by.

The highest religious court in Israel, of course, was the Great Sanhedrin, consisting of seventy-one judges (all religious leaders deemed experts in both Old Testament law and oral tradition). Their power, as we know from the New Testament, was oppressive and often unjust. Of course, the Great Sanhedrin devised and carried out the conspiracy that led to Jesus' crucifixion, so we know that body was riddled with injustice and corruption.

There was another layer of religious courts under the Great Sanhedrin. Larger cities throughout Israel each had their own ruling bodies, known as lesser Sanhedrin, consisting of twenty-three judges in each city. Like the chief rulers in Jerusalem, they were strongly influenced by the doctrine of the Pharisees and the politics of the Sadducees.** They were therefore given to perfunctory rulings; swayed by man-made rules and traditions; and prone to harsh or hasty judgments fueled by the Pharisees' twisted interpretations and faulty applications of Old Testament statutes. (We have seen the classic example of this already in their overzealous applications of ceremonial Sabbath restrictions.)

---

** Alfred Edersheim writes, "It deserves notice, that the special sin with which the house of Annas is charged is that of 'whispering'—or hissing like vipers—which seems to refer to private influence on the judges in their administration of justice, whereby 'morals were corrupted, judgment perverted, and the Shekhinah withdrawn from Israel.'" *The Life and Times of Jesus the Messiah*, 2 vols. (London: Longmans, Green & Co., 1896), 1:263.

Judges themselves were steeped in Pharisaical self-righteousness. Having risen to the top rungs of a highly politicized rabbinical hierarchy, they were often notoriously corrupt.

But in addition to all those judges, Rome had appointed local magistrates and village judges—municipal authorities who judged criminal cases and looked after the interests of Caesar. They were the worst of all—notoriously lacking in both morals and scruples. They were paid large salaries out of the temple treasury, even though they typically were Gentiles and unbelievers. The Jews generally regarded them with the same utter disdain typically shown to tax collectors. Their official title was "Prohibition Judges," but—changing just one letter in the Aramaic term—the Jews referred to them as "Robber-judges."[2]

From Jesus' description of this judge, it seems clear that he was one of these Roman appointees. He "did not fear God nor regard man" (Luke 18:2). That is a well-chosen characterization. Similar expressions are fairly common in literature from ancient times, even outside the Bible. Such a word portrait was used to depict a notoriously unscrupulous person. This was someone who showed no true reverence for God, His will, or His law. Furthermore, he was completely indifferent to the needs of people and their just causes. This man had become a judge because he loved the status and the money, not because he loved justice. He was unmoved by compassion or understanding. And to compound the gravity of his wicked character, we discover that he was not naive or self-deceived; he was fully aware of how thoroughly debauched his character had become. He freely acknowledged *to himself*, "I do not fear God nor regard man" (v. 4). By his own confession, he lived in open defiance of both the First and Second Great Commandments (cf. Matt. 22:37–40). He was an utterly amoral human being, and his wickedness had all kinds of tragic implications because he was making daily decisions that affected people's lives.

Jesus referred to him by a terse epithet: "the unjust judge" (Luke 18:6). This man was totally disregarding the duties of his office, because a judge is supposed to dispense justice according to the law of God and the needs of people.*** This man could hardly care less about either. He simply had no shame—and nothing was more supremely wicked than that kind of brazenness in a Middle Eastern culture where honor and shame are everything. In short, this judge was bereft of basic decency; lacking in nobility; devoid of natural affection, and without regard for either God or humanity. His own character was so barren of virtue that most would consider him inhuman. He seemed impervious to any appeal.

And yet this parable is told to teach a positive lesson about God and how He answers our prayers—using the wicked behavior of this unrighteous judge as an illustration. This is very similar to the parable of the unjust steward in that Jesus was using a wicked person's actions to depict something pure and righteous.

## The Woman's Dilemma

The only other character in this parable is a poor widow, the victim of some injustice or oppression, whose only recourse was to seek redress in the courts. Someone had defrauded her. She was apparently destitute and alone. In that culture the courts belonged exclusively to men. No woman would have appealed to a judge in the first place if there were a man in her life. Not only was her husband dead; she evidently had no brother, brother-in-law, father, son, cousin, nephew, distant male relative, or close neighbor who could plead her case. She represents those who are dirt poor, powerless, helpless, deprived, lowly, unknown, unloved, uncared for, or otherwise desperate.

Jesus built this illustration around a widow because as far as the Old Testament goes, her case ought to have been clear-cut. Regardless of the legal merits of her claim, the judge should have done something to care for her purely on the grounds of mercy. Moses' law was explicit on this

***

*** The Old Testament records how when King Jehoshaphat appointed judges "city by city" throughout Judah, he told them, "Take heed to what you are doing, for you do not judge for man but for the LORD, who is with you in the judgment. Now therefore, let the fear of the LORD be upon you; take care and do it, for there is no iniquity with the LORD our God, no partiality, nor taking of bribes. . . . Thus you shall act in the fear of the LORD, faithfully and with a loyal heart" (2 Chron. 19:5–9).

point. God Himself said, "You shall not afflict any widow or fatherless child. If you afflict them in any way, and they cry at all to Me, I will surely hear their cry; and My wrath will become hot, and I will kill you with the sword; your wives shall be widows, and your children fatherless" (Ex. 22:22–24). The principle is echoed in Isaiah 1:17:

> Learn to do good;
> Seek justice,
> Rebuke the oppressor;
> Defend the fatherless,
> Plead for the widow.

The law was full of similar special provisions for widows: "You shall not pervert justice due the stranger or the fatherless, nor take a widow's garment as a pledge" (Deut. 24:17). Widows were to be cared for, and legal authorities had a particular duty to see that their needs were met.

Apparently this woman also had a solid case on legal grounds alone, because she was pleading for justice, not special treatment. And she was relentless. The verb tense in the middle of Luke 18:3 signifies repeated action. "She *kept* coming to him" (NASB, emphasis added). She came back again and again and again, saying, "Get justice for me from my adversary"—literally, "Vindicate me!" It seems she was seeking redress for some injustice that had already been done to her. And her desperation suggests that everything had been taken from her. She had nothing left to lose.

But the judge's initial response to the woman was unbelievably cold. He simply refused her—dismissed her case with extreme prejudice and without any real consideration (v. 4). Perhaps whatever fraud or theft had been committed against her seemed paltry to him, but it was a threat to her very existence. The utter lack of any concern or compassion in his reaction to her is shocking.

Here we see once more Jesus' amazing skill at painting vivid pictures with a minimum of words. Like the unjust steward and the prodigal son in his rebellion, this judge is breathtakingly diabolical—and Jesus makes the point very simply, as usual, without piling on layers of adjectives or colorful phrases. He merely describes an act of callous, coldhearted, but casual cruelty. The judge simply brushed this poor woman away as if she were a troublesome gnat.

## The Turning Point

This went on "for a while" (Luke 18:4). But then the judge suddenly had a change of heart—not because he repented of his wickedness or admitted the righteousness of the widow's cause, but because he grew weary of hearing her pleas.

He utters a brief soliloquy, like that of the prodigal son when he came to his senses (15:17–19). It's even more reminiscent of how the unjust steward spoke to himself when it dawned on him what he needed to do to avert disaster (16:3–4). In a similar manner, the unjust judge spoke to himself: "Though I do not fear God nor regard man, yet because this widow troubles me I will avenge her, lest by her continual coming she weary me" (18:4–5).

Again, he knew he was a wretch; he held nothing back. But the widow was irritating him. He could easily silence her by simply granting her appeal. So he resolved to do that, just so she would not keep coming all the time. The word *continually* translates a two-word phrase in the Greek text: *eis telos*. It literally means, "to the end," or "endlessly." It's a common expression in the Bible meaning "forever." To paraphrase, the judge was thinking, *She will keep coming forever, and she will wear me out.*

The New King James Version uses the expression "lest . . . she weary me." That's more benign than the Greek term: *hup piaz*. It's a boxing term. It means to strike someone with a full blow just under the eye. It is the same word the apostle Paul uses in 1 Corinthians 9:27, where he describes himself as fighting, not like one who shadow boxes, but—in the words of the 1599 Geneva Bible: "I beate downe my body, & bring it into subjection." This woman's repeated pleas were like a verbal cudgel. She was not merely troublesome; she was painful to him. So this powerful and impervious judge was defeated by a helpless woman, merely through her persistence.

He still had no regard for God or man; he was looking out for his own self-interests. He needed to get rid of her. So he finally ruled in her favor.

## The Meaning

The point of this parable is clearly stated at the very start: "to show that at all times they ought to pray and not to lose heart" (Luke 18:1 NASB). But the point Jesus makes is especially about a particular kind of praying.

Bear in mind the context. This parable is a postscript to the prophetic discourse at the end of Luke 17. The theme of that passage is horrific judgment, "just as it happened in the days of Noah . . . the same as happened in the days of Lot" (vv. 26, 28 NASB). "It will be just the same on the day that the Son of Man is revealed" (v. 30 NASB). Christ will come again with a vengeance. His appearing will create death and devastation. "Out of His mouth goes a sharp sword, that with it He should strike the nations. And He Himself will rule them with a rod of iron. He Himself treads the winepress of the fierceness and wrath of Almighty God" (Rev. 19:15). Verse 19 says the kings of the earth and their armies will be gathered together to make war against Christ at His return. This will be the final war for all humanity—the battle sometimes called Armageddon. Christ will destroy all His enemies, "and all the birds [will be] filled with their flesh" (v. 21). That, of course, is precisely the scene referred to at the end of Luke 17:37: "Where the body is, there also the vultures will be gathered" (NASB).

The parable of the unjust judge follows immediately. The chapter break does not signify any change of scene or audience. The parable is told while the theme of Jesus' second coming (with all the apocalyptic imagery of bodies and vultures) is still on the minds of His listeners. The point Jesus is making is that while His disciples await His return—especially as the world seems to grow more wicked and more doomworthy—He wants His elect to keep praying and not lose heart. So this is a call to eschatological prayer. It's an encouragement to pray that the Lord will come, and to pray for the strength to endure to the end. The gist of the exhortation is summarized nicely in the words of Luke 21:36: "Watch therefore, and pray always that you may be counted worthy to escape all these things that will come to pass, and to stand before the Son of Man."

As we saw in an earlier chapter, Jesus taught the disciples that His coming was imminent—meaning that He *could* return at any time. On the other hand, He might come later than anyone expects. During His earthly ministry, even Jesus Himself, in the scope of His finite human consciousness, did not know the precise timetable: "But of that day and hour no one knows, not even the angels in heaven, *nor the Son,* but the Father alone" (Matt. 24:36 NASB, emphasis added). As God, of course He knows (and has always known) all things (John 16:30; 21:17). But it is evident that during His earthly life, He willingly abstained from the full and sovereign use of His divine omniscience. He was truly human, not superhuman. His life and experience as a man were authentic (Heb. 4:15). Thus He grew and learned things like any human (Luke 2:52). That means certain facts were kept for a time by God's plan from the forefront of His human consciousness. There is nothing remarkable about that.

But as we saw when we examined the parables of Matthew 24–25, without specifically revealing any timetable, He encouraged the disciples both to watch eagerly and to wait patiently for His return. Here He is encouraging them to pray faithfully until that day comes. He uses this parable that illustrates relentless persistence. It was an appropriate encouragement for the disciples in the first century. It is even more timely for us as we see the day approaching.

The difference between a long time and a short time is nothing in God's timing. "With the Lord one day is as a thousand years, and a thousand years as one day" (2 Peter 3:8). All history is a blink of the eye compared to eternity. But from our perspective, time often seems to drag. To this widow, the time span between the injustice she suffered and the judge's final vindication probably seemed like an aeon. To the apostle John, when Jesus did not return in his lifetime, that must have seemed like an interminable delay. For believers nearly two thousand years later, Jesus' admonition "to pray and not lose heart" is just the encouragement we need.

Today, at a rapidly accelerating pace worldwide, the Word of God is mocked, vilified, and censured. Christians are routinely maligned, persecuted, and oppressed, even in supposedly advanced Western cultures. In the Middle East, Africa, and parts of Asia Christians live in constant danger of martyrdom. Even by the most conservative measure, thousands are killed every year for their faith.

We long for Christ to come back and put an end to ungodliness and oppression—destroying sin forever and establishing His kingdom in righteousness. Jesus Himself taught us to pray, "Thy kingdom come" (Luke 11:2 KJV). Here, He encourages us to pray that prayer relentlessly, and not to lose heart.

The expression "lose heart" in the Greek text is *ekkakeō*, which speaks of giving up from exhaustion, or worse, turning coward. Luke 18:1 is the only place the word appears outside the Pauline epistles, but Paul uses it five times: "We do not lose heart" (2 Cor. 4:1, 16). "Let us not grow weary while doing good" (Gal. 6:9). "Do not lose heart at my tribulations for you" (Eph. 3:13). "Do not grow weary in doing good" (2 Thess. 3:13). The underlying meaning is always the same: don't give up hope that Jesus is coming.

God, of course, is nothing like the unjust judge. The argument Jesus is making is, again, an argument from the lesser to the greater. If such a depraved and wicked magistrate can be coaxed by sheer perseverance to grant justice to a widow for whom he has no regard and no compassion whatsoever, "shall God not avenge His own elect who cry out day and night to Him, though He bears long with them? *I tell you that He will avenge them speedily*" (Luke 18:7–8, emphasis added). When Christ *does* return, God's vengeance against the wicked will be swift and complete.

Meanwhile, He does not delay justice out of apathy or indifference. He delays because He is merciful. In the same context where Peter reminds us that "with the Lord one day is as a thousand years, and a thousand years as one day," the apostle immediately adds this: "The Lord is not slack concerning His promise, as some count slackness, but is longsuffering toward us, not willing that any should perish but that all should come to repentance" (2 Peter 3:8–9). The apparent delay is the measure of God's longsuffering. He is gathering "a people for His name" (Acts 15:14), and He will not shorten the time until every last one of His elect is saved—though their number be "a great multitude which no one could number, of all nations, tribes, peoples, and tongues" (Rev. 7:9).

Here's proof that the parable of the unjust judge pertains to the Second Coming, urging us to pray faithfully and persistently for that day. The end of Luke 18:8 is the key: "Nevertheless, when the Son of Man comes, will He really find faith on the earth?" Will He find His people persevering in prayer and expectation? Or will many "lose heart"? The parable is an encouragement to hold fast and keep praying.

The widow in this parable represents all true Christians—the elect. We are, in a sense, helpless—"poor in spirit" (Matt. 5:3); "not many wise according to the flesh, not many mighty, not many noble" (1 Cor. 1:26). We are totally at the mercy of the Judge.

But our heavenly Judge is nothing at all like the judge in the parable. He is the embodiment of perfect righteousness; He cannot do wrong. "Does God subvert judgment? Or does the Almighty pervert justice?" (Job 8:3). *Of course not.* "Shall not the Judge of all the earth do right?" (Gen. 18:25).

> *He is the Rock, His work is perfect;*
> *For all His ways are justice,*
> *A God of truth and without injustice;*
> *Righteous and upright is He. (Deut. 32:4)*

> *He is coming to judge the earth.*
> *With righteousness He shall judge the world,*
> *And the peoples with equity. (Ps. 98:9)*

Meanwhile, we live longingly, pleading like those under the altar in Revelation 6:10: "How long, O Lord, holy and true, until You judge and avenge our blood on those who dwell on the earth?" We are among those described in 1 Thessalonians 1:10, who "wait for [God's] Son from heaven . . . even Jesus who delivers us from the wrath to come."

It is impossible to live the Christian life faithfully unless it is in the light of the Second Coming. Knowing the end of the story gives us confidence and stability. As Paul says, "Be steadfast, immovable, always abounding in the work of the Lord, knowing that your labor is not in vain in the Lord" (1 Cor. 15:58).

Jesus' question in Luke 18:8, "When the Son of Man comes, will He really find faith on the earth?" ought to provoke us to self-reflection, and it is a perfect note on which to end our study. Are we faithfully praying for His return? I suspect that if He were to come right now, He would find multitudes who call themselves Christians who are totally unprepared for Him, not particularly eager for Him to come, and too enthralled with this life and worldly values to think much about it.

That is the antithesis of real faith. The heart-cry of the true believer is *Maranatha!* "O Lord, come!" (1 Cor. 16:22).

We who love Christ and long for His appearing must not lose heart. "Be patient, brethren, until the coming of the Lord. See how the farmer waits for the precious fruit of the earth, waiting patiently for it until it receives the early and latter rain. You also be patient. Establish your hearts, for the coming of the Lord is at hand" (James 5:7–8).

Meanwhile, we continue to pray and plead for the return of Christ— not merely because we want to be vindicated, but also because we want Christ to be glorified. And when you live that way and pray that way and plead that way, it changes everything about your life.

After two thousand years, our hope still burns brightly; our love for Christ is still true and pure; and our confidence that He keeps His Word is fast and firm. Therefore we pray persistently, calling on Him to come in order to vindicate His people, glorify Himself, punish sinners, dethrone Satan, establish a righteous kingdom, and bring everlasting peace on the earth. We pray relentlessly for Him to come and reign as King of kings and Lord of lords and create the eternal new heaven and the new earth. And we echo the closing plea of Scripture, "Even so, come, Lord Jesus!"

That prayer *ought* to be on our lips perpetually. And those hopes *should* govern all our thoughts. That is Jesus' point in the parable of the unjust judge.

Live in that kind of anticipation until He comes. And watch how it changes your life.

# Acknowledgments

One of the treasured rewards of pastoring the same church for nearly fifty years is the enduring loyal love and friendship of the congregation and its faithful shepherds. No one among them has been more valuable to me in extending my preaching than Phil Johnson. He has been at my side for more than thirty of those years to provide partnership and leadership in myriad ways to me and Grace Church. Beyond that, he has edited most all of my major books, starting with the sermon material preached and refining it into prose, leaving me to do some final touches. Only eternity will reveal the impact of his labors in making the truth known.

# Appendix
## Storied Truth: Objective Meaning in Narrative[1]

*"It has been given to you to know the mysteries."*

—MATTHEW 13:11

What is the significance of Jesus' use of stories as a medium for His teaching? Thirty years ago the typical evangelical could have easily answered that question in three sentences or less. As a matter of fact, it is not really a difficult question at all, because Jesus Himself answered it plainly when He said He employed parables for a dual reason—to illustrate the truth for those who were willing to receive it, and to obscure the truth from those who hated it anyway:

> But when He was alone, those around Him with the twelve asked Him about the parable. And He said to them, "To you it has been given to know the mystery of the kingdom of God; but to those who are outside, all things come in parables, so that 'Seeing they may see and not perceive, And hearing they may hear and not understand;

Lest they should turn, And their sins be forgiven them.'" (Mark 4:10–12)

So the short, simple answer to our opening question is that the parables are tools with which Jesus taught and defended the *truth*.

Do a simple survey and you'll notice that when Jesus explained His own parables to the disciples, He always did so by giving definite, objective meanings for the symbols He used: "The seed is the word of God" (Luke 8:11). "The field is the world" (Matt. 13:38). Sometimes His symbolism is perfectly obvious without any explanation, such as the shepherd in Luke 15:4–7 (who is obviously a figure of Christ Himself). Other times the meaning takes more careful thought and exegesis, but the true meaning can still be understood and explained clearly. A little bit of hard work and conscientious reflection always yields rich rewards in the study of parables. That, of course, is the very thing we have endeavored to do throughout this book.

Whether the true meaning of a story's symbolic features is obvious or one that requires some detective work, the point is still the same: Jesus' parables were all *illustrative* of gospel facts. The stories were not (as some people nowadays like to suggest) creative alternatives to propositional truth statements, designed to supplant certainty. They were not dreamy fantasies told merely to evoke a feeling. And they certainly weren't mind games contrived to make everything vague. Much less was Jesus employing fictional forms in order to displace truth itself with mythology.

Above all, He was not inviting His hearers to interpret the stories any way they liked, and thus let each one's own personal opinions be the final arbiter of what is true for that person. The conviction that the Bible itself is the final rule of faith (and the corresponding belief that Scripture itself should govern how we interpret Scripture) is a long-standing canon of biblical Christianity. Deny it, and you have in effect denied the authority of Scripture.

That's not to suggest that all Scripture is *equally* clear. Some of the parables in particular are notoriously difficult to interpret. It takes care, hard work, and the Holy Spirit's help to get it right. No one has ever seriously disputed that.

But on the question of whether each parable actually *has* a single divinely inspired sense and therefore a proper interpretation—an *objectively* true sense—there has never been any serious dispute among people who take the authority of Scripture seriously. The corollary of that idea is an equally sound principle: every possible interpretation that contradicts the one true meaning of a passage is false by definition.

In these postmodern times, however, there seems to be an abundance of voices denying those simple principles. They often suggest that since Jesus made such lavish use of parables and storytelling in His public ministry, He must not have thought of truth the same way modern men and women think of it. Is truth ultimately an objective reality, fixed and immutable, or is it soft and pliable and subjective?

This is more than just an interesting footnote to the rest of the book. It's a crucial matter to raise and examine—especially just now. We live in a generation where traces of fact and reality are sometimes deliberately blended together with elements of myth, guesswork, theory, falsehood, fiction, and feeling—and then released in the form of a dark mist, in order to make the concept of truth itself seem like a murky, mysterious vapor with no real substance.

Some who actually prefer this cloudy notion of truth are trying to tell us Jesus took precisely that approach to teaching. They say the main reason He frequently turned to storytelling was in order to stress the inscrutability of divine truth and thereby confound the spiritual arrogance and hypocrisy of His day. The Pharisees, for example, thought they had truth all figured out—even though they did not agree with the equally overconfident Sadducees. Jesus' parables simply put the whole concept of truth right back where it belongs: in the unfathomable realm of sheer mystery.

At least that's what those who have drunk deeply from the postmodern spirit of our age would have us believe. They insist it is a mistake to subject our Lord's narratives to serious systematic analysis in search of a precise interpretation, because to do that is to miss the real purpose of the stories. Instead, we're told, it's better to enjoy and admire and adapt Jesus' stories in whatever way makes them most meaningful to us. According to this way of thinking, since stories are inherently subjective, we should be less concerned with asking what the parables *mean*—and more concerned with finding ways of making the stories of the Bible our own.*

I was recently shown an essay posted on the Internet by an anonymous author (presumably a pastor), who reimagined the parable of the prodigal son from a feminist perspective and thereby intentionally turned the entire story on its head. In this person's freehanded reinterpretation, we're encouraged to visualize the father as an aloof family patriarch who thoughtlessly drives his younger son away by neglect. This one new facet of the story "changes everything," the unknown writer solemnly (and shamelessly) informs us. The son's demand for the early inheritance now "alludes to a prior and perhaps long-standing family strain, [and] the boy's dissolute living may be his effort to 'buy' . . . affiliation and belonging," which he had long craved but did not have because the father had so carelessly marginalized him. Rather than a self-indulgent "plot to sow his wild oats," the prodigal's pursuit of a reckless lifestyle thus becomes a desperate cry for help.[2]

Further observing that Jesus' own telling of the prodigal son parable ends without resolution, the article suggests that this "reveals the open-endedness of the Kingdom of God." What's more, the story's *true* ending "is the end of my story, your story, and everyone's story—beyond our wildest dreams."

By such a wholly subjective approach, Jesus' stories become playthings to be bent and shaped into whatever form suits the hearer's fancy. Jesus' whole message becomes versatile, subjective, and infinitely adaptable to the felt needs and personal preferences of each hearer.

---

* I've responded in much greater detail to the current wave of postmodern influences among evangelicals in *The Truth War* (Nashville: Thomas Nelson, 2007).

That is a very popular way to deal with Jesus' teaching these days: as if His parables were given mainly to create a mood and set the stage for a billion uniquely personal dramas. It's considered okay to admire the setting, but it's not okay to hold the story up to the light and attempt to discover any objective or universal meaning in it. Instead, we are supposed to try to experience the story for ourselves by living within it, or by retelling it in our own words, using little more than our own imaginations. That's how we can make Jesus' stories into *our* stories. It means, in effect, that the interpretation, the lesson, and the ending of each story are ultimately ours to determine.

In contemporary academic circles, such an approach would be recognized as a rather extreme form of "narrative theology." That's a fashionable buzzword these days, used to describe a large family of novel ideas about how we should interpret the Bible (with special emphasis on "the story" rather than the *truth claims* of Scripture). The stylishness of narrative theology has led to vast amounts of discussion—and a considerable measure of confusion—about Jesus' role as a storyteller. What did He mean to convey in His stories? Why did He use so many parables? How are we supposed to understand them? Does the narrative form itself alter or nullify the normal rules for interpreting Scripture?

On an even broader scale, does Jesus' frequent use of stories constitute a valid argument against the systematic approach to doctrine Christians have historically taken? Do we really even *need* to analyze Scripture, categorize truth, and attempt to understand biblical doctrine in any kind of logical fashion—or is it okay just to appreciate the stories and embellish them with our own plot twists and real-life endings? In very simple terms: Is Jesus' own style of teaching actually incompatible with our doctrinal statements, confessions of faith, and systematic approach to theology?

Those are all important questions, but they are not really difficult questions to answer if we simply accept at face value what the Bible itself says about Jesus' use of parables.

## Stories as Effective Vehicles for Truth

Jesus was a master storyteller, but He never told a story merely for the story's sake. Every one of His parables had an important lesson to convey.

That is a crucial fact to keep in mind, because it explains how *truth* (as we understand the concept) is compatible with storytelling. Even pure fiction is not altogether incompatible with our conventional ideas of truth—because every well-told story ultimately makes a point. And the point of a good story is supposed to be true (or at least true to life on *some* level), even when the story itself paints a totally imaginary scenario.

That is the very nature of parables. It is the main reason why one central lesson is always the most important feature of every parable and we should focus on that, rather than seeking hidden meaning in all the peripheral details of the story. When you see the key point of a parable, you have understood the essence of whatever truth the story aims to convey. That lesson itself is sometimes filled out or embellished by plot elements, characters, and other details in the story. But there's no need to look for multiple layers of secret meaning or suppose that some deeper symbolism or different dimension of truth has been hidden in the incidental features of the tale. As we noted in the introduction, parables aren't allegories, full of symbols from top to bottom. They highlight one important truth—just like the moral of a well-told story.

That explains why the vital truth contained in a parable is fixed and objective—not a metaphysical glob of modeling clay we can bend and shape however we like. Remember that when Jesus began to use parables in His public ministry, He was alone with the disciples and carefully explained the parable of the sower to them (Matt. 13:18–23). It had a clear, simple, single, straightforward, *objective* meaning, and as Jesus explained it to them, He indicated that all the parables could be understood through a similar method of interpretation: "Do you not understand this parable? How then will you understand all the parables?" (Mark 4:13). Thus there is absolutely no reason to surmise that Jesus' use of parables is somehow an indication that truth itself is so entangled in mystery as to be utterly unknowable.

Quite the contrary: as we noted at the start of this appendix, Jesus used parables to make certain truths clear to believers while obscuring the meaning from unbelievers. Have you ever considered *why* He did that?

Obscuring the truth from unbelievers was (in a very important sense) an act of mercy, because the more truth they heard and spurned, the worse it would be for them in the final judgment.

But Jesus' use of parables was also itself a temporal sign of judgment against them, sealing their own stubborn unbelief by removing the light of truth from them. They had already hardened their own hearts:

> For the hearts of this people have grown dull.
> Their ears are hard of hearing,
> And their eyes they have closed,
> Lest they should see with their eyes and hear with their ears,
> Lest they should understand with their hearts and turn,
> So that I should heal them. (Matt. 13:15)

But now their unbelief was irreversible. Jesus' use of parables both highlighted that reality and stood as a warning sign to others, encouraging them not to harden their hearts also, but rather to seek the truth.

And yet, Jesus told the disciples, "Blessed are your eyes for they see, and your ears for they hear" (v. 16). Jesus was making it clear that the parables *do* have objective meaning, and that meaning can indeed be apprehended. "It has been given to you to know the mysteries of the kingdom" (v. 11). Thus He plainly indicated that the parables contained eternal spiritual truth, which can actually be seen and heard and *known* by anyone with spiritual eyes and ears.

So even though the parables concealed Jesus' meaning from *unbelievers*, it's not as if He was forever encasing the truth itself in hopeless, impenetrable mystery. Truth is actually being unveiled and illustrated in every one of His parables. It is vital, timeless, unchanging, unadulterated, and unequivocal truth—not some ethereal or inaccessible truth. On the contrary, it is all simple enough that through the due use of ordinary means any believer should be able to come to a sound and sure understanding of it.

## The Wealth of Truth in Jesus' Parables

Jesus' stories were remarkable for both their simplicity and their sheer abundance. In Matthew and Luke, multiple parables are sometimes given in rapid-fire fashion, one after another, with little or no interpretive or elaborative material interspersed between them. Extended discourses containing virtually nothing but parables sometimes fill chapter-length portions of Matthew and Luke. (For example, Matthew 13; Matthew 24:32–25:30; and of course, Luke 15:4–16:13.) The selections recorded by Matthew and Luke were probably representative samples rather than exhaustive catalogues of Jesus' parables. Nevertheless, it seems reasonable to conclude that the parable-upon-parable pattern closely approximates Jesus' actual style of discourse.

Jesus clearly *liked* to teach by telling stories rather than by giving a list of raw facts for rote memorization, or by outlining information in a neatly catalogued systematic layout. He was never stiff and pedantic when He taught, but always informal and conversational. The parables contained familiar figures, and sometimes they stirred raw emotions. These things were what made Jesus' preaching most memorable, rather than tidy lists or clever alliteration.

That's not a novel observation, by the way; it's a fact that stands out on the face of the New Testament text—especially in the three Synoptic Gospels (Matthew, Mark, and Luke). And of course, all four gospels plus the book of Acts are likewise recorded almost completely in narrative form. In certain academic circles today, the sudden burst of enthusiasm over "narrative theology" and "narrative preaching" might give some students the impression that scholars have only recently discovered that the Bible is full of stories. Read some recent books and journals on the subject and you might even come away with the idea that the church has been kept largely in the dark (at least since the dawn of the modern era) until scholars reading the Bible through postmodern lenses suddenly noticed the true implications of Christ's narrative style of teaching.

Actually, Jesus' preference for narrative devices has been duly noted and strongly emphasized by practically every competent teacher in the history of the church, starting with the gospel writers themselves, through the best of the early church fathers, down to and including every important Protestant biblical commentator of the past four centuries.

But the fact that Jesus showed such a preference for narrative forms *still* doesn't nullify either the didactic purpose of the parables or the unchanging truth content they were meant to convey.

In fact, Matthew 13:34–35 sums up the proper perspective on the parables and their truth-value in very simple terms: "Jesus spoke to the multitude in parables; and without a parable He did not speak to them, that it might be fulfilled which was spoken by the prophet, saying: 'I will open My mouth in parables; I will utter things kept secret from the foundation of the world.'" He was quoting Psalm 78:2–4, which describes the primary purpose of the parables as a means of *revelation*, not *obfuscation*. The only context in which the parables deliberately conceal the truth or cloak it in mystery is in the face of willful, hostile unbelief.

## Stories and Propositions

One vital and related issue needs to be addressed briefly in this discussion, and that's the question of whether we violate the whole point of Jesus' storytelling when we summarize the truths we learn from the parables and restate them in propositional form.

That's a question frequently raised by people who take their cues from popular postmodernity. They conceive of *stories* and *propositions* as completely separate categories—virtually contradictory ways of thinking about truth. In the words of one author, "The emerging gospel of the electronic age is moving beyond cognitive *propositions* and linear formulas to embrace the power and truth of *story*."[3]

According to that way of thinking, the truth value of a story cannot and should not be reduced to a mere proposition.

Propositions are the building blocks of logic. They are inherently simple, not complex. A *proposition* is nothing more than an assertion that either affirms or denies something. "Jesus Christ—He is Lord of all" (Acts 10:36) is a classic biblical proposition that expresses one of the foundational truths of all Christian doctrine. Another is "Nor is there salvation in any other" (Acts 4:12). The first example is an affirmation of Jesus' supremacy and exclusivity; the second is a denial of the converse. Both are simple propositions declaring the same basic biblical truth, but in slightly different ways.

The truth value of every proposition is binary: it can only be either true or false. There is no middle value. And there is the rub as far as postmodern thinking is concerned: propositions do not allow for any ambiguity.

Since the form of a proposition demands either an affirmation or denial, and postmodern thinking prefers obscurity and vagueness rather than clarity, it is no wonder that the very notion of propositional truth has fallen out of favor in these postmodern times. Stories, by contrast, are widely perceived as fluid, subjective, and not necessarily emphatic— just like the postmodernist view of truth itself.

So it is more and more common these days to hear people express the belief that the brand of truth embodied in stories is somehow of an altogether different nature from the kind of truth that we can express in propositions. What they generally are arguing for is a fluid, subjective, ambiguous concept of truth itself.

To embrace that perspective is in effect to make mincemeat of the very notion of truth. Truth cannot be verbally expressed or formally affirmed at all—even in story form—without recourse to propositions. So the postmodern attempt to divorce truth from propositions is nothing more than a way of talking about truth, toying with the idea of truth, and giving lip service to the existence of truth—without actually needing to affirm anything as true or deny anything as false.

That is why the church has historic creeds and confessions in the first place—and they are all chock-full of propositions. I've heard Al Mohler say repeatedly that while the biblical notion of truth is always *more* than propositional, it is never *less*. He is exactly right. We are not to think Jesus' use of stories and parables in any way diminishes the importance of accuracy, clarity, historical facts, objective realities, sound doctrine, or propositional truth claims.

As a matter of fact, not all of Jesus' parables were full-fledged stories. Some of the shortest ones were stated in straightforward, simple propositional form. "The kingdom of heaven is like leaven, which a woman took and hid in three measures of meal till it was all leavened" (Matt. 13:33). Or, "Every scribe instructed concerning the kingdom of heaven is like a householder who brings out of his treasure things new and old" (v. 52). And, "[The Kingdom] is like a mustard seed, which a man took and put in his garden; and it grew and became a large tree, and the birds of the air nested in its branches" (Luke 13:19).

Furthermore, propositions are used as building blocks in every one of the parables Jesus gave in extended story form. Take the prodigal son, for example. The very first sentence, "A certain man had two sons," is a simple proposition. The closing phrase of the parable is likewise a barebones proposition: "Your brother was dead and is alive again, and was lost and is found" (Luke 15:11, 32). Those are statements about the facts of the story rather than the central truth claim the story aims to teach, but they serve to illustrate that it is hardly possible to communicate either raw truth or complex story at all without using propositions. Moreover, it's well nigh impossible to think of a truth that's authentically *knowable* that isn't capable of being expressed in propositional form.

To give another example, consider once more the three harmonious parables of Luke 15 (the lost sheep, the lost coin, and the prodigal son). The only exposition Jesus offers as a clue to their meaning is a single propositional statement: "There will be more joy in heaven over one sinner who repents than over ninety-nine just persons who need no repentance" (Luke 15:7). Thus Jesus Himself in one verse succinctly boiled down the whole point of the entire chapter into a simple proposition.

Notice: *That verse states a truth that is by definition objective.* It describes what occurs in heaven when someone repents. It discloses a reality that is not in any way affected by any earthly person's personal perspective. On the contrary, it is a fact that is true regardless of how someone perceives it. In fact, it has been true from the beginning, before any earthly creature perceived it at all. That is precisely what we mean when we say truth is "objective."

Why is all this important? Because truth itself is critically important, and the church today is in imminent danger of selling her birthright in exchange for a postmodern philosophy that in effect would do away with the very idea of truth.

That is ground we cannot yield. We must be willing to submit our minds to the truth of Scripture, and we must refuse to subject Scripture to whatever theories or speculations happen to be currently popular in the realm of secular philosophy.

> Beware lest anyone cheat you through philosophy and empty deceit, according to the tradition of men, according to the basic principles of the world, and not according to Christ. (Col. 2:8)

# Notes

*Introduction*

1. Janet Litherland, *Storytelling from the Bible* (Colorado Springs: Meriwether, 1991), 3.
2. Eugene L. Lowry, *The Homiletical Plot: The Sermon as Narrative* (Louisville: Westminster John Knox, 2001), xx–xxi.
3. John MacArthur, *Ashamed of the Gospel* (Wheaton, IL: Crossway, 2010).
4. Richard Eslinger, *A New Hearing: Living Options in Homiletic Method* (Nashville: Abingdon, 1987), publisher's description.
5. Ibid., 11.
6. William R. White, *Speaking in Stories* (Minneapolis: Augsburg, 1982), 32.
7. Charles W. Hedrick, *Many Things in Parables: Jesus and His Modern Critics* (Louisville: Westminster John Knox, 2004), 102.
8. Ibid.
9. Ibid.
10. Richard Chenevix Trench, *Notes on the Parables of Our Lord* (New York: Appleton, 1878), 26.
11. Part 3: "Jesus Illustrates His Gospel," in John MacArthur, *The Gospel According to Jesus* (Grand Rapids: Zondervan, 1988), 117–55.
12. John MacArthur, *A Tale of Two Sons* (Nashville: Thomas Nelson, 2008).
13. Harvey K. McArthur and Robert M. Johnston, *They Also Taught in Parables: Rabbinic Parables from the First Centuries of the Christian Era* (Grand Rapids: Zondervan, 1990), 165–66.
14. Simon J. Kistemaker, "Jesus As Story Teller: Literary Perspectives on the Parables," *The Masters Seminary Journal* 16, no. 1 (Spring 2005), 49–50.
15. Charles Haddon Spurgeon, *The Metropolitan Tabernacle Pulpit*, vol. 53 (London: Passmore & Alabaster, 1907), 398.

## Chapter 3: A Lesson About the Cost of Discipleship

1. Ruben Vives, "California Couple's Gold-Coin Find Called Greatest in U.S. History," *Chicago Tribune,* February 26, 2014, sec. A.
2. William Whiston, trans., *The Genuine Works of Flavius Josephus,* 4 vols. (New York: William Borradaile, 1824), 4:323.
3. Jacob Neusner, *The Halakah: An Encyclopedia of the Law of Judaism,* vol. 3: *Within Israel's Social Order* (Leiden: Brill, 2000), 57.
4. "Like a River Glorious," by Frances Ridley Havergal, 1876.
5. "Rock of Ages" Augustus M. Toplady and Thomas Hastings, "Rock of Ages, Cleft For Me," 1775; 1830.

## Chapter 6: A Lesson About Justification by Faith

1. Kenneth Bailey, *Poet and Peasant and Through Peasant Eyes: A Literary-Cultural Approach to the Parables in Luke* (Grand Rapids: Eerdmans, 1983), 394.
2. James I. Packer in James Buchanan, *The Doctrine of Justification* (Edinburgh: Banner of Truth, 1961 reprint of 1867 original), 2.

## Chapter 10: A Lesson About Persistence in Prayer

1. Luke 15 is surveyed in chapter 2 of John MacArthur, *A Tale of Two Sons* (Nashville: Nelson, 2008), 19–39.
2. Alfred Edersheim, *The Life and Times of Jesus the Messiah,* 2 vols. (London: Longmans, Green & Co., 1896), 2:287.

## Appendix:

1. This appendix originally appeared in John MacArthur, *A Tale of Two Sons* (Nashville: Nelson, 2008), 199–211.
2. The essay, titled "Check Out This Chick-Flick," was posted anonymously at the blog of First Trinity Lutheran Church (ELCA), Indianapolis, http://firsttrinitylutheran.blogspot.com/2007/03/check-out-this-chick-flick.html.
3. Shane Hipps, *The Hidden Power of Electronic Culture* (Grand Rapids: Zondervan/Youth Specialties, 2006), 90 (emphasis added).

# Index

# Scripture Index

# About the Author

John MacArthur has served as the pastor-teacher of Grace Community Church in Sun Valley, California, since 1969. His ministry of expository preaching is unparalleled in its breadth and influence; in more than four decades of ministry from the same pulpit, he has preached verse by verse through the entire New Testament (and several key sections of the Old Testament). He is president of The Master's College and Seminary and can be heard daily on the *Grace to You* radio broadcast (carried on hundreds of radio stations worldwide). He has authored a number of bestselling books, including *The MacArthur Study Bible, The Gospel According to Jesus, Twelve Ordinary Men,* and *One Perfect Life.*

For more details about John MacArthur and his Bible-teaching resources, contact Grace to You at 800–55-GRACE or www.gty.org.

# Also Available from Bestselling Author John MacArthur

Join master expositor and Bible commentator John MacArthur as he draws on his years of studying the Bible to guide readers through the most famous and influential short stories that Jesus told, including:

- The Parable of the Soils (Matthew 13:2–23)
- The Good Samaritan (Luke 10:30–37)
- The Pearl of Great Price (Matthew 13:45–46)
- The Workers in the Vineyard (Matthew 20:1–15)
- The Parable of the Talents (Matthew 25:14–30)
- The Two Sons (Luke 15:11–32) . . . and many more.

Each of the sessions in this workbook contains an in-depth look at the key Bible passages in the parables Jesus told, commentary to give you background on each, and study questions to help you explore Jesus' teachings in greater depth. This workbook will enhance your reading of *Parables* and is intended for both individuals and small groups.